Bloom's Modern Critical Views

Bloom's Modern Critical Views

HENRY DAVID THOREAU
Updated Edition

Edited and with an introduction by
Harold Bloom
Sterling Professor of the Humanities
Yale University

BLOOM'S
LITERARY CRITICISM
An imprint of Infobase Publishing

Bloom's Modern Critical Views: Henry David Thoreau—Updated Edition

Copyright ©2007 Infobase Publishing

Introduction © 2007 by Harold Bloom

Bloom's Literary Criticism
An imprint of Infobase Publishing
132 West 31st Street
New York NY 10001

ISBN-10: 0-7910-9348-4
ISBN-13: 978-0-7910-9348-1

Library of Congress Cataloging-in-Publication Data
Henry David Thoreau / Harold Bloom, editor. — Updated ed.
    p. cm. — (Bloom's modern critical views)
  Thoreau: the quest and the classics / Ethel Seybold — Naturalizing Eden: science and sainthood in Walden / John Hildebidle — From a week to Walden / Robert Sattelmeyer — Revolution and renewal: The genres of Walden / Gordon V. Boudreau — Paradise (to be) regained / David M. Robinson — Thoreau, Homer and community / Robert Oscar Lopez — Thoreau, crystallography, and the science of the transparent / Eric G. Wilson —"The life excited": faces of Thoreau in Walden / Steven Hartman."
  Includes bibliographical references and index.
  ISBN 0-7910-9348-4
  1. Thoreau, Henry David, 1817-1862—Criticism and interpretation. I. Bloom, Harold. II. Title. III. Series.
  PS3054.H38 2007
  818'.309—dc22   2006034841

Contributing Editor: Janyce Marson

Cover designed by Takeshi Takahashi

Cover photo © The Granger Collection, New York

Printed in the United States of America

Bang EJB 10 9 8 7 6 5 4 3 2 1

This book is printed on acid-free paper.

Contents

Editor's Note

My Introduction suggests that Thoreau remains one of Emerson's major works.

Ethel Seybold traces the literary foregrounding of Thoreau's career, while John Hildebidle seeks the balance between the transcendental and the naturalistic in *Walden*.

Thoreau's movement from his earlier *A Week on the Concord and Merrimack Rivers* to *Walden* is charted by Robert Sattelmeyer as a progress through reading, after which Gordon V. Boudreau sees the mythology of nature as the heart of *Walden*.

Thoreau's Wordsworthian, over-influenced poetry is studied by Lance Newman, while David M. Robinson proposes *Walden*'s prose as its author's truest poetry.

Homeric thematic influence upon Thoreau is stressed by Robert Oscar López, after which Eric G. Wilson exalts Thoreau's metamorphic mastery of the image of the crystal.

In this volume's final essay, Steven Hartman analyzes Thoreau's many roles in *Walden*.

HAROLD BLOOM

Introduction

I

All of us, however idiosyncratic, begin by living in a generation that overdetermines more of our stances and judgments than we can hope to know, until we are far along in the revisionary processes that can bring us to a Second Birth. I myself read *Walden* while I was very young, and "Civil Disobedience" and "Life without Principle" soon afterwards. But I read little or no Emerson until I was an undergraduate, and achieved only a limited awareness of him then. I began to read Emerson obsessively just before the middle of the journey, when in crisis, and have never stopped reading him since. More even than Freud, Emerson helped change my mind about most things, in life and in literature, myself included. Going back to Thoreau, when one has been steeped in Emerson for more than twenty years, is a curious experience. A distinguished American philosopher, my contemporary, has written that he underwent the reverse process, coming to Emerson only after a profound knowing of Thoreau, and has confessed that Emerson seemed to him at first a "second-rate Thoreau." I am not tempted to call Thoreau a second-rate Emerson, because Thoreau, at his rare best, was a strong writer, and revised Emerson with passion and with cunning. But Emerson was for Thoreau even more massively what he was for Walt Whitman and all Americans of sensibility ever since: the metaphor of "the father," the pragmatic image of the ego ideal, the inescapable precursor, the literary hero, the mind of the United States of America.

My own literary generation had to recover Emerson, because we came after the critics formed by the example and ideology of T. S. Eliot, who had proclaimed that "the essays of Emerson are already an encumbrance." I can recall conversations about Emerson with R. P. Blackmur, who informed me that Emerson was of no relevance, except insofar as he represented an extreme example for America of the unsupported and catastrophic Protestant sensibility, which had ruined the Latin culture of Europe. Allen Tate more succinctly told me that Emerson simply was the devil, a judgment amplified in my single conversation with the vigorous Yvor Winters. In many years of friendship with Robert Penn Warren, my only disputes with that great poet have concerned Emerson, upon whom Warren remains superbly obdurate. As these were the critical minds that dominated American letters from 1945 to 1965 (except for Lionel Trilling, who was silent on Emerson), it is no surprise that Emerson vanished in that era. From 1965 through the present, Emerson has returned, as he always must and will, because he is the pragmatic origin of our literary culture. Walt Whitman and Emily Dickinson, Robert Frost and Wallace Stevens, Hart Crane, Elizabeth Bishop, and John Ashbery have written the poems of our climate, but Emerson was and is that climate.

How does Thoreau now read in our recovered sense of the Emersonian climate? Is the question itself unfair? Rereading *Walden* and the major essays, I confess to an experience different in degree, but not in kind, from a fresh encounter with Thoreau's verse. As a poet, Thoreau is in the shadow of Wordsworth, towards whom his apotropaic gestures are sadly weak. In prose, conceptually and rhetorically, Thoreau strongly seeks to evade Emerson, wherever he cannot revise him directly. But this endless agon, unlike Whitman's, or the subtler subversion of Emerson by Dickinson and by Henry James, is won by the image of the father. Rereading Thoreau, either I hear Emerson overtly, or more darkly I detect him in what Stevens called "the hum of thoughts evaded in the mind."

II

During that 1945–1965 heyday of what then was called "the New Criticism," only *Walden*, among all of Thoreau's works, was exempt from censure. I have never understood the New Critical tolerance for *Walden*, except as a grudging bit of cultural patriotism, or perhaps as a kind of ultimate act of revenge against Emerson, the prophet who organized support for John Brown, cast out Daniel Webster because of the Fugitive Slave Act, and burned himself into a premature senility by his fierce contempt for the South and its culture throughout the Civil War. Thoreau, no less an enthusiast for John Brown, and equally apocalyptic against the South, somehow escaped the wrath of Tate, Warren, and their cohorts. This may have something to do with the myth of Thoreau as a kind of American Mahatma Gandhi, a Tolstoyan hermit practicing native arts and crafts out in the woods. Homespun and reputedly naive, such a fellow may have seemed harmless enough, unlike the slyly wicked Sage of Concord, Ralph Waldo Lucifer, impediment to the United States somehow acquiring a Southern and Latin culture.

The merely actual Thoreau has been so prettified that one does best to begin a consideration of the man with the opening paragraphs of Leon Edel's pungent pamphlet, in which an amiable disenchantment with our American Narcissus is memorably expressed:

> Of the creative spirits that flourished in Concord, Massachusetts, during the middle of the nineteenth century, it might be said that Hawthorne loved men but felt estranged from them, Emerson loved ideas more than men, and Thoreau loved himself. Less of an artist than Hawthorne, less of a thinker than Emerson, Thoreau made of his life a sylvan legend, that of man alone, in communion with nature. He was a strange presence in American letters—we have so few of them—an eccentric. The English tend to tolerate their eccentrics to the enrichment of their national life. In America, where democracy and conformity are often confused, the nonconforming Thoreau was frowned upon, and for good reason. He had a disagreeable and often bellicose nature. He lacked geniality. And then he had once set fire to the Concord woods—a curious episode, too lightly dismissed in the Thoreau biographies. He was, in the fullest sense of the word, a "curmudgeon," and literary history has never sufficiently studied the difficulties his neighbors had in adjusting themselves to certain of his childish ways. But in other ways he was a man of genius—even if it was a "crooked genius" as he himself acknowledged.
>
> A memorable picture has been left by Hawthorne's daughter of the three famous men of Concord skating one winter's afternoon on the river. Hawthorne, wrapped in his cloak, "moved like a self-impelled Greek statue, stately and grave," as one might expect of the future author of *The Marble Faun*. Emerson, stoop-shouldered, "evidently too weary to hold himself erect," pitched forward, "half lying on the air." Thoreau, genuinely skillful on

his skates, performed "dithyrambic dances and Bacchic leaps," enchanted with himself. Their manner, of skating was in accord with their personalities and temperaments.

Behind a mask of self-exaltation Thoreau performed as before a mirror—and first of all for his own edification. He was a fragile Narcissus embodied in a homely New Englander. His life was brief. He was born in 1817, in Concord; he lived in Concord, and he died in Concord in 1862 shortly after the guns had spoken at Fort Sumter. A child of the romantic era, he tried a number of times to venture forth into the world. He went to Maine, to Staten Island, to Cape Cod, and ultimately to Minnesota, in search of health, but he always circled back to the Thoreau family house in Concord and to the presence of a domineering and loquacious mother. No other man with such wide-ranging thoughts and a soaring mind—it reached to ancient Greece, to the Ganges, to the deepest roots of England and the Continent—bound himself to so small a strip of ground. "He was worse than provincial," the cosmopolitan Henry James remarked, "he was parochial."

Edel's Jamesian slight can be dismissed, since Edel is James's devoted biographer, but the rest of this seems charmingly accurate. The great conservationist who set fire to the Concord woods; the epitome of Emersonian Self-Reliance who sneaked back from Walden in the evening to be fed dinner by Lidian Emerson; the man in whom Walt Whitman (whom Thoreau admired greatly, as man and as poet) found "a morbid dislike of humanity"—that, alas, was the empirical Thoreau, as contrasted to the ontological self of Thoreau. Since, to this day, Thoreau's self-mystifications continue to mystify nearly all of Thoreau's scholars, I find myself agreeing with Edel's judgment that the best discussions of Thoreau continue to be those of Emerson, James Russell Lowell, and Robert Louis Stevenson. Magnificent (and subtly balanced) as Emerson's funeral eulogy is, and brilliant as Lowell's much-derided essay continues to be, the best single remark on Thoreau remains Stevenson's: "It was not inappropriate, surely, that he had such close relations with the fish."

Lowell, sympathetic enough to Emerson, had little imagination to countenance the even more extreme disciple, Thoreau:

This notion of an absolute originality, as if one could have a patent-right in it, is an absurdity. A man cannot escape in thought, any more than he can in language, from the past and the present. As no one ever invents a word, and yet language somehow grows by general contribution and necessity, so it is with thought. Mr.

Thoreau seems to me to insist in public on going back to flint and steel, when there is a match-box in his pocket which he knows very well how to use at a pinch. Originality consists in power of digesting and assimilating thoughts, so that they become part of our life and substance. Montaigne, for example, is one of the most original of authors, though he helped himself to ideas in every direction. But they turn to blood and coloring in his style, and give a freshness of complexion that is forever charming. In Thoreau much seems yet to be foreign and unassimilated, showing itself in symptoms of indigestion. A preacher-up of Nature, we now and then detect under the surly and stoic garb something of the sophist and the sentimentalizer. I am far from implying that this was conscious on his part. But it is much easier for a man to impose on himself when he measures only with himself. A greater familiarity with ordinary men would have done Thoreau good, by showing him how many fine qualities are common to the race. The radical vice of his theory of life was that he confounded physical with spiritual remoteness from men. A man is far enough withdrawn from his fellows if he keep himself clear of their weaknesses. He is not so truly withdrawn as exiled, if he refuse to share their strength. "Solitude," says Cowley, "can be well fitted and set right but upon a very few persons. They must have enough knowledge of the world to see the vanity of it, and enough virtue to despise all vanity." It is a morbid self-consciousness that pronounces the world of men empty and worthless before trying it, the instinctive evasion of one who is sensible of some innate weakness, and retorts the accusation of it before any has made it but himself. To a healthy mind, the world is a constant challenge of opportunity. Mr. Thoreau had not a healthy mind, or he would not have been so fond of prescribing. His whole life was a search for the doctor. The old mystics had a wiser sense of what the world was worth. They ordained a severe apprenticeship to law, and even ceremonial, in order to the gaining of freedom and mastery over these. Seven years of service for Rachel were to be rewarded at last with Leah. Seven other years of faithfulness with her were to win them at last the true bride of their souls. Active Life was with them the only path to the Contemplative.

It is curious that Lowell should have directed this attack upon Emersonian Self-Reliance at the disciple, not the master, yet Lowell, as he shows abundantly in his fine essay "Emerson the Lecturer," was overcome by the great lecturer's charisma, his mysterious but nearly universally acknowledged personal charm. Even Lowell's argument against Transcendentalist "solitude" would have been better directed against the author of *Society and Solitude* than the recalcitrant author of *Walden*. Lowell's essay survives, despite its unfairness, because of its accuracy, and even because of its ultimate judgment of Thoreau.

> We have said that his range was narrow, but to be a master is to be a master. He had caught his English at its living source, among the poets and prose-writers of its best days; his literature was extensive and recondite; his quotations are always nuggets of the purest ore: there are sentences of his as perfect as anything in the language, and thoughts as clearly crystallized; his metaphors and images are always fresh from the soil; he had watched Nature like a detective who is to go upon the stand; as we read him, it seems as if all-out-of-doors had kept a diary and become its own Montaigne.

To be the Montaigne of all-out-of-doors ought to have been distinction enough for anyone, yet Emerson confessed that he had hoped for more from this rugged and difficult disciple:

> His virtues, of course, sometimes ran into extremes. It was easy to trace to the inexorable demand on all for exact truth that austerity which made this willing hermit more solitary even than he wished. Himself of a perfect probity, he required not less of others. He had a disgust at crime, and no worldly success would cover it. He detected paltering as readily in dignified and prosperous persons as in beggars, and with equal scorn. Such dangerous frankness was in his dealing that his admirers called him "that terrible Thoreau," as if he spoke when silent, and was still present when he had departed. I think the severity of his ideal interfered to deprive him of a healthy sufficiency of human society.
> The habit of a realist to find things the reverse of their appearance inclined him to put every statement in a paradox. A certain habit of antagonism defaced his earlier writings,—a trick of rhetoric not quite outgrown in his later, of substituting for the obvious word and thought its diametrical opposite. He praised wild mountains and winter forests for their domestic air, in snow and ice he would find sultriness, and commended the wilderness

for resembling Rome and Paris. "It was so dry, that you might call it wet."

The tendency to magnify the moment, to read all the laws of Nature in the one object or one combination under your eye, is of course comic to those who do not share the philosopher's perception of identity. To him there was no such thing as size. The pond was a small ocean; the Atlantic, a large Walden Pond. He referred every minute fact to cosmical laws. Though he meant to be just, he seemed haunted by a certain chronic assumption that the science of the day pretended completeness, and he had just found out that the *savans* had neglected to discriminate a particular botanical variety, had failed to describe the seeds or count the sepals. "That is to say," we replied, "the blockheads were not born in Concord; but who said they were? It was their unspeakable misfortune to be born in London, or Paris, or Rome; but, poor fellows, they did what they could, considering that they never saw Bateman's Pond, or Nine-Acre Corner, or Becky Stow's Swamp; besides, what were you sent into the world for, but to add this observation?"

Had his genius been only contemplative, he had been fitted to his life, but with his energy and practical ability he seemed born for great enterprise and for command; and I so much regret the loss of his rare powers of action, that I cannot help counting it a fault in him that he had no ambition. Wanting this, instead of engineering for all America, he was the captain of a huckleberry-party. Pounding beans is good to the end of pounding empires one of these days; but if, at the end of years, it is still only beans!

Emerson's ironies are as beautiful here as anywhere, and their dialectical undersong is wholly in Thoreau's favor. Henry Ford, a fervent and overt Emersonian, engineered for all America; and clearly Emerson himself, like many among us, would have preferred Thoreau to Ford, and a huckleberry-party to a car factory.

III

Thoreau's crucial swerve away from Emerson was to treat natural objects as books, and books as chunks of nature, thus evading all literary tradition, Emerson's writings not excepted. Unfortunately, Thoreau was not really an oppositional or dialectical thinker, like Emerson, though certain an oppositional personality, as the sane and sacred Emerson was not. Being also something of a prig and an elitist, again unlike Emerson, Thoreau could not always manage Emerson's insouciant praxis of building up a kind of Longinian discourse by quoting amply without citation. Self-consciousness kept breaking in, as it rarely does with Emerson, unless Emerson wills it thus. But, if you cannot achieve freedom in quotation, if you cannot convert the riches of others to your own use without a darkening of consciousness, then what can it mean to demand that books and natural objects interchange their attributes? *Walden*, for all its incessant power, is frequently uneasy because of an unspoken presence, or a perpetual absence that might as well be a presence, and that emerges in Thoreau's Journal:

> Emerson does not consider things in respect to their essential utility, but an important partial and relative one, as works of art perhaps. His probes pass one side of their center of gravity. His exaggeration is of a part, not of the whole.

This is, of course, to find the fault that is not there, and qualifies only as a weak misreading of Emerson. Indeed, it is to attribute to Emerson what is actually Thoreau's revision of Emerson, since it is Thoreau who considers things as books, not Emerson, for whom a fact was an epiphany of God, God being merely what was oldest in oneself, that which went back before the Creation-Fall. Emerson, like the considerably less genial Carlyle, was a kind of Gnostic, but the rebel Thoreau remained a Wordsworthian, reading nature for evidences of a continuity in the ontological self that nature simply could not provide.

Thoreau on "Reading" in *Walden* is therefore chargeable with a certain bad faith, as here in a meditation where Emerson, the Plato of Concord, is not less than everywhere, present by absence, and perhaps even more absent by repressed presence:

> I aspire to be acquainted with wiser men than this our Concord soil has produced, whose names are hardly known here. Or shall I hear the name of Plato and never read his book? As if Plato were my townsman and I never saw him,—my next neighbor and I never heard him speak or attended to the wisdom of his words. But how actually is it? His Dialogues, which contain what was immortal in him, lie on the next shelf, and yet I never read them. We are under-bred and low-lived and illiterate; and in this respect I confess I do not make any very broad distinction between the illiterateness of my townsman who cannot read at

all, and the illiterateness of him who has learned to read only what is for children and feeble intellects. We should be as good as the worthies of antiquity, but partly by first knowing how good they were. We are a race of tit-men, and soar but little higher in our intellectual flights than the columns of the daily paper.

It is not all books that are as dull as their readers. There are probably words addressed to our condition exactly, which, if we could really hear and understand, would be more salutary than the morning or the spring to our lives, and possibly put a new aspect on the face of things for us. How many a man has dated a new era in his life from the reading of a book. The book exists for us perchance which will explain our miracles and reveal new ones. The at present unutterable things we may find somewhere uttered. These same questions that disturb and puzzle and confound us have in their turn occurred to all the wise men; not one has been omitted; and each has answered them, according to his ability, by his words and his life. Moreover, with wisdom we shall learn liberality. The solitary hired man on a farm in the outskirts of Concord, who has had his second birth and peculiar religious experience, and is driven as he believes into silent gravity and exclusiveness by his faith, may think it is not true; but Zoroaster, thousands of years ago, travelled the same road and had the same experience; but he, being wise, knew it to be universal, and treated his neighbors accordingly, and is even said to have invented and established worship among men. Let him humbly commune with Zoroaster then, and, through the liberalizing influence of all the worthies, with Jesus Christ himself, and let "our church" go by the board.

The wisest man our Concord soil has produced need not be named, particularly since he vied only with Thoreau as a devoted reader of Plato. The second paragraph I have quoted rewrites the "Divinity School Address," but with the characteristic Thoreauvian swerve towards the authority of books, rather than away from them in the Emersonian manner. The reader or student, according to Emerson, is to consider herself or himself the text, and all received texts only as commentaries upon the scholar of one candle, as the title-essay of *Society and Solitude* prophesies Wallace Stevens in naming that single one for whom all books are written. It may be the greatest literary sorrow of Thoreau that he could assert his independence from Emerson only by falling back upon the authority of texts, however recondite or far from the normative the text might be.

One can read Thoreau's continued bondage in *Walden*'s greatest triumph, its preternaturally eloquent "Conclusion":

> The life in us is like the water in the river. It may rise this year higher than man has ever known it, and flood the parched uplands; even this may be the eventful year, which will drown out all our muskrats. It was not always dry land where we dwell. I see far inland the banks which the stream anciently washed, before science began to record its freshets. Every one has heard the story which has gone the rounds of New England, of a strong and beautiful bug which came out of the dry leaf of an old table of apple-tree wood, which had stood in a farmer's kitchen for sixty years, first in Connecticut, and afterwards in Massachusetts,— from an egg deposited in the living tree many years earlier still, as appeared by counting the annual layers beyond it; which was heard gnawing out for several weeks, hatched perchance by the heat of an urn. Who does not feel his faith in a resurrection and immortality strengthened by hearing of this? Who knows what beautiful and winged life, whose egg has been buried for ages under many concentric layers of woodenness in the dead dry life of society, deposited at first in the alburnum of the green and living tree, which has been gradually converted into the semblance of its well-seasoned tomb,—heard perchance gnawing out now for years by the astonished family of man, as they sat round the festive board,—may unexpectedly come forth from amidst society's most trivial and handselled furniture, to enjoy its perfect summer life at last!
>
> I do not say that John or Jonathan will realize all this; but such is the character of that morrow which mere lapse of time can never make to dawn. The light which puts out our eyes is darkness to us. Only that day dawns to which we are awake. There is more day to dawn. The sun is but a morning star.

The first of these paragraphs echoes, perhaps unknowingly, several crucial metaphors in the opening pages of Emerson's strongest single essay, "Experience," but more emphatically Thoreau subverts Emerson's emphasis upon a Transcendental impulse that cannot be repressed, even if one sets out deliberately to perform the experiment of "Experience," which is to follow empirical principles until they land one in an intolerable, more than skeptical, even nihilistic entrapment. Emerson, already more-than-Nietzschean in "Experience," is repudiated in and by the desperately energetic, indeed apocalyptic Transcendentalism of the end of *Walden*, an end that refuses Emersonian (and Nietzschean) dialectical irony. But the beautiful, brief final paragraph of *Walden* brings back Emerson anyway, with an unmistakable if doubtless involuntary allusion to the rhapsodic conclusion of *Nature*, where however the attentive reader always will hear (or overhear) some acute Emersonian ironies. "Try to live as though it were morning" was Nietzsche's great admonition to us, if we were to become Overmen, free of the superego. Nietzsche was never more Emersonian than in this, as he well knew. But when Thoreau eloquently cries out: "The sun is but a morning star," he is not echoing but trying to controvert Emerson's sardonic observation that you don't get a candle in order to see the sun rise. There may indeed be a sun beyond the sun, as Blake, D. H. Lawrence, and other heroic vitalists have insisted, but Thoreau was too canny, perhaps too New England, to be a vitalist. *Walden* rings out mightily as it ends, but it peals another man's music, a man whom Thoreau could neither accept nor forget.

ETHEL SEYBOLD

Thoreau: The Quest and the Classics

I

PROTEUS

"The fact is I am a mystic, a transcendentalist, and a natural philosopher to boot."

Criticism has given us no integrated interpretation of Thoreau. Certain of his friends and early biographers came close to recognizing him for what he was but they made no statements precise and convincing enough to transmit their information. Nor have other critics been more successful. Too many have been willing to believe that "the whole of Thoreau, the objective and subjective man—is to be found in the two books he saw through the press."[1] Others have read the journals, but usually to "cull out the significant things here and there"[2] to prove their own special theses. And so we have Thoreau in one after another Protean disguise: Thoreau the hermit; Thoreau the naturalist; Thoreau the scholar, student of the classics, of oriental lore, of New England legend and history, of the life of the North American Indian; Thoreau the primitivist, the "apostle of the wild"; Thoreau the man of letters, writer of perfect prose; even Thoreau the walker.

From *Thoreau: The Quest and the Classics*, pp. 1–21. © 1969 by Yale University Press.

Certainly Thoreau appeared in each of these roles, but his life is not explained by any one of them. And when we examine him closely in any one role we find always that he did not quite fit the part, that he exhibited certain peculiar aberrations and deficiencies: a partial, intermittent, temporary hermit, who spent a good part of two years in semiseclusion, who rather liked to eat out, who said of himself even, "I am naturally no hermit";[3] a naturalist whose ornithology was never quite trustworthy and who contributed no new fact of importance to natural history; a scholar who believed that men had a respect for scholarship much greater than its use and spoke of the great reproach of idle learning; a classicist who preferred the agricultural writers to the literary authors; a reader of oriental philosophy who genuinely disapproved of any system of philosophy; a student of New England history who found genealogy ridiculous and the facts of history unimportant; an expert on the North American Indian whose experience came largely from books, from Joe Polis, and from gathering arrowheads while the red man still roamed the West; a primitivist who might talk of devouring a raw woodchuck but who also talked of abstaining from animal food; a man of letters who published little and was relieved when it did not sell; a writer who believed that a man's life was the perfect communication; a walker of whom Emerson said that if he did not walk he could not write but who spent his last months in composition and never even referred to his former outdoor life.

Certainly Thoreau was not basically or primarily any one of these. Was he then simply a Jack-of-all-trades, interested superficially or whimsically in a wide variety of things—or, in more complimentary terms, a man of extreme versatility? For there does not seem at first sight any way to reconcile such apparently divergent interests as his. John King, the classicist, was surprised that a man could love both Homer and nature, and although we may group together the hermit, the primitive, and the Indian lover, what common denominator can we find, say, for the classics and the North American Indian? In the face of such difficulties it has become a habit for scholars to conclude that Thoreau is an enigma and his life full of paradoxes. Yet judgment revolts against that conclusion. If we know Henry Thoreau at all, we are convinced that there was no contradiction within the man himself and that he lived no aimless life of shifting interest and activity, but that here was a man with a purpose in his life, one who knew what he was about and who went steadily and persistently about it.

He spoke often of the value and necessity of a serious occupation. He knew himself seriously occupied and was annoyed that others did not seem to realize it. His working hours were inviolable. Why should a huckleberry party feel that he had leisure to join the excursion simply because he was not shut up in a school room?[4] Could not his friends understand the impossibility of interrupting his work in order to visit them? "Not that I could not enjoy such visits, if I were not otherwise occupied. I have enjoyed very much my visits to you ... and am sorry that I cannot enjoy such things oftener; but life is short, and there are other things also to be done."[5] Especially as he grew older did he feel the shortness of life and the pressure of work. "I have many affairs to attend to, and feel hurried these days."[6]

These affairs were part of a single, lifelong enterprise. In "Life without Principle," completed in the last year of Thoreau's life, he gave testimony to the fact that he had known what he would do with his life even before he was of proper age to carry out his project. Marveling again that men could often have supposed him idle and unoccupied, available for their trivial undertakings, he corrected the error: "No, no! I am not without employment at this stage of the voyage. To tell the truth, I saw an advertisement for able-bodied seamen, when I was a boy, sauntering in my native port, and as soon as I came of age I embarked."[7]

But for what port, or by what route, is not so clearly stated. Thoreau referred obliquely and mysteriously to the nature of his enterprise in such public announcements as *The Week* and *Walden*: "I cut another furrow than you see,"[8] and "If I should attempt to tell how I have desired to spend my life in years past, it would probably surprise those of my readers who are somewhat acquainted with its actual history; it would certainly astonish those who know nothing about it. I will only hint at some of the enterprises which I have cherished."[9]

He would have liked to tell the world what he was doing, had it been possible: "... there are more secrets in my trade than in most men's, and yet not voluntarily kept, but inseparable from its very nature. I would gladly tell all that I know about it, and never paint 'No Admittance' on my gate."[10] Certainly he tried hard enough to communicate with his friends. He was even willing, he said, "to pass for a fool" in his "desperate, perhaps foolish, efforts to persuade them to lift the veil from off the possible and future, which they hold down with both their hands, before their eyes."[11] Communication involves comprehension as well as expression.

It was, as we should expect, only in the private record of the journal that Thoreau made a plain statement of his business in life. He had been asked by the Association for the Advancement of Science to state that branch of science in which he was particularly interested. He complained that he would not be taken seriously were he to make a public confession.

> ... I felt that it would be to make myself the laughing-stock of the scientific community to describe ... that branch of science ... inasmuch as they do not believe in a science which deals with the higher law. So I was obliged to speak to their condition and

describe to them that poor part of me which alone they can understand. The fact is I am a mystic, a transcendentalist, and a natural philosopher to boot. Now that I think of it, I should have told them at once that I was a transcendentalist. That would have been the shortest way of telling them that they would not understand my explanations.[12]

He was right in saying that the scientists would not understand him if he called himself a mystic, a transcendentalist, and a natural philosopher. Burroughs even misunderstood the last term, assuming that Thoreau meant naturalist or natural historian, which was certainly not his thought, as anyone who has read the endless distinctions between poet and scientist in the journals of the 1850's should know. But Thoreau might well have widened the class of scientists, for often as these words have been quoted, many earnest students of Thoreau are still refusing to take them earnestly. We regard them as an instance of Thoreau's perversity and exaggeration, qualities always to be dealt with in trying to find Thoreau. Or, identifying transcendentalism with Hawthorne's mist, moonshine, and raw potatoes, we simply refuse to believe that anyone who seems as practical and down to earth as Thoreau could be in any real sense transcendental. But Thoreau was not afraid to wear the label or to defend the faith, even to defend its practicality. He talks about lecturing on the subject of reality "rather transcendentally treated."[13] He understands that people complain that his lectures are transcendental, but he comments caustically that if you call a lecture "Education" the audience will pronounce it good, while if you call it "Transcendentalism" the same audience will find it moonshine.[14] As for his outward appearance of practicality, he warns that it cannot be trusted; pushed too far, "I begin to be transcendental and show where my heart is."[15] And in more serious vein he asserts repeatedly that the practicality of the world is delusion and the so-called impracticality of the poet, the philosopher, the transcendentalist is the only true practicality. The values of the banker are subject to fluctuation; the poet's values are permanent. Who would be willing to "exchange an absolute and infinite value for a relative and finite one,—to gain the whole world and lose his own soul!"[16]

It is worth noting that Thoreau calls John Brown a practical man and a transcendentalist: "A man of rare common sense and directness of speech, as of action; a transcendentalist above all, a man of ideas and principles,—that was what distinguished him. Not yielding to whim or transient impulse, but carrying out the purpose of a life."[17]

But probably the major obstacle in the way of our accepting Thoreau's own definitive statement of himself is that the word "transcendentalist" does not constitute for us a definition. It says either too little or too much. There were, of course, all degrees and grades of transcendentalists just as there are all varieties of Christians. We classify as Christians all those who profess a Protestant or Catholic faith; we apply the term to good men, churchgoers, those who abstain from the major vices. So do we classify as transcendentalists all to whom transcendentalism meant nothing more than a new and hopeful view of life, permitting them to substitute a god of love for a god of wrath, the dignity of the soul for natural depravity, conscience for law, and the warm sense of personal conviction for the emptiness of the unknown and unknowable. We think of "Christian" specifically in connection with the professionally religious: ministers, Sunday-school superintendents, missionaries. In the same way when we say "transcendental" we think at once of such leaders of the movement as Emerson and Alcott, preachers and missionaries of the faith, those who wrote the sermons and carried the gospel into the wilderness of the West. Used in such ways the terms must be rejected as definitive or identifying; they are only vaguely descriptive.

Both words have, however, real meanings, meanings which we almost never use because they seem to us impossibilities. Thoreau spoke of the wide gap between the accepted and the real meanings of the word "Christian" and of the difficulty of finding a real Christian. "It is not every man who can be a Christian," he said, "even in a very moderate sense ..."[18] And speaking of the New Testament, the embodiment of Christian doctrine, he commented thus:

> I know of no book that has so few readers. There is none so truly strange, and heretical, and unpopular. To Christians, no less than Greeks and Jews, it is foolishness and a stumbling block. There are, indeed, severe things in it which no man should read aloud more than once. "Seek first the kingdom of heaven." "Lay not up for yourselves treasures on earth." "If thou wilt be perfect, go and sell that thou hast, and give to the poor, and thou shalt have treasure in heaven." "For what is a man profited, if he shall gain the whole world, and lose his own soul? Or what shall a man give in exchange for his soul?" Think of this, Yankees! "Verily, I say unto you, if ye have faith as a grain of mustard seed, ye shall say unto this mountain, Remove hence to yonder place, and it shall remove; and nothing shall be impossible unto you." Think of repeating these things to a New England audience! ... They never *were* read, they never *were* heard.[19]

Where is the Christian who does these things? Where is the man who believes enough to practice? Call a man a Christian in this sense, and no one will credit the statement.

So we have refused again and again to credit Thoreau's statement that he was a transcendentalist. In one sense it means nothing; in another it is incredible; we ignore it. We are no different in this respect from his friends, who consistently ignored and denied the significance of his life, insisting on seeing "parts, not wholes." Alcott said of him, "He is less thinker than observer; a naturalist in tendency but of a mystic habit, and a genius for detecting the essence in the form and giving forth the soul of things seen."[20] But the terms are in reverse order; Thoreau was a mystic first and a naturalist second.

Sanborn could see all the parts of Thoreau and refuse to state the whole: "... Thoreau, though a naturalist by habit, and a moralist by constitution, was inwardly a poet ... His mind tended naturally to the ideal side."[21] "Thoreau's business in life was observation, thought, and writing, to which last, reading was essential."[22] Such statements are reminiscent of one of Thoreau's own: "Have not we our everlasting life to get? and is not that the only excuse at last for eating, drinking, sleeping, or even carrying an umbrella when it rains?"[23] His friends could see him eating, drinking, sleeping, even carrying the familiar umbrella through the woods, but they could not perceive that he was "getting his everlasting life." They could say that the business of his life was reading, observation, thought, and writing; they could recognize him as naturalist, poet, mystic; but they refused, even in that credulous and optimistic time, to add up the terms. They, like us, did not believe in real Christians or real transcendentalists.

But it was in the real meaning of the term that Thoreau called himself a transcendentalist. He said it as one might say, "I am a bricklayer." It was the occupation of his days and the pattern of his life. He was that rare phenomenon, a practitioner of his faith. "*Philosophia practica est eruditionis meta,*" he quoted, "Philosophy practiced is the goal of learning ..."[24] And again, "We are shown fair scenes in order that we may be tempted to inhabit them, and not simply tell what we have seen."[25] Transcendental doctrine showed him fair scenes and he meant to dwell in them. He made in *Walden* a clear distinction between himself and his fellow transcendentalists in his distinction between philosophers and professors of philosophy.

> There are nowadays professors of philosophy, but not philosophers.... To be a philosopher is not merely to have subtle thoughts, nor even to found a school, but so to love wisdom as to live ... a life of simplicity, independence, magnanimity, and trust. It is to solve some of the problems of life, not only theoretically, but practically.[26]

Why should not a man's faith determine his work? Newspaper editors might think John Brown insane because he believed himself divinely appointed for his work, but

> They talk as if it were impossible that a man could be "divinely appointed" in these days to do any work whatever; as if vows and religion were out of date as connected with any man's daily work ...[27]

What is more urgent for any man than the attainment of the great and certain promises?

> Yet the man who does not betake himself at once and desperately to sawing is called a loafer, though he may be knocking at the doors of heaven all the while, which shall surely be opened to him.[28]

Why should it be impossible for a man to *know*?
Surely, we are provided with senses as well fitted to penetrate the spaces of the real, the substantial, the eternal, as these outward are to penetrate the material universe.[29]

The truth, the quite incredible truth about Thoreau, the truth that we resist in spite of his own repeated witness, is that he spent a quarter of a century in a quest for transcendent reality, in an attempt to discover the secret of the universe. It is, after all, a matter only of belief. If one believed that the riddle could be solved, the mystery penetrated, the secret laid bare, who would choose to remain in ignorance? Thoreau believed; he accepted the conditions;[30] he claimed the promises. He had the map to the hidden treasure, and his whole life was spent in the search. Only when we see him and his life in this light do the pieces of the puzzle fall into place; his divergent interests are reconciled and all his paradoxes are resolved by the simple fact of his transcendentalism.

It is unnecessary to be scholarly or philosophical about transcendentalism. We are not concerned with its sources, system, and influences; only with its general pattern in New England in Thoreau's time. The best place to find what transcendentalism meant to its followers is the *Dial*,[31] the little family journal, the quarterly round robin which held them all together, which sounded the message of encouragement to the initiate and the advertisement of hope to the rest of the world. Thoreau expressed what the *Dial* meant to him in a letter to Emerson written from New York in 1843: "I hear the sober and the earnest, the sad and the cheery voices of my friends, and to me it is a long letter of encouragement and reproof; and no doubt so it is to many another in the land."[32]

The message it carried to its readers was simple, and simply and fervently, although somewhat repetitiously, stated. It proclaimed belief in an all-good Creator who wished to be accessible to all his creatures, who made no special revelations to special groups, entrusting the truth to any exclusive religion or philosophy, but who kept the channel of communication open from himself to every soul. The soul was able of itself to recognize and communicate with the Spirit of which it was made, to perceive the infinite and absolute, to understand its own relation "to all being and all eternity." Since every soul must possess this power, it was not a matter of sense perception or of logic or intellect but a matter of intuition. Man had only to seek God in solitude, reverence, and faith in order to find him. Every man was potentially a mystic.

Within man himself, then, lay all the answers, but not in man alone. Man was only part of the creation, and the pattern and principles of the universe existed in every part, had so existed always and everywhere, in the commonest phenomenon of nature and the smallest unit of matter. Essentially nature never changed, and if man would know the secret of the universe he had only to observe her "visible aspects." Insight and sympathy would show him "the unseen in the visible, the ideal in the actual," the real and eternal creation behind the apparent and temporary. He who so observed and discovered might be called a natural philosopher. But whether through mysticism or through nature, when a man discerned "the open secret of the universe" he then became "a prophet, a seer of the future," and his utterance was inspired. The word "prophet" was synonymous with the word "poet." Poet or prophet possessed not only "the gift of insight" but "the faculty of communication, instruction, persuasion ... a profound faith, and earnest eloquence ..." Not only did the poet know, but it was his function to speak.

There have been such men in all ages, men who perceived truth and transmitted it. Moses was such a man to the Hebrews, and Orpheus and Homer to the Greeks and "through them to all modern civilization." The great books of all cultures contain the fragments and glimpses of truth revealed to their authors. Yet, however valuable these may be as guides, the final test of truth lies in the individual soul. Every man should be poet.

When we try the pattern to Thoreau, it fits.

A hermit? Not at all; but one who needed solitude, the solitude that was the primary requirement of the poet, the solitude essential for the mystic state in which revelation comes. This insistence upon solitude was so characteristic of youthful transcendentalists that Emerson expressed a mild regret that so many promising young people should feel the necessity of withdrawal and retreat.[33] It was so much a commonplace of the times that it made the plot of Ellery Channing's half-autobiographical narrative, *The Youth of the Poet and the Painter*, in which the hero, like his author, escapes from college and establishes himself in a rural retreat, to the bewilderment of his devoted but conventional family and to his own great satisfaction.[34] This epistolary novel was published in the *Dial* during the year when Thoreau was doing much of the editing and may possibly have given energy to his already expressed desire to withdraw to Walden. Not a hermit, but a mystic.

Not a naturalist, but a natural philosopher. Thoreau was very jealous of the distinction and expressed it over a period of many years at great length and in a variety of ways. "Man cannot afford to be a naturalist," he announced flatly, "to look at Nature directly, but only with the side of his eye. He must look through and beyond her."[35] Emerson contributed much to Thoreau's reputation as a naturalist, but Emerson did not know very clearly what a naturalist was; and Burroughs, who did know, also knew that Thoreau was not one.

> Emerson says Thoreau's determination on natural history was organic, but it was his determination on supernatural history that was organic.... Thoreau was not a born naturalist, but a born supernaturalist.... The natural history in his books is quite secondary.... He was more intent on the natural history of his own thought than on that of the bird.... he was looking too intently for a bird behind the bird—for a mythology to shine through his ornithology.[36]

Burroughs knew that Thoreau was looking for something, but being no more a natural philosopher than Emerson was a naturalist, he was never quite certain what it was: "He cross-questions the stumps and the trees as if searching for the clue to some important problem, but no such problem is disclosed.... In fact, his journal is largely the record of a search for something he never fully finds ..."[37]

He was searching, of course, for that true and ideal world of which this is but the reflection, and Burroughs made a more accurate statement than he perhaps realized when he said, "Natural history was but one of the doors through which he sought to gain admittance to this inner and finer heaven of things."[38]

Scholarship was another door, for the utterances of other poets and prophets were the third avenue to truth. Histories, chronologies, traditions were all "written revelations."[39] Some poet might already have found, might at any time find, what he had missed.

> The book exists for us, perchance, which will explain our miracles and reveal new ones. The at present unutterable things we may find somewhere uttered. These same questions that disturb and puzzle and confound us have in their turn occurred to all the wise men; not one has been omitted; and each has answered them, according to his ability, by his words and his life.[40]

The last phrase is also significant. The lives of great men were as interesting to Thoreau as their books. He wished to know how they lived. In fact, he seemed often to investigate a man's life before he read his works; the commonplace books record biography before they record quotation.

But books were not only "the simplest and purest channel by which a revelation may be transmitted from age to age";[41] they served a second use, as a check on one's own experience. The poor hired man who had had "his second birth and peculiar religious experience" might know that Zoroaster, "thousands of years ago, travelled the same road and had the same experience," and might thus be assured of the authenticity and universality of his own.[42] Thoreau himself spoke of searching books for confirmation of the reality of his own experiences.[43]

Thoreau's reading, aside from that in natural history, falls into certain clearly marked categories: the Greek and Latin classics, the oriental scriptures, the English poets, New England history and legend, data on the North American Indian, and early accounts of travel, adventure, and exploration. It would be difficult to say in which field he read most or which he enjoyed most, but anyone who has read *Walden* will be aware that he valued the classics most. "For what are the classics but the noblest recorded thoughts of man? They are the only oracles which are not decayed, and there are such answers to the most modern inquiry in them as Delphi and Dodona never gave."[44]

The oriental scriptures also had a high place in his esteem. They, like the classics, were required reading for the transcendentalist, and one of Thoreau's chores for the *Dial* was the arrangement of collections of oriental quotations and sayings. Their elements of mysticism and contemplation naturally appealed to him; but probably the source of their greatest interest for him was the same as it was in the case of Orpheus and Homer—their antiquity. "They seem to have been uttered," he said, "with a sober morning prescience, in the dawn of time."[45]

All antiquities had a great attraction for Thoreau. They seemed to him not so much old as early, not so far removed from the present as near to the beginning. There is, to be sure, a slight inconsistency between the belief that all things are everywhere and always the same and the suspicion that the further back you are in time, the closer you are to reality. But that suspicion was always with Thoreau. He fancied that the message shone a little clearer in the beginning.

English poetry he found derivative, imitative, and tame, lacking "the rudeness and vigor of youth." It was characteristic that he should approve Chaucer most, since he might be regarded as "the Homer of the English poets" and "the youthfullest of them all."[46] But despite his extensive reading in the field and his frequent quotation, he was more inclined to be critical than admiring, going so far even as to wonder whether he might not have contracted a lethargy from his attempt to read straight through Chalmers' *English Poets!*[47]

Thoreau's concern with the primitive was only another manifestation of his interest in antiquities. Primitive man is not necessarily old in time, but he is young in nature, which amounted to the same thing for Thoreau. He was delighted to find in Maine a man living "in the primitive age of the world, a primitive man.... He lives three thousand years deep into time, an age not yet described by poets. Can you well go further back in history than this?" he asks.[48] Therien, the woodchopper, fascinated him, as did Rice, the mountaineer, and Joe Polis, the Indian guide, descendant of still more primitive man. As the early man must have been closer to his Creator and to direct revelation, so the primitive or natural man must be closer to nature and to natural insight. Thoreau said of the Indian, "By the wary independence and aloofness of his dim forest life he preserves his intercourse with his native gods, and is admitted from time to time to a rare and peculiar society with Nature. He has glances of starry recognition to which our saloons are strangers."[49]

Thoreau found the same satisfaction in the study of the early history of the American colonies. When he read such books as John Smith's *General Historie of Virginia* he thought himself "in a wilder country, and a little nearer to primitive times."[50] Reading Wood's *New England's Prospect*, he remarked, "Certainly that generation stood nearer to nature, nearer to the facts, than this, and hence their books have more life in them."[51]

He believed that the truest accounts of things were given by those who saw them first,[52] and for that reason he enjoyed the early naturalists, explorers, and travelers. Within himself he tried to feel the sensations of earlier man and earlier times. He cultivated his own wildness. The scent of the Dicksonia fern translated him to the Silurian Period.[53] The sight of a toadstool carried him "back to the era of the formation of the coal-measures—the age of the saurus and pleiosaurus and when bullfrogs were as big as bulls."[54] He might become one with God through the mystic trance; he might become one with nature by surrendering himself completely to natural influences, by becoming himself a primitive man.

He was trying always to get back to the beginning of things, to "anticipate, not the sunrise and the dawn merely, but, if possible, Nature herself!"[55] There surely he would find the answer. The last years of his life found him reading Herodotus and Strabo, the one commonly classified as a historian, the other as a geographer, but he did not read them for the history of nations or the geography of countries; he read them for the history of the human race and the geography of the globe. That was as far back as he could go.

Thoreau's philological interests should be classified as scholarly. He made charts of the language families; he collected dictionaries of foreign languages, even Rasle's dictionary of the Abenaki tongue; he spoke often of the value of language training; his writing is full of speculation about word derivation and meaning, classical, Anglo-Saxon, French, Indian. But he was very skeptical about the learning of languages per se; his interest in words and languages was transcendental, semantic rather than etymological:

> Talk about learning our *letters* and being literate! Why, the roots of *letters* are *things*. Natural objects and phenomena are the original symbols or types which express our thoughts and feelings ...[56]

> As in the expression of moral truths we admire any closeness to the physical fact which in all languages is the symbol of the spiritual, so, finally, when natural objects are described, it is an advantage if words derived originally from nature, it is true, but which have been turned (*tropes*) from their primary signification to a moral sense, are used ...[57]

With Emerson's little diagram in his head and a dictionary—more often Latin than any other language—in his hand, he went looking for spiritual facts.

Not a writer merely—but a poet, he who receives and communicates the truth. The paradox of a man of letters who published so little is solved. If all that a man writes must be truth, his production will be limited. In his youth Thoreau felt very strongly the poet's obligation to make his report: "An honest book's the noblest work of man. It will do the world no good, hereafter, if you merely exist, and pass life smoothly or roughly; but to have thoughts, and write them down, that helps greatly."[58]

Thoreau's endless revision served two purposes: to clarify his thoughts and experiences in his own mind, reducing them to their essence, and to eliminate rather than to achieve style. This also was transcendental conviction: "... the matter is all in all, and the manner nothing at all."[59] So strenuously did he try to reduce the communication to essentials that he could finally say, "the theme is nothing, the life is everything."[60] This idea that the life, the force, the vitality which the communication carried was all important is very close to Thoreau's speculation whether truth was not simply sincere being and living its only perfect communication.

A walker? Yes, but not so much a walker in Walden Woods as a saunterer to the Holy Land. In "Walking" it was not the physical act which was his subject. "We would fain take that walk, never yet taken by us through this actual world, which is perfectly symbolical of the path which we love to travel in the interior and ideal world ..."[61] His walking was the material manifestation of his journey through life, his quest for "the other world" which was, as he said, "all my art."[62]

And so at last we see him whole: Thoreau, practicing transcendentalist. His solitude, his natural history, his scholarship, his writing, his walking were not ends but instruments. He forged them well and kept them sharp, but he frequently laid down one to pick up another, and he used them practically and efficiently toward one end only and without concern for other uses which they might serve.

If we cannot believe either Thoreau's repeated statements or the evidence of our own logical demonstration, we have another and better proof, that which Thoreau considered the perfect communication: the life of the man himself. "Some men's lives are but an aspiration, a yearning toward a higher state, and they are wholly misapprehended until they are referred to, or traced through all their metamorphoses."[63] There is only one way to trace Thoreau's life and that is through the journals. If we have misapprehended the life it is quite possibly because we have misapprehended the journals. They are not notebooks from which the best has been extracted. They are not, as Burroughs would have them, "merely negative," without human interest, a mass of irrelevant details. They are not, intrinsically, *Early Spring in Massachusetts*. They are a man's spiritual autobiography, a "record of experiences and growth,"[64] addressed to himself and to the gods.[65] "Is not the poet bound to write his own biography?" he asks, "Is there any other work for him but a good journal?"[66]

It is not a "circumstantial" journal, one that deals with fact and deed, with the trivia of everyday life, but a "substantial" one of truth and thought; yet not the truth and thought of the public documents, modified, simplified, and presented as conclusions, but truth and thought in the process of evolution. In the journal we can follow Thoreau on every step of his expedition, through one experiment after another, accumulating evidence, testing theories, building hypotheses. We can see him hopeful, disappointed, successful, desperate, acquiescent.

We can follow him better if we adopt for our use one of the instruments by which he implemented his investigation. It would be difficult to say which of these was his favorite, which he used most, or which he found most efficient. Probably he would have considered the mystic state the truest means of discovering reality, and quite likely he would have placed the study of nature second. But mysticism belonged largely to the period of his youth, and his recorded observation of nature especially to the decade after Walden. If we choose one of these we cannot use it to full advantage throughout his life. There was a tool, however, a phase of his scholarship, which he used in youth and in age and to the value of which he gave frequent enthusiastic testimony, both public and private; this was his classicism. There were intervals in his life, it is true, when he did not read in the classics, but these were intervals when he was not actively engaged in the quest, when it seemed to him either that he might have reached his goal or that he had lost his way. The classics seem never to have been absent from his thought.

Thoreau's classicism recommends itself for our use not only for these reasons but also because it has not been so thoroughly analyzed as have most of Thoreau's other channels of investigation. It has, indeed, usually been either exaggerated or ignored. Thoreau's contemporaries, out of their admiration for him and their ignorance of the classics, and possibly because of their failure to recognize his real distinction and their eagerness to create a distinction for him, made for him impossible claims, crediting him with reading the works of authors whose works exist only in scattered fragments in secondary sources and assuming that he read and admired every work which he even mentioned. Later critics, no doubt bewildered by a man who considered flour, sugar, and lard luxuries but regarded the *Iliad* as a necessity, have been content to leave the subject alone and to generalize vaguely from the statements of their predecessors.[67] It will be instructive, therefore, to make some preliminary examination of the nature, scope, and quality of Thoreau's classicism.

We have already said the fundamental thing about the purpose of Thoreau's classical reading: that the classics were to him the most pertinent and valuable source of past revelation. It is possible to identify most of the classical works which Thoreau either owned or read not only by author and title but even by exact edition;[68] and it is possible through a study of his classical quotation, reference, and comment to discover what authors and subjects he found of special interest, what ideas and concepts appealed to him, and what influence the classics left upon his writing.[69] In brief summary we can say here that his postcollege reading fell generally into three periods.

The first was a literary period; he began by rereading authors which he had read in college and by making little explorations into fields suggested by that reading. Among the Greeks he read Homer[70] and Orpheus;[71] the Greek lyrists, especially Anacreon and Pindar; in drama, Aeschylus' *Prometheus Bound* and *Seven against Thebes*. He investigated also Plutarch's *Lives* and *Morals*, Jamblichus' *Life of Pythagoras*, and Porphyry's *On Abstinence from Animal Food*. Among the Latin authors he read Vergil, Horace, Persius, and Ovid. In the second period, after Walden, in the early 1850's, he made the acquaintance of the agricultural writers, Cato, Varro, Columella, and Palladius, and confined himself to them with two exceptions, Sophocles' *Antigone* and a brief excursion into Lucretius. He did no new reading in Greek during this period.[72] In the late 1850's he discovered the early naturalists—the Roman Pliny and among the Greeks, Aristotle, Theophrastus, and Aelian. His last reading was in Herodotus and Strabo.[73]

Such reading is not standard classical fare; it is a personal selection directed toward Thoreau's special purpose. The basis of selection is not so obvious in the first period as in the later ones, but the young investigator had to begin where he was with what he knew. He was misled also by general literary ambition during the *Dial* days, but he quickly eliminated certain authors who did not fulfill his requirements. Persius he found lacking in the true poetical qualities, and he referred to his reading of Persius as "almost the last regular service which I performed in the cause of literature."[74] He wished that Pindar were "better worth translating."[75] Homer and Orpheus had for him the common attraction of their antiquity, Orpheus of an immeasurable antiquity. Each had besides his special attraction: Orpheus, mysticism; Homer, myth and nature. The Greek lyrics appealed to him simply as music, fine, remote, delicate, the true accompaniment of true poetry, the music of the spheres, the singing of the blood, the ringing in the ears, the harmony to which the universe was tuned. Plutarch's *Lives* and the plays of Aeschylus appealed to his admiration of the heroic, a strong transcendental characteristic. Jamblichus and Porphyry, from their neo-Platonic character, were required reading for all transcendentalists. Ovid Thoreau apparently read for the mythology and Vergil for his nature descriptions, for his representation of man's primitive closeness to the soil, and for his picture of the pastoral age, the Golden Age of the world.

The reading of the last two periods is self-explanatory, with the possible exceptions of Lucretius and the *Antigone* of Sophocles. Lucretius attempted in his poem, *De rerum natura*, the same thing that Thoreau was attempting, an explanation of the universe, and it was reasonable that Thoreau should be curious about it; but Lucretius' materialistic explanation could never interest a transcendentalist, and Thoreau found out of the first two hundred lines only two which interested him—a flaming description of the heroic Prometheus.[76]

The *Antigone*, however, cannot be so summarily dismissed. Although other classical works left much more specific quotation and reference in Thoreau's writing, the *Antigone* is probably responsible for one whole section of Thoreau's thought and public expression. From it must have come his concept of the divine law as superior to the civil law, of human right as greater than legal right. Its concepts lie behind the body of Thoreau's writing on government and politics; it is implicit in "Civil Disobedience" and in the articles on John Brown.

Other works yielded Thoreau minor images and symbols, figures, and myths that occur again and again in his writing: Homer's woodchopper, Anacreon's cricket with its earth song; the *oestrus*, stinging to frenzy Io, men, and poets, and perhaps only a grub after all; Vergil's swelling buds and evening cottage smoke, the fable of Apollo and Admetus.

Much has been said of the influence of the classics on Thoreau's prose style. Latinity produces prolixity as often as it does compactness; involution as often as clarity. Thoreau's compactness and clarity are probably the result of his innumerable revisions; his Latinity is obvious, if at all, in his accuracy of word usage and perhaps in his neat and precise pronoun reference. But Thoreau could write in classical fashion when he chose to do so; he was a clever imitator of individual styles. He wrote four exquisite little Orphics, two versions of the poem "Fog," and two others, "Smoke" and "Haze."[77] They consist of the usual series of imaginative epithets addressed to some natural phenomenon but they have somewhat more body and solidity than the Greek Orphics. To these should be added the mad Orphic extravaganza to his moon-sister Diana,[78] the really lovely little Vergilian pastoral of the beautiful heifer[79] with all its fragmentary forerunners and reflections in the journal, and that delightful Catonian essay on "How to Catch a Pig."[80] Successful imitations indicate thorough familiarity with the models.

Although Thoreau believed that works should be read in the language in which they were written, he did not do all his classical reading in the original. He read some of the Greek texts in Latin translations; Aristotle in Greek and French. He read English translations also, although these were few.[81] He read a number of books which, although not classics, were written in the Latin language, such books as the Latin Linnaeus and the Latin Gray. It is quite obvious that his Latin is better than his Greek, but it is also obvious that his Greek is adequate, adequate enough to enable him to compare information from different sources and to make cross references from one text to another.

Both the Latin and the Greek vocabularies are on the tip of his tongue, although Latin oftener than Greek. Once he forgets the Greek word for "waves" and has to substitute "sea" for it;[82] still he calls those same waves "social, multitudinous," ἀνήριθμον.[83] Running water reminds him of the Greek word ἔαρ;[84] the konchus tree makes him think of κόγχη,[85] and he starts speculating on a possible connection between the two.

We have spoken of this continual speculation on the origin, meaning, and relation of words in connection with the transcendental theory of language. Thoreau's philology seems fairly dependable. He allows his imagination to raise rather fanciful suggestions but he is careful not to make incorrect statements. He was quite aware of the pitfalls which philology offers to the amateur and once commented that the chief difference between an educated lecturer and one who had not had the advantages of formal education was that the educated man would "if the subject is the derivation of words ... maintain a wise silence."[86]

Thoreau's translations from the classical languages into English show both his facility with the languages and the transcendental bias which colored all his study. The major translations, those of Aeschylus, Pindar, and Anacreon, belong to the literary period and partake of the nature of literary exercises. The *Prometheus Bound*[87] is very literally and exactly and unimaginatively rendered; word order is sometimes painfully preserved. There have been worse translations of the play, but Thoreau's does not rise above what it purported to be: a faithful and literal transcript. The Pindar and Anacreon selections are more poetically done. Even though the Pindar was announced as a literal translation, there are passages of nature description and of heroism which are beautiful and stirring:

> With the javelin Phrastor struck the mark;
> And Eniceus cast the stone afar,
> Whirling his hand, above them all,
> And with applause it rushed
> Through a great tumult;
> And the lovely evening light
> Of the fair-faced moon shone on the scene.[88]

Thoreau achieved here the economy and clarity of phrase of the Greek.

The Anacreon translations, taken as a whole, are the best of the published ones; Thoreau seems to have caught in them what he called their chief merit, "the lightness and yet security of their tread."[89] They are at the same time both literal and free, faithful to both the precision and the luxurance of the originals.

Thoreau polished his translations in much the same way that he polished his English prose. We see the finished product in publication, but in a discarded manuscript fragment of the journal there exists Thoreau's work sheet for the translation of Ovid's version of the Phaethon story, showing many revisions, deletions, insertions, substitutions.[90] In the manuscript Thoreau worked through the whole story; only a few lines of it appeared in print.[91]

But the printed translations were meant for publication, and they necessarily answer with varying degrees of excellence certain orthodox standards of accuracy and fidelity to source. It is in the fragmentary translations scattered throughout Thoreau's works that we see what his own standards of translation were. The snowflake simile from the *Iliad* is an excellent illustration. As most readers will recall, Homer is comparing the battle of the Achaeans and the Trojans to a snowstorm. The passage runs like this:

> And as flakes of snow fall thick on a winter's day, when the counselor Zeus rouses himself to snow, revealing these arrows to men, and he lulls the winds, and showers down the flakes steadily until he has covered the tops of the high mountains and the headlands, and the meadows and the fertile fields of man; yes, and the harbors and the shores of the gray sea, too, though the beating waves wash it away, but all other things are clothed with the snow when the fury of Zeus drives it on; so from both sides the stones flew thick, both on the Trojans and from the Trojans upon the Achaeans, as they hurled them at each other, and the tumult rose up over the wall.[92]

This is what Thoreau does with it:

> The snowflakes fall thick and fast on a winter's day. The winds are lulled, and the snow falls incessant, covering the tops of the mountains, and the hills, and the plains where the lotus tree grows, and the cultivated fields. And they are falling by the inlets and shores of the foaming sea, but are silently dissolved by the waves.[93]

It is beautiful poetry, reminiscent both of Alcman's "Night" and of Goethe's "Night Song," both of which Thoreau may quite possibly have known.[94] But the interesting thing about it is that Thoreau has taken from the original only what spoke to him. He has stripped the passage of circumstance, all that was local and temporal and particular, and has kept only the universal. A battle between the Achaeans and the Trojans is a trivial matter, but the blanketing peace of the snow is an eternal reality.

When Thoreau read and translated for himself, he was not at all concerned with fidelity to the original; he was not concerned with verb tenses or with completeness of content. As he omitted, so he patched, putting together into one context widely separated lines.[95] He wanted the heart of the matter. And to a transcendentalist the heart of the matter was what answered to a man's individual genius. The prophet from the past spoke his revelation, but each man weighed the revelation in his own heart and accepted that which was for him. A very slight extension of this practice permits a man to read his own meaning into another's words. Thoreau once remarked that he suspected that the Greeks were commonly innocent of the meanings attributed to them;[96] he made a much more definite statement to that effect about the Orientals. Speaking of the Rig Veda, he said that it meant "more or less as the reader is more or less alert and imaginative," and added, "... I am sometimes inclined to doubt if the translator has not made something out of nothing,—whether a real idea or sentiment has been thus transmitted to us from so primitive a period." But he considered the matter quite unimportant, "for I do not the least care where I get my ideas, or what suggests them."[97]

It was a philosophy like this which enabled him not only to select from the classics whatever he wanted but even to read into the classics ideas which were strictly his own. Of Anacreon's poems he made the remarkable statement that "they are not gross, as has been presumed, but always elevated above the sensual."[98] The statement is possibly half true, depending upon the definition of "sensual"; certainly their exquisite expression elevates them above the sensual in the most unfavorable meaning of the word, but just as certainly their whole basis is sensual in any meaning of the word, and only a very innocent mind could deny it.

Horace and Persius Thoreau deliberately mistranslated, knowing quite well that the lines meant one thing as Horace and Persius wrote them but finding a second meaning more acceptable to himself.[99]

Certainly Thoreau was a classicist; he was competent in language and grammar; his reading was wide; his translation was dependable according to his purpose. But he was not a classicist for the sake of classicism. He was a classicist, just as he was a naturalist or a hermit or a writer, only because and as far as his classicism furthered his search for reality. It was only as the classics were related to the quest that they had meaning and value for Thoreau.

NOTES

1. William Lyon Phelps, *Howells, James, Bryant, and Other Essays* (New York, Macmillan, 1924), p. 79.

2. John Burroughs, "Another Word on Thoreau," *The Last Harvest* (Boston and New York, Houghton Mifflin, 1922), p. 148.

3. *Writings*, ii, 155.

4. *Ibid.*, xviii, 333; journal of September 16, 1859.

5. *Ibid.*, vi, 353; letter to Daniel Ricketson, November 4, 1860.

6. *Ibid.*, xviii, 344; journal of September 24, 1859.

7. *Ibid.*, iv, 460.

8. *Ibid.*, i, 54.

9. *Ibid.*, ii, 28.

10. *Ibid.*

11. *Ibid.*, xv, 495; journal of July 29, 1857.

12. *Ibid.*, xi, 4; journal of March 5, 1853.

13. *Ibid.*, vi, 189; letter to T. W. Higginson, April 2–3, 1852.

14. *Ibid.*, xix, 145; journal of February 13, 1860. See also *ibid.*, xiii, 197.

15. *Ibid.*, viii, 228; journal of June 7, 1851. See also *ibid.*, vi, 32, 81.

16. *Ibid.*, vi, 216; letter to Harrison Blake, February 27, 1853. See also *ibid.*, xx, 283–4.

17. *Ibid.*, iv, 413; "A Plea for Captain John Brown."

18. *Ibid.*, iv, 445; "The Last Days of John Brown."

19. *Ibid.*, i, 73–4; *The Week*.

20. *The Journals of Bronson Alcott*, ed. Odell Shepard (Boston, Little, Brown, 1938), p. 318: journal of July 3, 1850.

21. F. B. Sanborn, *Henry D. Thoreau*, ed. Charles Dudley Warner, "American Men of Letters Series" (Boston and New York, Houghton Mifflin, 1891), p. 284.

22. *Ibid.*, p. 300.

23. Writings, vi, 214; letter to Harrison Blake, February 27, 1853.

24. *Ibid.*, iv, 344; "Thomas Carlyle and his Works."

25. *Ibid.*, xvi, 202; journal of November 24, 1857.

26. *Ibid.*, ii, 16.

27. *Ibid.*, iv, 436; "A Plea for Captain John Brown."

28. *Ibid.*, x, 433; journal of December 28, 1852.

29. *Ibid.*, ii, 412; *The Week*.

30. The conditions were solitude, poverty, and the public opprobrium of failure and possibly of insanity. See *Writings*, viii, ii: "Referred to the world's standard, the hero, the discoverer, is insane, its greatest men are all insane." One of the reasons we have been slow to admit the truth about Thoreau is that it seems to us the equivalent of calling him "insane."

31. Read particularly "The Editors to the Reader," *Dial*, Vol. i, No. 1 (July, 1840); "Prophecy—Transcendentalism—Progress," *ibid.*, Vol. ii, No. 1 (July, 1841); and Emerson's "Lectures on the Times," *ibid.*, Vol. iii, Nos. 1–3 (July, October, 1842; January, 1843). The summary and all quoted phraseology come from these articles.

32. Writings, vi, 94; letter to Emerson, July 8, 1843.

33. "The Transcendentalist," *Dial*, iii, No. 1, 303–4.

34. *Dial*, Vol. iv, Nos. 1–4 (July, 1843–April, 1844).

35. *Writings*, xi, 45; journal of March 23, 1853.

36. John Burroughs, "Henry D. Thoreau," *Indoor Studies* (Boston and New York, Houghton Mifflin, 1893), and "Another Word on Thoreau," *The Last Harvest, passim*.

37. *Ibid.*

38. Burroughs, "Henry D. Thoreau," *op. cit.*, p. 33. Burroughs' antecedent for "inner and finer heaven of things" is vague. It seems to be "supernatural history."

39. *Writings*, ii, 342; *Walden*.

40. *Ibid.*, ii, 120; *Walden*.

41. *Ibid.*, vii, 370; journal of 1845.

42. *Ibid.*, ii, 120; *Walden.*

43. *Ibid.*, viii, 307; journal of July 16, 1851.

44. *Ibid.*, ii, 112; *Walden.*

45. *Ibid.*, vii, 277; journal of August 30, 1841. For slight variant of this statement see *ibid.*, i, 155; *The Week.*

46. *Ibid.*, x, 395, 393; *The Week.*

47. *Ibid.*, ii, 285; *Walden.*

48. *Ibid.*, iii, 87; "Ktaadn."

49. *Ibid.*, i, 55; *The Week.*

50. *Ibid.*, x, 494; journal of February 23, 1853.

51. *Ibid.*, xiii, 109; journal of January 9, 1855.

52. *Ibid.*, xv, 232; journal of January 27, 1857.

53. *Ibid.*, xviii, 346–7; journal of September 24, 1859.

54. *Ibid.*, xi, 271; journal of June 18, 1853.

55. *Ibid.*, ii, 19; *Walden.*

56. *Ibid.*, xviii, 389; journal of October 16, 1859.

57. *Ibid.*, xix, 145; journal of February 15, 1860.

58. *Ibid.*, vi, 31; letter to his sister Helen, January 23, 1840.

59. *Ibid.*, ix, 86; journal of November 1, 1851.

60. *Ibid.*, xv, 121; journal of October 18, 1856.

61. *Ibid.*, v, 216–17.

62. *Ibid.*, i, xxiii; Emerson in his biographical sketch of Thoreau quotes him as saying in his youth, "The other world is all my art: my pencils will draw no other; my jackknife will cut nothing else ..."

63. *Ibid.*, ix, 71; journal of October 14, 1851.

64. *Ibid.*, xiv, 134; journal of January 24, 1856.

65. *Ibid.*, xvii, 120; journal of August 23, 1858; ix, 107; vii, 206–7.

66. *Ibid.*, xvi, 115; journal of October 21, 1857.

67. Clarence Gohdes, "Henry Thoreau, Bachelor of Arts," *Classical Journal*, xxiii (February, 1928), 323 ff., and Norman Foerster, "The Intellectual Heritage of Thoreau," *Texas Review*, ii (April, 1917), 192 ff., have made commendably factual, although brief and general, statements on Thoreau's classicism.

68. Appendix A of this work contains bibliographical identification of the classical books which it is known that Thoreau either owned or read. Identification of each book is accompanied by a description of content and by any information available on the disposition of the book after Thoreau's death or on its present location. Books are arranged chronologically in the order of Thoreau's acquisition or use, which is also the general order of their discussion in the text. The reader is urged to consult Appendix A for specific information on any classical book mentioned in the text as used or owned by Thoreau.

69. Appendix B of this work lists and identifies quotation in the published works of the major classical authors which Thoreau read. It includes quotation from Thoreau manuscript when such quotation adds anything to the knowledge of Thoreau's classicism. Authors are arranged alphabetically, and the quotations are arranged chronologically by date of use. The reader is urged to refer to this appendix for more specific and complete information than is admissible to text discussion.

Appendix C is a classical index to the published works of Thoreau. The reader can, by using this index, locate all classical translation, quotation, or reference made by Thoreau in the twenty volumes of his *Writings.*

70. How much reading Thoreau did in the *Odyssey* is debatable. It was the *Iliad* which he studied at Harvard, and it is the *Iliad* from which nearly all his references and quotations come. While in college he withdrew from the library an English translation of both the *Iliad* and the *Odyssey* (see App. A, No. 24); but his only quotation from the *Odyssey* (see App. B, "Homer") occurs in "Wild Apples" and is almost certainly taken from a secondary source; his references (see App. C) would not necessarily involve reading. The current popularity of the *Odyssey* as a source of literary themes did not prevail in Thoreau's time.

71. Orpheus was regarded by the Greeks as one of the inventors of music and poetry. He was mentioned as early as the sixth century B.C. as a historical rather than a mythological figure. A number of poems were attributed to him and collected by later writers. These, dating at least as far back as the fifth century, were collected along with a far greater number of Alexandrine forgeries under Orpheus' name and were until recently accepted as the genuine productions of one man. It was this collection of largely spurious items, now known as the pseudo-Orpheus, which Thoreau read.

72. Thoreau had read the *Antigone* at Harvard and had probably reread it by 1849. This would constitute a third reading.

73. The reader is reminded that such generalized information as the above may be made complete and specific by the use of the appendices.

74. *Writings*, i, 327; *The Week*.

75. *Ibid.*, vi, 102; letter to Emerson, August 7, 1843.

76. *Ibid.*, xiv, 312; journal of April 26, 1856.

77. *Collected Poems of Henry Thoreau*, ed. Carl Bode (Chicago, Packard, 1943), pp. 27, 56, 59, 150.

78. *Writings*, viii, 78; journal of 1850.

79. *Ibid.*, viii, 67–8; journal of September, 1850.

80. *Ibid.*, xv, 260; journal of February 15, 1857.

81. Consult App. A for descriptions of classical books translated into other languages.

82. *Writings*, xii, 247; journal of May 8, 1854.

83. *Ibid.*, xvi, 127; journal of October 26, 1857.

84. *Ibid.*, ix, 363; journal of March 29, 1852.

85. *Ibid.*, iii, 120; "Chesuncook."

86. *Ibid.*, xix, 83; journal of January 8, 1860.

87. *Ibid.*, v, 337–75.

88. *Ibid.*, v, 378; Pindar, *Olympia* 10, 85–92.

89. *Writings*, i, 239; *The Week*.

90. *Huntington Journal Fragments* (HM13182).

91. *Writings*, viii, 144–5; journal of 1851.

92. Homer, *Iliad*, xii, 278–89.

93. *Writings*, vii, 61; journal of October 24, 1838; also iii, 181–2, "A Winter Walk."

94. Thoreau owned two books (App. A, Nos. 37, 40) which included the poems of Alcman. He did not mention Alcman or quote from him. He also read extensively in Goethe, but he made no mention of this lyric.

95. See App. B, "Horace," for an example of this. See his treatment of the last two chapters of Tacitus' *Agricola* in "After the Death of John Brown," *Writings*, iv, 452–4, as an example of taking liberties with classical text.

96. *Writings*, xvi, 227; journal of December 27, 1857.

97. *Ibid.*, xiv, 135; journal of January 24, 1856.

98. *Ibid.*, i, 240; *The Week*.

99. This is discussed and illustrated in Chap. ii.

JOHN HILDEBIDLE

Naturalizing Eden:
Science and Sainthood in Walden

The late essays of Thoreau demonstrate that he had not lost his conviction that the methods of the scientist were both personally congenial to him and of great use in the transcendent tasks he wished to accomplish. Scholars who argue that one can, by viewing Thoreau's work chronologically, see a growing negativism in his attitude toward science, seem to miss his basic consistency. Thoreau is always aware of the limits of science; and in his last years he seems especially aware of the possibility that the decay of the modern world will leave the schooled eye with nothing worth observing. But he also maintains the belief that training the observer in a recognizably scientific way, and through recognizably scientific means, is a task of fundamental importance.

So much can be learned from looking at those of his works which announce themselves as being about the data of natural history—leaves, fruits, seeds, trees. The role of natural history in his more elaborate and more wide-ranging works is, not surprisingly, more complex. The limitations of science, in Thoreau's view, arise not just because of the threat of extinction or the weakness of any single route to understanding the full and ultimately mystical richness of nature. He is certain that there are states of consciousness concerning which science has no relevance, and to which science contributes little insight. His task, then, would seem to be to teach mankind enough science so that they could, in the end, move beyond science into that condition

From *Thoreau: A Naturalist's Liberty*, pp. 97–125. © 1983 by the President and Fellows of Harvard College.

of Transcendental elevation or sainthood which is his great goal and the particular focus of his greatest work. To the saint, science is of little use. But Thoreau knows, all too painfully, that this elevated state is not the normal condition of man, not even of Transcendental man, in this fallen world. In the day-to-day fallen state, natural history has very great importance, as a discipline which prepares the mind for blessedness, as a means of finding those mystical facts which may provoke blessedness, and as a vehicle for describing the pursuit of blessedness. This distinction between two radically different states of being tends to produce the apparent paradox of a Thoreau who is an antiscientific scientist.

Sherman Paul summarizes Thoreau's attitude in the late journals as a "steadfast rejection of science."[1] The odd thing about Paul's argument is that it seems to develop toward an exactly opposite conclusion. Having allowed that Thoreau's science was "merely a discipline to the end of greater familiarity"—a qualification, I think, which deserves more than a passing notice—Paul goes on to assert, not a rejection of science, but the *usefulness* of science to Thoreau:

> Instead of signifying his failure, his reliance on science signified a greater maturity and success: to be scientific for Thoreau was not to abandon the ultimate poetic use of the fact, but to be public and objective. He was driven by his studies to know the entire natural environment, and in this great labor, science was an economy ... His science, his insistence on accuracy, was also an act of social faith; he was a "natural historian" because he used science in the way he did history.[2]

How this squares with a "steadfast rejection of science" is not at all apparent. But it is clear that at the center of the problem lies the issue of method, of finding or devising a way in which the potentially overwhelming "multitude of detail" which comprises "the entire natural environment" can be observed, learned, understood, and used. "Why do precisely these objects which we behold make a world?" is one of Thoreau's central questions in *Walden* (p. 225). It cannot be answered until some certainty is attained about the existence and nature of those objects, and some reliable vantage point is reached from which to behold them. And both preliminary problems can at least be attacked, if not solved, by using the supposedly objective and disciplined methods of science.

Paul, however, insists that Thoreau rejected from the first even the *method* of the naturalist: "This is not to say that the method of the naturalist is a bad method, but rather that for Thoreau it was the wrong method, and that his distrust of it, indeed the guilt he felt in consciously employing it, banished the 'presence' that he hoped to find."[3] "Distrust" is a fair word for it; but the distrust need not necessarily lead to repudiation. In "The Natural History of Massachusetts" Thoreau remarks, "What an admirable training is science for the more active warfare of life!" (*Excursions*, 106). And, lest we think that he means science only in "the most comprehensive sense possible," he goes on to observe how even such a particular and specialized science as "entomology extends the limits of being in a new direction" (p. 107). There is always in Thoreau a strong element of the notion (heretical, for a native of Puritan New England) that insight, and along with it redemption, are earned. To get to know beans requires hours of hoeing; and the value of "an admirable training" is not therefore to be dismissed lightly. But science offers as well something less onerous and demanding: "I would keep some book of natural history always by me as a sort of elixir" (p. 105).

The significant fact is that the value of science does not, to Thoreau, depend ultimately upon the accuracy or even the inherent interest of the scientific source. He acknowledges in his review that the books he considers "are such as imply more labor than enthusiasm ... measurements and minute descriptions, not interesting to the general reader" (*Excursions*, 129–130). Thoreau can "detect several errors ... and a more practiced eye would no doubt expand the list" (p. 130). But still he reads the books, and others like them; and still he finds a value there. Much has been made of the fact that Thoreau's review very nearly ignores entirely the volumes which are its supposed subject—a peculiar way to evaluate even the dullest book. But what the essay does, again and again, is demonstrate exactly how to *use* volumes of natural history. The pattern is represented by the following passage:

> It appears from the report that there are about forty quadrupeds belonging to the State, and among these one is glad to hear of a few bears, wolves, lynxes, and wildcats.
>
> When our river overflows its banks in the spring, the wind from the meadows is laden with a strong scent of musk, and by its freshness advertises me of an unexplored wilderness. (*Excursions*, 114)

The paragraph proceeds, rather fitfully, to a consideration of muskrats and some word-play involving the Musketaquid River. The connection between the list of quadrupeds which Thoreau finds in the report and the sight of a muskrat swimming across the Concord River is, at first glance, so tenuous as to be nearly nonexistent; and indeed, even by Thoreau's standards, "The Natural History of Massachusetts" is hardly a model of careful and effective transition. But the connection is there: the reading of natural history leads Thoreau inevitably back to thinking about his own observations of nature. It is in this way that facts, even in dull written form, can teach; as later Thoreau finds a "singular fact" in the "Report on Invertebrate Animals ... which teaches [him] to put a new value on time and space" (*Excursions*, 129). Science, then, teaches us to look ("Nature will bear the closest inspection," p. 107), even if late in his life Thoreau's journal records at times his worry that he is looking too closely, too "microscopically."[4] Science, however, provides at the same time the opportunity for transcendence of that realm of fact with which science is normally concerned. The essay is, in part, an assertion of the former value of science, and a demonstration of the latter.

Thoreau is, however, unequivocal on one point; while the facts stored up by natural history may teach, nature itself is the better teacher: "Nature has taken more care than the fondest parent for the education and refinement of her children" (*Excursions*, 124). Whatever the virtues of measurements and minute descriptions, "Nature is mythical and mystical always" (p. 125). The essay rests on a final distinction between science (the discipline and method) and true science, science in its broadest, its etymological and Transcendental sense, which is a state of consciousness: "The true man of science will know nature better by his finer organization; he will smell, taste, see, hear, feel, better than other men"[5] (p. 131).

The same distinction is to be found in the body of the essay. Thoreau begins by observing that "books of natural history make the most cheerful winter reading" (*Excursions*, 103). But later he insists that, even in winter when observation is most trying and uncomfortable, it is better to observe than to read: "In the winter, the botanist need not confine himself to his books and herbarium, and give over his outdoor pursuits, but may study a new department of vegetable physiology, what may be called crystalline botany, then" (p. 126). Cheerful reading has its limits; and he who is willing (not, we notice, by abandoning, but rather by extending the name and method of the scientist) to go beyond "the accession of health" to be found in the written "reminiscences of luxuriant nature" (p. 103) will find not only something worth observing at first hand, but in fact something fundamental. In crystals, the botanist will discover a new and indeed a more profound science: "Vegetation has been made the type of all growth; but as in crystals the law is more obvious, their material being more simple, and for the most part more transient and fleeting, would it not be as philosophical as convenient to consider all growth, all filling up within the limits of nature, but a crystallization more or less rapid?" (p. 128).

That the distinction between natural history and nature itself, between the sciences and true science, is fundamental to Thoreau is of course not in question. But that this distinction rests on the assumption that the more ordinary sciences are in any way to be rejected as invalid or wrong, seems to be a considerable overstatement of the case. It is this early essay, we remember, that closes by praising even the pioneer who raises no flowers. As he grew older, Thoreau seems to have found increasingly frequent occasion on which to wonder if perhaps he himself could do no more than sow the seeds of another man's crop; and thus it is not surprising that he seemed at times restless and unsatisfied to be no more than a natural historian. But he never completely lost the conviction that science provided at least a vehicle of approach to the "mystical and mythical." Indeed at times he seems to have found in the very materials of science an almost magical transforming power. Here, late in his life, he considers the value of scientific names:

> How hard one must work in order to acquire his language,— words by which to express himself! I have known a particular rush, for instance, for at least twenty years, but have ever been prevented from describing some of its peculiarities, because I did not know its name nor anyone in the neighborhood who could tell me it. With the knowledge of the name comes a distincter recognition and knowledge of the thing. That shore is now more describable, and poetic even. My knowledge was cramped and confined before, and grew rusty because not used,—for it could not be used. My knowledge now becomes communicable and grows by communication. I can now learn what others know about the same thing. (*Journal*, XI, 137; 29 Aug. 1858)

Even allowing for its roots in Part IV of Emerson's *Nature*, the emotional force of the passage seems in excess of its explicit meaning. Precisely how the learning of the name of the plant enlarges Thoreau's ability to describe its peculiarities is not at first clear. But the tremendous importance placed on the finding of names, which at first seems a violation of the kind of calm and objectivity we expect of the scientist, has its roots in naturalism as well as in Transcendentalism. We remember Linnaeus assigning the task of naming as one of the most important obligations of the natural historian; Michel Foucault has argued that this unwavering interest in the correct *words*, the names of things, is a crucial and determining step in the very origins of natural history as a science.[6] What is clear in this case is the importance not only of observing, but of recording and communicating that observation—Thoreau had *known* the plant for years, but now he can describe it and make that description communicable; and it is science that allows the expression.

Perhaps it was his difficulty in establishing a form by which he could fully express, in a generally useful way, the knowledge he spent those last years assembling, that led Thoreau to doubt his accustomed methods. But he had long been aware that there were states of consciousness to which science had no apparent applicability. A long journal entry dating from 1851 attempts to pin down the condition of mind and soul which represents the final leap beyond any mundane science:

> July 16. Wednesday. Methinks my present experience is nothing; my past experience is all in all. I think that no experience which I have to-day comes up to or is comparable with, the experiences of my boyhood. And not only this is true, but as far back as I can remember I have unconsciously referred to the experiences of a previous state of existence. "For life is a forgetting," etc. Formerly, methought, nature developed as I developed, and grew up with me. My life was ecstasy. In youth, before I lost any of my senses, I can remember that I was all alive, and inhabited my body with an inexpressible satisfaction; both its weariness and its refreshment were sweet to me. This earth was the most glorious musical instrument, and I was audience to its strains. To have such sweet impressions made on us, such ecstasies begotten of the breezes! I can remember how I was astonished. I said to myself,—I said to others,—"There comes into my mind such an indescribable, infinite, all-absorbing, divine, heavenly pleasure, a sense of elevation and expansion, and I have nought to do with it. I perceive that I am dealt with by superior powers. This is a pleasure, a joy, an existence which I have not procured myself. I speak as a witness on the stand, and tell what I have perceived." The morning and the evening were sweet to me, and I led a life aloof from the society of men. I wondered if a mortal had ever known what I knew. I looked in books for some recognition of a kindred experience, but, strange to say, I found none. Indeed, I was slow to discover that other men had had this experience, for it had been possible to read books and to associate with men on other grounds. The maker of me was improving me. When I detected this interference I was profoundly moved. For years I marched as to a music in comparison with which the military music of the streets is noise and discord. I was daily intoxicated, and yet no man could call me intemperate. With all your science can you tell me how it is, and whence it is, that light comes into the soul? (*Journal*, II, 306–307; 16 July 1851)

Leaving aside for the moment Thoreau's reference to science, the last sentence is a clear restatement, similar in syntax and imagery as in import, of one of the central questions of Romanticism: "Whither is fled the visionary gleam?" It is indeed surprising to find Thoreau claiming that his search in books for "some recognition of a kindred experience" proved unavailing, since he himself acknowledges by misquotation the work which seems most directly to demonstrate "some recognition of a kindred experience," Wordsworth's "Ode: Intimations of Immortality." But in place of the continuous falling away from glory which Wordsworth describes, Thoreau suggests an extended and apparently unchanging, if now lost, state of consciousness: "*For years I marched,*" he says, employing a metaphor more familiar in its present-tense version in *Walden*, "as to a music in comparison with which the military music of the streets is noise and discord." The ecstasy is recurrent ("I was *daily* intoxicated"); and it is this elevated state—I will call it Transcendental Sainthood—for which science has no explanation.

Elsewhere Thoreau makes it clear that the state of elevation and expansion is not inevitably lost as one grows older. In an 1841 letter to Isaiah Williams, Thoreau insists on the possibility of "a revelation fresher and director than that" in the New Testament "if any soul look abroad even today" (*Correspondence*, 52; 8 Sept. 1841). In *Walden*, which I take to be Thoreau's most elaborated account of this blessed condition, Thoreau twice recalls youthful visits to the pond; neither case supports the contention that "my present experience is nothing; my past experience is all in all" (*Walden*, 175 and 191). *Walden* as a whole is, to borrow Emerson's term, prospective, full of reawakenings, ranging from that of each morning ("After a partial cessation of his sensuous life, the soul of man, or its organs rather, are reinvigorated each day," (p. 89) to the great reawakening of all Nature in spring ("Walden was dead and is alive again," p. 311). His recasting, from the past to the present tense, of his image of the elevated life as a march is indicative then of the whole course of his thinking.

What is apparent in both the journal and in *Walden* is that to Thoreau there are at least two distinct states of being, the elevated and the fallen, the saintly and quotidian. In the journal entry he locates these two states in time, in the past and the present; in *Walden* he acknowledges that time is not the appropriate framework for such a distinction. In both cases, however, the question that concerns him is, "how it is, and whence it is, that light comes into the soul." More than that, *Walden* takes up the problem of finding adequate expression for the saintly condition. "Heaven speaks, but what language does it use to preach to men?" he had asked, paraphrasing Confucius in 1843 (*Dial*, III, 494; April 1843). His answer then was silence and action; but neither will serve a writer. In *Walden*, as we will see, one of Thoreau's greatest difficulties lies not so much in achieving sainthood, but in preaching from that condition to the fallen state of men around him. The normal means of discourse will not precisely serve, any more than the normal means of accumulating knowledge—science, history—will suffice to explain the nature of sainthood. But Thoreau writes in the everyday world; the condition of sainthood is after all usually silent. As J. L. Shanley has conclusively documented, the account of the holy year was not (as Thoreau repeatedly claimed it was) composed at the time. The journal entry of July 1851 was written in fact very near the time when Thoreau was about to take up his manuscript again, after putting it aside when *A Week* proved such a commercial disappointment.[7] What the experience of writing and rewriting *Walden* seems to have proven to Thoreau is that the pastness of the elevated moment is not altogether a reason to lament. The Transcendental event may be most clear and most comprehensible—and thus most communicable, most useful as literary material—after the fact: "Often I can give the truest and most interesting account of any adventure I have had after years have elapsed, for then I am not confused, only the most significant facts surviving in my memory. Indeed, all that continues to interest me after such a lapse of time is sure to be pertinent, and I may safely record all that I remember" (*Journal*, IX, 311; 28 March 1857).

I have perhaps been overindulgent in applying a religious terminology to the "existence which I have not procured myself." But the suggestion for such terminology lies in Thoreau's own language. In the July 1851 journal entry he shies away from identifying specifically the "superior powers" at work and refuses to dignify the "maker of me" with capitalization. In this way he keeps his feet firmly in the natural and earthly, without necessarily involving the supernatural. But the manner in which his ecstasy is described is both implicitly and explicitly religious. "The morning and the evening were sweet to me" carries a weight of allusive reference to Genesis and to Revelation; and "an indescribable, infinite, all-absorbing, divine, heavenly pleasure" granted by "superior powers" is a state perilously close to an old-style conversion experience.

But if it is religious, the moment lacks a recognizable God. Even if Thoreau's brand of blessedness may at times seem to him to be unprocured, it is usually a clear result of activity and, as Emerson would have it, of self-reliance. Thoreau says (speaking particularly of chastity, "the flowering of man" of which "Holiness, and the like, are but various fruits") that "Nature is hard to be overcome, but she must be overcome" (*Walden*, 219–221). And he could hardly be accused of having that strong and consistent sense of personal inadequacy which is inherent in more traditional (and especially Protestant) descriptions of the Pentecostal moment. In his repeated lists of cardinal virtues in *Walden* he never overlooks simplicity (which is to him an active and deliberate, not a passive and accidental virtue) and never mentions humility.[8] More orthodox writers would agree with him that "the maker of me was improving me" only if they chose to ignore Thoreau's equation of subject and object.

To assert, in any case, that there are transcendent states of consciousness does not resolve the problems of understanding and expressing those states. The July 1851 journal entry, not unexpectedly, will not answer its own questions. If the experience was "improving," why does it leave behind such a sense of present loss? Where, and why, in other words, did the progress stop and the decline begin? Does his youthful sense that "nature developed as I developed, and grew up with me" represent a profound sense of communion, now lost, or a childish solipsism? In *Walden*, being all alive, inhabiting the body with inexpressible satisfaction, takes on a coloring of animality and brutishness—it is closer to the ecstasy of Alek Therien than to Thoreau's. The entry turns, in a way, on the phrase which refers to losing one's senses. Strictly construed, the loss is a bad thing; the true man of science does not lose his senses, and the colloquial meaning of the phrase connects it with simple madness, a loss, rather than a gain, in understanding. But in *Walden* Thoreau considers the profit to be gained by "being beside ourselves in a sane sense," by being "completely lost" as a way of, indeed as a necessary first step toward, appreciating the "vastness and strangeness of Nature" (*Walden*, 135, 171). That is not quite the same as losing one's senses, but it tends that way, and suggests that Thoreau would have us continue to hope for (and not only to lament the loss of) "that light [which] comes into the soul."

It is in relation to this state of elevation and expansion that Thoreau expresses his doubts about the value of science, specifically about the ability of science to offer an explanation of ecstasy. What keeps Thoreau from generalizing this skepticism to a wholesale rejection of "your science" is the awareness that the blessed condition, in which revelation, rather than investigation or explanation, is the operative and informing force, is at best occasional and customarily short-lived, and that it touches only the small number of the Elect. In those periods—July 1851 was apparently one of them—when the light fails, one can at least fall back on the more mundane pursuits of knowledge which, after all, do still constitute "an admirable training ... for the more active warfare of life." Thoreau frames his assertion of his own holiness with a certain Yankee irony, and he too has his times of self-doubt, although usually in a curiously generalized way: "We are conscious of the animal within us, which awakens in proportion as our higher nature slumbers. It is reptile and sensual, and perhaps cannot be wholly expelled; like the worms which, even in life and health, occupy our bodies. Possibly we may withdraw from it, but never change its nature. I fear that it may enjoy a certain health of its own; that we may be well, yet not pure" (*Walden*, 219). Thoreau set himself, as Perry Miller put it, the task of discovering "how to be conscious of the self in a commonplace, prosperous American town"—which I take to be the Transcendental equivalent of living a holy life in a fallen world.[9] Miller cannot, in the end, forgive Thoreau his apparent arrogance: "[He] fought ... to be a partner with the Almighty. Obviously he who strives to play the drama of such arrogance on the solid soil of Massachusetts is heading as recklessly as Tamburlaine or Faust toward catastrophe."[10] One wonders where, precisely, to seek the catastrophe; surely not in "Wild Apples" or the other late essays. Miller misses the degree to which the arrogance was turned against the self; the contemptuous tone of "with all your science" is surely directed as much toward Thoreau himself as toward the world. In any case, the effort toward sainthood, of his own sort, was for Thoreau "a distinct profession," even, as Sherman Paul argues, a vocation.[11]

It was this admittedly and intentionally eccentric sense of profession which contributed as well to Thoreau's refusal to accept at common value the name of scientist or historian. Asked to describe himself for a tenth-year report of his Harvard class, Thoreau insisted on the inadequacy of those professional labels which a more worldly soul might have accepted willingly:

> I don't know whether mine is a profession, or a trade, or what not. It is not yet learned, and in every instance has been practiced before being studied. The mercantile part of it was begun here by myself alone.
>
> —It is not one but legion. I will give you some of the monster's heads. I am a schoolmaster—a Private Tutor, a Surveyor—a Gardener, a Farmer—a Painter, I mean a House Painter, a Carpenter, a Mason, a Day-laborer, a Pencil-Maker, a Glass-paper Maker, a Writer, and sometimes a Poetaster. (*Correspondence*, 186; 30 Sept. 1847)[12]

As at the top of Ktaadn, Thoreau chooses to identify himself with the evil spirits, in this case the demon whose name is Legion (Mark V:1–13). Thoreau declines the honor, not only of a profession, but even of the use of the *word* profession. But we should not let the harsh manner of the letter obscure the fact that he might, on the basis of skill or remunerative employment or, indeed, careful study, have accepted most if not all of the names he lists. His refusal of labels—even, most surprisingly, of the title writer or poet—

represents less a turning away from these "trades or what not" than a clear assertion that he is all these, and more if he wishes.

So too with the name of scientist or historian or natural historian; if he adopts none of them as wholly and all-inclusively his own, still he practices the methods and professions they encompass seriously, in his own way. Hawthorne, who insisted that "Mr. Thorow is a keen and delicate observer of nature—a genuine observer, which, I suspect, is almost as rare a character as even an original poet," also recognized that his then young friend would live "in a way and method of his own."[13] That way would be inclusive, not exclusive; and even "in Arcadia when I was there" (*Walden*, 57), even on the shores of mystic Walden, dead and born again like Christ in the Creed, he could find a way to employ science, if not as a source of explanations, then at least as a mode of inquiry. As a man who knows carpentry and hoeing, Thoreau knows too the proper use of any tool, as of any method—what it will do and what it will not do: "No method nor discipline can supersede the necessity of being forever on the alert. What is a course of history, or philosophy, or poetry, no matter how well selected, or the best of society, or the most admirable routine of life, compared with the discipline of looking always at what is to be seen? Will you be a reader, a student merely, or a seer? Read your fate, see what is before you, and walk into futurity" (p. 111).[14] One of the many peculiarities of *Walden* is that it is a book which carries within it the hope that one day, if it is read properly, it will not need to be read at all.

Thoreau's attitude toward science, then, is not so much a repudiation as it is a constant wariness. Robert Langbaum has remarked that "The Romanticist is not against science. He is merely trying to limit the applicability of its findings."[15] In this regard, as in others, Thoreau is clearly Romantic. In *Walden* he is concerned with the blessed condition and the blessed place—a condition and a place in which the applicability of science is especially limited. The question he had raised in his journal in July 1851 is thus peculiarly relevant: "With all your science can you tell me how it is, and whence it is, that light comes into the soul?" Remarkably enough, the science of natural history is to be found, and even used, in Eden, as a closer look at *Walden* may help to demonstrate.

Thoreau's most direct answer in *Walden* to the "very particular inquiries ... made by my townsmen concerning my mode of life" (p. 3) is this: "I went to the woods because I wished to live deliberately, to front only the essential facts of life, and to see if I could not learn what it had to teach" (p. 90). This combines two tasks in one formula: observation (fronting the facts) and discrimination (fronting only the essential). The nature of living deliberately thus calls directly for the habits of the naturalist, and of course in addition the frame of mind of the mystic. And, since Thoreau sets himself the added task of speaking precisely to and about the condition of "you who read these pages, who are said to live in New England" (p. 4), he must be an evangelist, the effect of whose speech would, in the ideal, be utterly transforming: "There are probably words addressed to our condition exactly, which, if we could really hear and understand, would be more salutary than the morning or the spring to our lives, and possibly put a new aspect on the face of things for us" (p. 107).

This peculiar combination of roles—naturalist, mystic, evangelist—is not an easy one; as mystic, Thoreau distrusts the very methods he must employ as a naturalist. As a preacher, he finds the record of observed phenomena to be, at the least, a useful vehicle of communication; but he also knows that many of the things of which he must speak are incommunicable. He ends up, paradoxically, writing a natural history of Eden, or at least a natural history of bliss.

Repeatedly he insists on the *possibility* of blessedness—"man's capacities have never been measured; nor are we to judge of what he can do by any precedents, so little has been tried" (*Walden*, 10). So much then for authority and received wisdom—"What old people say you cannot do you try and find that you can. Old deeds for old people, and new deeds for new" (p. 8). But it is not, unfortunately, enough to assert the necessity for a new way of life, nor to repeat the virtues of the new dispensation, "simplicity, independence, magnanimity, and trust" (p. 15). Even though the place and the state of salvation are, at bottom, simple, symmetrical, *not* detailed ("Our life is frittered away by detail," p. 91), salvation can, in the present world, only be pursued and described by means of detail—names, measurements, accounts, arithmetic. And as we will see, it is inherent in the kind of resolutely *individual* revelation which Thoreau finds that it cannot be passed on. The most he can hope to offer his readers is the inspiration and reassurance which they may draw from being shown that the goal is attainable and has indeed been attained. At the same time he produces a cautionary record of how difficult the path will be.

Walden is a book, then, that not only contradicts but criticizes itself.[16] Much is made, as I have said, of Thoreau's arrogance, of the Transcendental egotism which allows him to write a saint's life of himself. His apology—"I should not talk so much about myself if there were any body else whom I knew as well" (*Walden*, 3)—is too disingenuous and rather too quickly gotten over to answer the charge satisfactorily. We are dealing with a peculiar kind of sainthood, one which includes among its aspects irony and anger and excludes the note of humility we find more usual and more to our taste. But it is a sainthood which does not insist, indeed does not expect or desire, emulation in any exact way; the arrogance of this saint's manner is in part a prophylaxis against the too easy path of simple imitation. Part of the science of this self-hagiographer is to establish for us the distance we need to observe saintliness safely and productively; there is, as Thoreau remarks in passing while considering the pickerel of Walden, great danger in being translated before our time "to the thin air of heaven" (p. 285).

I use the word saint with no more apology; I read *Walden* as, in part at least, an autobiographical saint's life. We must not take as absolutely true either the assertions we find in it (since many of the most direct and forthright statements in the book are explicitly contradicted elsewhere between its covers) or the often jocular self-deprecation which surrounds some of its most important moments. And we must never lose the paradoxical yardstick of approximation, no matter how many apparently hard, well-documented facts and numbers we find in it. The nature of this kind of sainthood is that it is achievable and definite, if rare, but not quite earnable. It is thus at once deliberate and accidental, procured and providential. And, if it is recurrent (like the rise and fall of Walden Pond, like the movement of seasons from Spring to Spring), it is also, in its recognizable form, passing and largely inexpressible except in the inadequate language of the fallen state. Indeed, the fundamental questions that continually drive Thoreau toward the Pentecostal insight he finds at Walden are a sign of his own fallen nature, his own unnaturalness:

> After a still winter night I awoke with the impression that some questions had been put to me, which I had been endeavoring in vain to answer in my sleep, as what—how—when—where? But there was dawning Nature, in whom all creatures live, looking in at my broad windows with serene and satisfied face, and no question on *her* lips. I awoke to an unanswered question, to Nature and daylight. The snow lying deep on the earth dotted with young pines, and the very slope of the hill on which my house is placed, seemed to say, Forward! Nature puts no question and answers none which we mortals ask. (*Walden*, 282)

The questions about which science has nothing to say (how it is, where it is, whence it is that light comes into the soul) are the questions which trouble this saint. The written answers to such questions will, looked at one way, be yet another second-hand account, an "authority" of sorts, useful only in "homeopathic doses" (p. 167), but useful nevertheless, if used warily. Having early on insisted that experience is invariably preferable to advice (p. 9), and having, as a beginning farmer, refused to be "in the least awed by many celebrated works on husbandry" (p. 55), Thoreau still loses few chances to study, "consulting such authorities as offered" even when he sets out to make bread (p. 62).

The precise connection between human knowledge and revelation, between science and sainthood, is played out in the sequence of chapters from "The Village" to "Baker Farm." The trip begins among the most fallen and moves to and just beyond one of the principal Pentecostal moments in *Walden*, Thoreau's attainment of his halo; at the same time Thoreau proceeds from naturalizing of various sorts to inspiration to attempted evangelism, when he tries to convert the Irishman John Field. The chapters are, in many ways, central in the book; most obviously, the chapter on "The Ponds," the middle of the three we will be considering, is the ninth of the seventeen chapters of *Walden*.

"The Village" follows Thoreau's extended discussion of how he earned his living, in the reformed sense, by hoeing beans, and tells how he spent the resulting "absolutely free" time (*Walden*, 167). We remember how much of *Walden* is intended to show us that we waste time getting and spending. "The Bean-Field" (and, of course, "Economy") demonstrates how little time we really need to fulfill our economic needs. That means we will have more time to spend elsewhere. It is at first surprising to discover that "every day or two [Thoreau] strolled to the village to hear some of the gossip which is incessantly going on there, circulating either from mouth to mouth, or from newspaper to newspaper" (p. 167). Earlier Thoreau had insisted, "I am sure that I never read any memorable news in a newspaper" (p. 94), and "Economy" makes it clear how little sympathy he has for that village in which man "has no time to be anything but a machine" (p. 6), and toward whose expectations he is deliberately antipathetic: "The greater part of what my neighbors call good I believe in my soul to be bad, and if I repent of anything, it is very likely to be my good behavior. What demon possessed me that I behaved so well?" (p. 10). But if we have been paying attention, we also know that Thoreau "love[s] society as much as most." "I am naturally no hermit, but might possibly sit out the sturdiest frequenter of the bar-room, if my business called me thither" (p. 140).

Still, a visit to the village is a visit, as it soon becomes apparent, to a fallen and dead world, the locus and visible sign of the deadening way of life detailed in "Economy." Thoreau goes to Concord as a naturalist: "As I walked in the woods to see the birds and squirrels, so I walked in the village to see the men and boys; instead of the wind among the pines I heard the carts rattle. In one direction from my house there was a colony of muskrats in the river meadows; under the grove of elms and buttonwoods in the other horizon was a village of busy men, as curious to me as if they had been prairie dogs, each sitting at the mouth of its burrow, or running over to a neighbor's to gossip" (*Walden*, 167). How seriously Thoreau intends the polarity suggested here by his talk of two horizons will be made clearer at the beginning of "Baker Farm" when he again walks to a grove of trees, and finds among its flora "the *Celtis occidentalis*, or false elm" (p. 202).[17] That grove, however, contains a shrine, not a village. In the present case, if we know Thoreau's favorite beasts, the polarity is the opposite of what a naive reader might think; the muskrat is an especially well-regarded animal to this naturalist, and village man is not. These brute neighbors might better be prairie dogs. As at John Field's house, where the only order of being explicitly identified as human is the chicken, not the Irish (p. 204), "animal nature" here in Concord is considerably more lively than man. The town has "digestive organs"—but only for news, which, of course, in this Nowhere is no news. The row of worthies Thoreau observes, despite their occasionally "voluptuous" expressions, are no more than stone caryatids (p. 168). The village moves but does not live; its "vitals" are stores, not heart and belly, and the most elaborately described activity—the "gantlet" which Thoreau escapes only "wonderfully" (pp. 168–169)—is, on close inspection, an activity not of men but of houses. The chapter, as it quickly turns out, is, despite its relatively warm and good-humored beginning, not about the village but about escaping from it.[18] The observer, by detailing the landscape of hell, learns how to avoid it. Having investigated the world of "machines" (p. 168), of lines, lanes, traps, and bizarre but clear-cut orderings, a world where the primary sense to be employed by the naturalist is the eye, Thoreau launches himself (the nautical image is his own) into the woods, where the only way to find one's route is to feel with feet and hands (p. 169) and where the "most surprising and memorable, as well as valuable experience" is to be invisible and lost. That experience is available, however, only to the enlightened; the villagers become lost frequently, without apparent gain (p. 170). The moral is clear and clearly pointed: "not till we have lost the world, do we begin to find ourselves" (p. 171). It is the version, in this Transcendental scripture, of the parable of the rich man and the eye of the needle (Matthew XIX: 16–30). The chapter ends, however, not with this text but rather with a very brief account of Thoreau's seizure for taxes—another warning sign of the dangerously entrapping force of the village and of men's "dirty institutions." The only safeguard (like the only means of escape from the gantlet, which was by "keeping my thoughts on higher things" (p. 169)), is to be found in "the virtues of the superior man" (p. 172).

The effect, then, of naturalizing hell is to warn; but what of naturalizing heaven? "The Ponds" is Thoreau's most extended description of Walden itself. He gets there—and away from "human society and gossip"—by proceeding in the mystical direction, westward, and by renewing his direct experience of nature, plucking and tasting blueberries on Fair Haven Hill (*Walden*, 173). Thoreau likes to begin his natural histories with instructive parables rather than facts.[19] Here he tells us of the Cenobitic fisherman, a kind of society less dangerous than the town of Concord; and then he recounts his youthful misunderstanding of Walden, at a time when he could still happily return from its banks to the "haunts of men."

Finally he describes in some detail an instance of escape (*Walden*, 173–175). Again the experience is "memorable and valuable." He leaves a "village parlor" and fishes by night, "partly with a view to the next day's dinner" but, more important, to restore his senses. The fable contains one of the better known moments in *Walden*: that time when, letting his thoughts "wander to vast and cosmogonal themes in other spheres," he has the great luck to "catch two fishes as it were with one hook." A real fish tugs at his line, destined for that next day's supper; a metaphysical one appears in the same moment, a sign of the productive loss of orientation and of the re-establishment of the link to Nature (pp. 174–175).

It is a reminder to us that the true scientist wants both fact and symbol and seeks those best moments when the two spheres meet. Having established a safe context, Thoreau now adopts the full-blown manner of the naturalist: "The scenery of Walden is on a humble scale, and though very beautiful, does not approach grandeur, nor can it much concern one who has not long frequented it or lived by its shore; yet this pond is so remarkable for its depth and purity as to merit a particular description" (*Walden*, 175).[20] The chapter proceeds to prove, and to disprove, this statement, and establishes, in hard detail, both the uniqueness and the symbolic typicality of the place. Nothing could be more matter-of-fact than Thoreau's initial description of the pond: "It is a clear and deep green well, half a mile long and a mile and three quarters in circumference, and contains about sixty-one and a half acres; a perennial spring in the midst of pine and oak woods, without any visible inlet or outlet except by the clouds and evaporation" (p. 175). But because this is Thoreau and not Gilbert White, one immediately begins to subject these facts to a pressure of interpretation. Clarity and depth point directly to the question of finding bottom in "The Pond in Winter" (pp. 282–298). The precision of the measurements here forewarn us about the astounding (and, to the layman's eye, unlikely) symmetry of the pond's shape (p. 289).[21] The question of inlet and outlet is raised again (p. 292) and related to a world-wide transmigration of waters (pp. 297–298); that the only apparent outlet is the sky raises the point that part of Walden's uniqueness is the way in which it *combines* elements into Sky Water (pp. 188–189). Most striking of all is the phrase "perennial spring," for it is the peculiar timelessness of Walden and its recurrent awakening in spring ("Walden was dead and is alive again") that lie at the heart of its symbolic value. The passage is, as promised, a particular description—color, size, shape, volume—as well as an introduction to a whole series of symbolic developments to come. Thoreau proceeds, in the short run, to develop each of the points raised, in proper sequence: color (pp. 176–177); transparency and purity (pp. 177–178); circumference (pp. 178–179); rise and fall, by whatever inlet or outlet (pp. 180–182).

Each step in the fully elaborated description is a repetition of the synthesis of detail and metaphor to be found in the introductory sentences. The question of color, for example, is related directly to known and observable phenomena—effects of light, weather, and distance. But quickly the larger point is established: in science as well as in symbol, the pond is intermediary, since, "lying between the earth and the heavens, it partakes of the color of both." And the pond, even in winter, is the "vivid green" of rejuvenation; so, later, the arrival of spring occurs in a chapter entitled "The Pond in *Winter*." And color, intimately related to vision, allows Thoreau, while describing the precise scientific reasons for Walden's thawing near the shore, to make the pond an Emersonian eyeball: "Such is the color of its iris." The development of that point he saves until a few pages later (p. 186). At the moment, the observation of the pond allows Thoreau to look "with divided vision," and thus to see twice at once, as he had just before in catching his two fish at once and as he will later be able, in puddles, to be beside himself in a sane sense by seeing himself stand on his head (p. 293). Finally, color involves purity, and the purity of this water is part of its ritual, baptismal effect. "The body of a bather" in Walden, unlike that of a bather elsewhere, "appears of an alabaster whiteness." The suggestion of baptism is both a clue and a puzzle; this baptism is, initially at least, "unnatural"—but it is also fruitful in art, "making fit studies for a Michel Angelo."

The color of Walden, then, as it is described by Thoreau, can serve as an exemplification of the way in which the macrocosm of the book is almost entirely contained within the microcosm of a paragraph, and of the way Thoreau proceeds *both* naturalistically and Transcendentally—and, in each case, to much the same point. The accumulation of facts establishes the general case of Walden's uniqueness, and the specific nature of that uniqueness—a task of definition and description, of natural history. But, at the same time, any individual fact, fronted deliberately and imaginatively, generates symbolic understanding. Thoreau insists that it is the *single* fact which will redeem: "When one man has reduced a fact of the imagination to be a fact to his understanding, I foresee that all men will at length establish their lives on that basis" (*Walden*, 11). And a single fact will be the test of our redemption: "If we knew all the laws of Nature, we should need only one fact, or the description of one actual phenomenon, to infer all the particular results at that point" (p. 280). Looked at either way—indeed looked at many ways at once, literally, scientifically, imaginatively, symbolically—the facts lead inexorably to the conclusion that Walden is unique and uniquely instructive,[22] both a mediator ("intermediate ... between land and sky," p. 199) and a standard of measurement ("how much more beautiful than our lives, how much more transparent than our characters," p. 199).

We have had in these two chapters natural history as warning, as a means of insight, and as a source of symbol. Having immersed himself in ponds (as he does, more literally, before daring to venture against the dangers of the village), Thoreau is ready to wander where the transforming spirit might find or follow him. That wandering takes him eventually to Baker Farm, home of, among others, John Field, his brave but slovenly wife, starveling sibylline brats, and chickens. But first he encounters a series of magic places, grove-temples, worthy of Druids and Norse gods (*Walden*, 201). "Baker Farm" begins with a compendium of mysteries—temples built by no human hand, fleets on dry land, Valhalla, and swamp gods, all appearing in one (admittedly long) sentence. At the same time the places are intensely real and detailed. The catalogue includes twenty different plants, each correctly and specifically named (pp. 201–202). As fits such a complex and, initially, puzzling place, it is disturbing and even ominous: "The wild-holly berries make the beholder forget his home with their beauty, and he is dazzled and tempted by nameless other wild forbidden fruits, too fair for mortal taste" (p. 201). That leaves moot the question of whether this is Eden or Lotus-Land; and it makes this place (which is, in good mystical form, many places) a suitable counterweight for the ambiguities of the village, which is also, in its own way, both alluring and dangerous. Unexpectedly, the Pentecostal moment occurs:

> Once it chanced that I stood in the very abutment of a rainbow's arch, which filled the lower stratum of the atmosphere, tinging the grass and leaves around, and dazzling me as if I looked through colored crystal. It was a lake of rainbow light, in which, for a short while, I dived like a dolphin. If it had lasted longer it might have tinged my employments and life. As I walked on the railroad causeway, I used to wonder at the halo of light around my shadow, and would fain fancy myself one of the elect. One who visited me declared that the shadows of some Irishmen before him had no halo about them, that it was only the natives that were so distinguished. Benvenuto Cellini tells us in his memoirs, that, after a certain terrible dream or vision, which he had during his confinement in the castle of St. Angelo, a resplendent light

appeared over the shadow of his head at morning and evening, whether he was in Italy or France, and it was particularly conspicuous when the grass was moist with dew. This was probably the same phenomenon to which I have referred, which is especially observed in the morning, but also at other times, and even by moonlight. Though a constant one, it is not commonly noticed, and, in the case of an excitable imagination like Cellini's, it would be basis enough for superstition. Beside, he tells us that he showed it to very few. But are they not indeed distinguished who are conscious that they are regarded at all? (pp. 202–203)

Thoreau has prepared himself—and us—for this visitation by going carefully over the ground of heaven and hell in the previous chapters. And we must not be misled by the self-deprecation here; this is indeed a visitation, and no mistake. In fact it is two visitations, one accidental, single, and improbable, the second constant and more commonly available. The first—Thoreau's moment at the end of the rainbow—apparently occurs in or near one of the shrines which he has just told us he "visited both summer and winter." It transforms both Thoreau and the whole "lower" world; it distorts his vision, which, as elsewhere, seems to be paradoxically a good thing. And of course, the visible sign is "a *lake* of rainbow light." That he dives like a dolphin suggests both the legend of Arion the poet (and, by extension, of Thoreau the poet) and, perhaps, the Pauline description of God: "In Him we live, and move, and have our being" (Acts XVII:28). By becoming a dolphin Thoreau succeeds in gaining the clearest sign of redemption offered in *Walden*: the confusion of elements. He has already tended this way by seeing the air as crystal; now he continues by identifying himself as an air-breathing water-beast, the only possible being able to survive in a lake of light, or in a pond which is sky-water.

    Rather abruptly, it seems, the moment passes. Thoreau moves on to another experience—a sign of the first having occurred, a kind of stigmatical aura?—the halo around his shadow. The associative links are clear enough, primarily light and Election, but the experiences are not necessarily related, even as phenomena of science. But if we recall Gilbert White's account of the shower of cobwebs or the leper of Selborne, we can at least recognize the familiar pattern of investigation. Thoreau begins with a striking, indeed unique ("*Once* it chanced ...") experience. He then looks abroad for any sort of analogous phenomenon, particularly a recurrent one (thus providing more evidence) and reviews his own experience (which is less susceptible to the distortion of report). The closest parallel to be found—and the initial event is so unusual that neither we nor he should expect a close match—occurs on the railroad causeway. In that way the Pentecostal moment is returned to the literal shores of Walden Pond, and to the very place which, although it is the lair of the "devilish Iron Horse" (*Walden*, 192), is to be the scene of the great final resurrection in "Spring" (pp. 304–309). The natural historian, keeping his mystical side alive by linking the phenomenon, ironically, to Election, finds in the more customary phenomenon the material of reasoned investigation. The sources of information are the expected ones: personal observation, second-hand contemporary report (from "one who visited me"), and historical document.[23] The lesson to be drawn by the naturalist is that the problem is one of observation, not of occurrence; that is, if those who had eyes to see *did* see, the constancy of such visitations would no longer be missed. There is no absence of such moments in the fallen world, but only a failure of fallen consciousness, which sets off the generality of men even from the superstitious souls who misinterpret the halo, but who nevertheless at least know the regard (that is, esteem) which any man could feel.

The passage, which has tried in the manner of the naturalist to separate sense from superstition, ends with a resolution that is also a verbal puzzle. Who is it who *regards* the distinguished few? If the word is taken to mean *observe*, then the observer is either the self (if the distinction is a personal recognition of election) or, perhaps, the world at large. The common run of men regard the saved as at least different, even if they can only see this as eccentricity; so Thoreau played the role of the town eccentric, or worse. That sort of regard is what lead to the writing of *Walden*: "I would not obtrude my affairs so much on the notice of my readers if very particular inquiries had not been made by my townsmen concerning my mode of life, which some would call impertinent" (*Walden*, 3). The sign of redemption seems, then, to be a combination of self-awareness and the wary, indeed often hostile observation of the saint by the lost.[24]

The style of the natural historian provides a vehicle whereby the complexities of the moment can be organized and expressed. Thoreau's description and the lesson he draws from it are, in intention, the least naturalistic points imaginable. The passage combines in a very short space many of the important elements of the book as a whole: sainthood, the railroad, the confusion of elements, the symbolism of limnology, the theme of the productive imprecision of the elevated senses. The visitor who offers Thoreau some information (apparently wrong, since Cellini is no native), raises at the same time the troublesome issue of the Irish (which will crop up again barely a page later when John Field appears) and the question of who is more saved or more redeemable, strangers or natives. The mention of Cellini's finding and recording the same phenomenon far distant in space and time, at first seems to undercut the identification of Walden as the holy place. But in fact the idea that such a visitation can occur even in France (a most fallen land, to judge from Thoreau's hostility to the French in *A Yankee in Canada*) emphasizes again that sainthood is a state of consciousness, and that Walden is a holy place only in the symbolic realm, not necessarily in the physical. Thoreau put the matter squarely in a letter to Isaiah Williams: "It is curious that while you are sighing for New England the scene of our fairest dreams should lie in the west—it confirms in me the opinion that places are well nigh indifferent. Perhaps you have experienced that in proportion as our love of Nature is deep and pure we are independent upon her" (*Correspondence*, 53; 8 Sept. 1841).[25] It is fitting that, wherever they occur, these moments are "especially observed in the morning," the time, throughout *Walden*, of awakening in both the physical and the spiritual sense (*Walden*, 282). Thoreau's problem as a writer is how to control so much complexity of reference, how to render an account of something that is, in its way, unaccountable; and the methods of the natural historian are readily at hand.

The problem of how to express the nature and accessibility, to the "conscious" being, of the redeemed condition, is the issue of the remainder of the chapter. Thoreau continues by recounting the story of one particular walk, to the meadow near Baker Farm. He remembers the days before he himself was in the least redeemed—"I thought of living there before I went to Walden. I 'hooked' the apples, leaped the brook, and scared the musquash and the trout" (*Walden*, 203). The day proves unpropitious for fishing, and Thoreau finds shelter in a hut "fabled" to be by "a poet builded" (pp. 203–204), but now the home of "John Field, Irishman." Field is an ideal subject for evangelism, if Thoreau is right about the "constancy" of sainthood, its availability to any man whose consciousness is altered. Field is a stranger, but he has clearly "settled," and one assumes he has lived near Walden about as long as Thoreau has actually been in residence. Field works hard, but altogether wrongly; just as the society scrutinized in "Economy" does. Thoreau is moved to preach—"I tried to help him with my experience" (p. 205)—and proceeds, in a long sentence, to summarize much of the matter of *Walden*. The sermon ends with the expected points: that redemption is not a place and that the real task is not hoeing but *self*-culture. The message fails to take hold: John Field and his wife will go on living "bravely, after their fashion, face to face," but still lost (p. 206).

That the sermon fails is not surprising; moreover, since its matter is so close to that of *Walden*, it is an omen of the possibility that *Walden* itself will fall on equally deaf ears. But after all, Thoreau knows that experience cannot be passed on—that the past, however recent, cannot be straightforwardly presented. What that means, to a writer who wishes to render a useful account of his own exemplary life, is problematical. At the very least, the product will not be a guidebook. In the immediate instance, Thoreau sets off after another rainbow (*Walden*, 206) and falls into some despair. He tries to look down the well, since bottom is always restorative to him, but cannot see it; instead he drinks water that is as unlike the pure fluid of Walden as one could imagine (p. 206). He wanders in the wilderness; and not the restorative wilderness, but that of ordeal, of the forty-days' test, full of "sloughs and bog holes ... forlorn and savage places" (p. 207). But the despair is not final; Thoreau finds, or rather gives himself ("my good Genius seemed to say ...") a prophecy. The language is unmistakably biblical, and the message is unmistakably individualistic: cultivate yourself. The prophecy is, like the sermon to Field, a summary in small of *Walden*; but now, not of the facts but of their meaning (pp. 207–208). The chapter ends with some hope even for the fallen John Field. He is moved to find Thoreau again, now "with an altered mind." The two men fish, and of course John catches nothing. Thoreau laments the Irishman's fate: "Poor John Field!—I trust he does not read this, unless he will improve by it,—thinking to live by some derivative old country mode in this primitive new country,—to catch perch with shiners" (p. 208). All hope is not lost—"It is good bait sometimes, I allow." Field, poor man that he is, but poor at least in the right way (pp. 34–35 and 196), is specifically identified with the first of the fallen, Adam, and so damned ("not to rise in this world, he nor his posterity")—but only, perhaps, provisionally ("till their wading webbed bog-trotting feet get *talaria* to their heels"). Thoreau will not in any case stop preaching; he proceeds, without more hesitation than a change of chapters, to make of his walk home from the fishing expedition a sermon on "Higher Laws."

Although science may not be able to tell us "how it is, and whence it is, that light comes into the soul," natural history has its use, even to the elect and even in Eden, as the source of instructive and admonitory information about the fallen, a way of uncovering facts to be studied Transcendentally, a means of description of the holy places, and a method of organization. Natural history is a way of speaking to the fallen, of providing the closest available approximation of the Celestial City to those not yet ready for its thin air. So, in "The Pond in Winter," Thoreau spends a great deal of time measuring Walden by the world's standards, and in the process emphasizes the more significant symbolic truth of the necessity of settling down to the bottom, while pointing out as well the usual limitations of man's vision and the final import of Walden's symmetry. The effect is natural history as parable, the physical act of measuring serving to exemplify the imaginative and spiritual act of fronting the essential facts, of overseeing all the details ourselves in person (*Walden*, 20). The science involved is not a source of insight so much as it is a vehicle for the representation of insight; the commonness of the reported experience (the plumbing, by the most obvious of means, of a humble pond which cannot much concern one who has not long frequented it) is a sign of the proximity of grace, which, though constant, is not commonly noticed. So, too, the recognizability of the methods—common sense and observation— allows to the fallen at least the possibility of comprehension. The result of the descent of the tongues of fire upon the heads of the Apostles at Pentecost was to let them speak in all the tongues of men; the listening multitude "were bewildered, because each one heard them speaking in this own language" (Acts II:6). There may be little hope for John Field or for those of us who are only said to live, but what little there is arises only because Thoreau talks to him and to us in our own tongue of tea, coffee, butter, and milk, of fishing and hoeing, of the most recognizable of "wild" life.

In speaking to the literate, the employment of the mundane (in several senses) and popular methods of the field naturalist serves a similar purpose. But what of history in the more strict sense? It can be argued that *Walden* is in most ways the least historical of Thoreau's longer works. Certainly by comparison to *Cape Cod* or *A Week*, where the written chronicles of New England are explicitly cited again and again, *Walden* is exceedingly sparing in its use of authorities. Such sources are not completely absent; we noticed that Cellini's autobiography was invoked in "Baker Farm." But, as a rough measure, Thoreau mentions in *Walden*, by my count, only four local histories, three of them in "Economy" when he is outlining the debased society he sees around him.[26] Compare this to *Cape Cod*, where the acknowledged authorities include, among others, Beverly's *History of Virginia*, *Mourt's Relation*, Champlain's *Voyages*, Wood's *New England's Prospect*, Morton's *New England's Canaan*, the *Collections of the Massachusetts Historical Society*, and, at great length, the church records of the town of Eastham.

There is of course history of a kind elsewhere in the book. The vicinity of Thoreau's chosen home near the pond has a past that is largely fable, which constitutes the material of the chapter "Former Inhabitants; and Winter Visitors," in which Thoreau is "obliged to conjure up the former occupants of these woods," slaves, drinkers, and squatters (*Walden*, 256). As conjuration or fable, the past frequently enters into *Walden*, even in the description of the pond itself, which includes, for example, the "Indian fable" of Walden's origin (p. 182). But the question of accuracy does not arise where fable is concerned, as it inevitably does in dealing with history. "The Ponds" offers at least three separate and not especially congruent fables about the origin and age of Walden, one of them purely of Thoreau's own making (p. 179). In the end what concerns him is not the source but the existence of the pond—"It is very certain, at any rate, that once there was no pond here, and now there is one" (p. 182).

Of historical facts of the more commonly valued sort, Walden Pond is blessedly innocent. The former inhabitants are members of that great mass of men of whom history, until very recently, took no notice. Concord's greatest moment of worldly fame, the Concord Fight, occurred only some two miles away, but the Battle Ground, "our only field known to fame," is invisible from Thoreau's seat "by the shore of a small pond" (*Walden*, 86). As for history in the abstract sense, as a field of study or a path to knowledge, Thoreau makes it clear that the redeemed need take no notice of it, for they live at the meeting of two eternities (p. 18) and in that spiritual spring where all histories are irrelevant (p. 310). If for some reason the saint employs history, he does so as a true natural historian would, warily and only as corroboration, always trying and measuring it against the observed present. As Gilbert White had said, "One cannot safely relate any thing from common report ... without expressing some degree of doubt and suspicion" (*NHS*, 11/28/1768).

History is most often mentioned in Walden in the abstract—"history" rather than "the history of"—and in the negative, as during the sermon to John Field: "For I purposely talked to him as if he were a philosopher, or desired to be one. I should be glad if all the meadows on the earth were left in a wild state, if that were the consequence of men's beginning to redeem themselves. A man will not need to study history to find out what is best for his own culture" (*Walden*, 205). That the dismissal of history follows, on the page, the beginning of redemption is not, I think, merely an accident of syntax. Once saved, indeed, man will not need to study history; the dictum is couched in what we might call the Revelatory Optative. Later, Thoreau dismisses "histories, chronologies, traditions, and all written revelations," but only at the moment of Resurrection, "the year beginning with younger hope than ever!" (p. 310). Alas, as he knows, the mass of men are far from redeemed as yet, the year is not all Spring, and there is still a place for written revelations, even for one called *Walden*. In the meantime, rubbish, especially the accumulation of written accounts, may still be put to use: "By such a pile we may hope to scale heaven at last" (p. 104).

Walden however is a book especially about the elect, rather than the fallen; and as such, it is only right that it should contain little history, and that what history there is should be most prevalent in "Economy," the part of the book in which the false way is being condemned on its own terms. *Cape Cod* by contrast is a journey to and among the fallen; and as we will see it is full of history. But still *Walden* is, in itself, a history—an account of specific events, compiled from first-hand reports and pretending, at least, to be full of the stuff of the most dull and detailed chronicles, a rendering of accounts in the numerical as well as in all other senses. It is in fact, in Emersonian terms, a history of the truest sort; the most accurate history, Thoreau repeatedly insists, that he could write—a history and natural history of the Self.

And, as a natural history should be, *Walden* is a settled, grounded, parochial book. But we remember from our consideration of Darwin that the natural historian can be a traveler as well as a settler. In one sense *Walden* rebuts this idea. Thoreau's assertion that he travels widely in Concord (*Walden*, 4) is a broad clue about the eccentric kind of book he intends. The book is an explicit alternative to books (and to human lives) which presume that discovery and travel are necessarily two words for the same thing. While getting to know beans, Thoreau observes "travellers bound westward"—in his favorite direction—and remarks how he was to them "a very *agricola laboriosus* ... the home-staying, laborious native of the soil" (p. 157). But that is by no means the conclusion of the book, either in pages or in argument. Indeed, almost the first words of Thoreau's "Conclusion" are, "Thank Heaven, here is not all the world" (p. 320). So much for the absolute virtue of parochialism.

The mistake Thoreau sees travelers making is to confuse activity with method. "Extra-vagance," being beside one's self in a good sense, is not to be confused with physical movement, although, indeed, to Thoreau himself, as to Wordsworth or Whitman or Stevens, true extra-vagance seems most easily to happen while one is walking. Exploration of the proper sort can be done as well or as poorly on the edge of Concord as on the coast of Tierra del Fuego.

We exaggerate, I think, in taking *Walden* too easily as Thoreau's characteristic book—especially that *Walden* which we tend to simplify, in remembrance, as a gospel of Transcendental parochialism. Geographical movement is the apparent organizing principle in the majority of his extended works; *A Week*, *Cape Cod*, the four selections of *Maine Woods*, and *A Yankee in Canada* are all, explicitly, travelogues. It is true that, as travelogues, they tend to follow the dictum laid down in *Walden*: "Our Voyaging is only great-circle sailing" (*Walden*, 320). The clearest example is *A Week*, which describes a trip from Concord to Concord to Concord (and perhaps to or at least toward concord). Nor does Thoreau, even while traveling, venture very far; Quebec and Truro are nowhere near as distant as Darwin's Chiloe or Patagonia. But Thoreau, interested in becoming "expert in home-cosmography" (p. 320), is also aware of the advantages to be gained by being a stranger, the man who "has just come out of the woods" and who as a result sees "with unprejudiced senses" that which is misperceived as beautiful only by "the weary traveller, or the returning native—or, perchance, the repentant misanthrope" (*Cape Cod*, 21). Asked to choose between the roles of stranger and native, of traveler and squatter, Thoreau, paradoxically but not surprisingly, wants both.

In Eden, the generalized written record of customary behavior over time—which we usually call history—is out of place, since the blessed condition, as Thoreau defines it, is individual, timeless, and only very approximately describable. The native of Eden, however, still finds natural history useful—as a way of assembling and documenting his case against the unholy world, as a way of finding corroboration for the transcendental moments of elevation and expansion, and as a vehicle for the communication of those moments to the fallen. But Thoreau is not always in Eden; and it will be worthwhile now to observe him when he is far away indeed from the holy place, on his trip to the wrecked world of Cape Cod.

NOTES

1. Sherman Paul, *The Shores of America* (Urbana: University of Illinois Press, 1972), p. 396.

2. Ibid., p. 396.

3. Ibid., p. 275; see also p. 105 for Thoreau's preference for "sympathy" over "scientific method" in "The Natural History of Massachusetts."

4. Ibid., p. 275, provides a summary of these entries.

5. Thoreau omits reading as a skill of the scientist: "Would you be a reader, a student merely, or a seer?" (*Walden*, 111)

6. Michel Foucault, *The Order of Things* (New York: Random House, 1973), pp. 130–131 and 157–161.

7. See J. L. Shanley, *The Making of Walden* (Chicago: University of Chicago Press, 1957), pp. 30–33.

8. See *Walden*, 15, 25, 57, 63, 88, 91, 131, and 164. The similarities—and differences—between this kind of "sainthood" and a more traditional Protestant variety, may be seen by considering the experience recounted in Jonathan Edwards' "Personal Narrative" and Edwards' description of "evangelical humiliation" as a necessary accompaniment of "gracious affections" in his *Treatise Concerning Religious Affections*, ed. J. E. Smith (New Haven: Yale University Press, 1959), p. 311.

9. Perry Miller, *Consciousness in Concord* (Boston: Houghton Mifflin, 1958), pp. 51–52.

10. Ibid., p. 34.

11. Paul, *Shores of America*, pp. 10–16 and 49–57.

12. Here as elsewhere, the (perhaps accidental) analogies between Thoreau and more traditional naturalists are striking. Joseph Kastner cites a similar list of "professions" in the case of the colorful Constantine Rafinesque; see *A Species of Eternity* (New York: Knopf, 1977), p. 242. Kastner's book as a whole persuasively demonstrates the degree to which the practice of naturalism in the early nineteenth century demanded an acquaintance with a wide variety of skills and occupations. Thoreau's disguise as hydra must also be considered as a part of the tradition of the boaster as an American comic type, as Constance Rourke demonstrated some years ago in her *American Humor* (New York: Harcourt Brace, 1931). Thoreau's picture of himself as a man of many skills and no profession goes hand in hand with his interest in the early settlers of New England. He must have realized that, when Concord was born, a man who could justly claim to be a carpenter, surveyor, painter,

schoolmaster, mason, and more besides would have been a prized addition to the town, not an eccentric or a ne'er-do-well.

13. Nathaniel Hawthorne, *American Notebooks*, ed. Claude M. Simpson (Columbus: Ohio University Press, 1972), pp. 353–354.

14. The same point is of course developed more fully in "Economy" (*Walden*, 49–52).

15. Robert Langbaum, *The Poetry of Experience* (New York: Norton, rev. ed. 1971), p. 23.

16. The contradiction is of course intentional, as a perusal of the various comments Thoreau makes about the railroad (*Walden*, 41, 52–54, 92, 97, 114–117, and 305) or about the "virtues" of cooperation (pp. 71 and 110) would show. It is, I think, arguable that contradiction is the peculiarly American genius.

17. The elm tree also stands as a premonitory pun on the heritage of that other *Celtis occidentalis*, John Field.

18. The chapter could, on this and other grounds, bear comparison to Hawthorne's similarly ambiguous "Custom House."

19. In exactly the same way, for instance, before measuring Walden he tells the fables of the ice-fishermen and the pickerel (*Walden*, 282–285).

20. How much this passage and the following paragraphs are literally in the style of the field naturalist can be seen clearly by a reading of Gilbert White's seventh introductory letter to *The Natural History of Selborne*, which describes ponds.

21. The layman would probably rely on some such reference as the maps included on pages 6, 8, and 9 of Robert Stowell's *A Thoreau Gazeteer*, ed. William L. Howarth (Princeton: Princeton University Press, 1970): and of course the layman would be wrong. As modern understanding of the nature and formation of glacial ponds has shown, Thoreau had his facts right. See Edward S. Deevey, Jr., "A Re-examination of Thoreau's *Walden*," *The Quarterly Review of Biology*, 17 (March 1942), pp. 1–11: and Eugene H. Walker, "Walden's Way Revealed," in *Man and Nature* (Lincoln: Massachusetts Audobon Society, 1971). I am indebted to William Howarth for correcting my own, exceedingly lay eye on this point.

22. Of course, one of the final surprises of the chapter is that Walden is not, after all, unique; there is always White's Pond if Walden fails (*Walden*, 197–200).

23. The particular document, Cellini's autobiography, is of course, in Emersonian terms, the perfect one—autobiography being the truest history.

24. This belief that the contempt and suspicion of the world are a sign of sainthood may be one reason why Thoreau takes such pleasure in *Cape Cod* in the fact that he was mistaken during his excursion for a bankrobber (*Cape Cod*, 101 and 177).

25. To the modern reader the letter takes on an unforeseen irony; that frontier paradise to which Williams had moved is Buffalo, New York.

26. See *Walden*, 29, 38, 39, and 198.

ROBERT SATTELMEYER

From A Week *to* Walden

EXIGENCIES AND OPPORTUNITIES, 1849–1850

Following the publication of *A Week on the Concord and Merrimack Rivers* in May 1849, Thoreau's life began a quiet transformation. Partly as a result of the reception of the book, but partly owing also to the development of new interests and a newfound stability in the routines of his life, his literary habits—his reading, especially—changed and began to settle into patterns that would remain more or less constant for the rest of his life. The failure of *A Week* to generate much critical or popular appreciation and the financial setback that its poor sales caused were both disappointing to Thoreau, but they were offset by other and compensating developments among his literary interests that made the next decade a busy and productive one—although the issue of the significance and value of his projects after *Walden* was published in 1854 is still capable of provoking lively critical debate.[1]

Nevertheless, there is a kind of quiet drama to be inferred from the record of his reading and writing during these years, for his studies of natural history, early American history, and the American Indian did progress far enough to suggest, at least in the essays that he managed to finish or cull from these projects late in life, the directions in which his thought was proceeding. His natural history work may be gauged from such late essays as "Wild Apples" and "The Succession of Forest Trees" (extracted from a

From *Thoreau's Reading: A Study in Intellectual History*, pp. 54–77. © 1988 by Princeton University Press.

longer manuscript on the dispersal of seeds); his ideas about American history from "Provincetown" in *Cape Cod*; and his engagement with the American Indian from the contrast between his reading on the subject and his firsthand experience with Joe Polis in Maine in 1857, narrated in "The Allegash and East Branch" in the posthumously published *The Maine Woods*. Before taking up the developments in his reading that helped to shape these late works and that mark his mature intellectual interests, however, it may be useful to consider first the new patterns of stability that began to cohere in his life around 1850 from a concatenation of circumstances as varied as the commercial failure of *A Week* and his partial estrangement from Emerson, the establishment of the Concord Town Library, and his resumption of regular reading notes and detailed, dated Journal entries.

The failure of *A Week* to sell well had at least three significant repercussions for Thoreau. First, since he had agreed to guarantee the costs of production, and since it was soon apparent that royalties from sales would not cover these costs, he incurred a debt of almost $300. He had to rely on other employment, especially surveying and pencil making, to meet his ordinary expenses and to pay off his publisher ("falsely so called," he observed mordantly). It was not until near the end of 1853, four and a half years after the book appeared, that he managed to discharge this obligation (JL 5.521). The extremely slow sales of the book (just over two hundred copies in four years) also dimmed Thoreau's chances of earning at least a nominal living from his pen and of following *A Week* with *Walden*, which he was confident by 1849 was nearly ready for publication.[2] He had to confront more directly than before the stark reality that, after nearly a decade of writing for various magazines, lecturing, and publishing a book, he was unlikely to be even moderately remunerated for his work. Like virtually all other serious American writers of his generation, he had to find some alternative arrangement for making a living if he wished to continue to write, and he also had to find some alternative forms of expression for his writing while his literary career reoriented itself to cultural and economic realities.

This is not to say that Thoreau abandoned the idea of lecturing or of writing for paying publications. Quite the contrary: There were occasional periods of brisk activity in lecturing, and he was, in Emerson's words, in "a tremble of great expectation" when *Walden* appeared in 1854.[3] In 1861 and 1862, he quite literally worked on his deathbed, dictating to his sister Sophia after he became too weak to write himself, in order to prepare as many essays as possible for publication. But in 1850 he had to accommodate himself to the truth that no reliable public outlet for his work existed, and as a consequence he turned increasingly to the Journal as a mode of private expression that served simultaneously as a record of his studies and observations and as a potential storehouse for his occasional public performances. This shift in his primary form of composition is vividly suggested by the proportions of his printed Journal in the 1906 edition: whereas two volumes suffice for the thirteen-year period from 1837 to 1849, twelve are required for the next dozen years, from 1850 to 1861. (The earlier Journal had been much longer, of course; much of it was used up or destroyed by Thoreau in the process of drafting his early literary works.) The summer of 1850 marks the beginning of this later phase of the Journal as a voluminous, regularly kept, and dated document that records in great detail Thoreau's studies—especially of natural history—during the rest of his life. Since he frequently noted his response to books he was reading in his Journal, his interests in the fifties are generally somewhat easier to trace than those of earlier decades.

The third consequence of *A Week* and its reception appears to have been a real rupture in Thoreau's relationship with Emerson. Thoreau's Journal records a deep and disturbed preoccupation with the subject of friendship in 1849, returning again and again to the idea of its failure or end. He goes so far as to associate the crisis and its aftermath with the friend's criticism of *A Week*: "I had a friend, I wrote a book, I asked my friend's criticism, I never got but praise for what was good in it; —my friend became estranged from me and then I got blame for all that was bad, & so I got at last the criticism which I wanted."[4] The critic is never explicitly named, but since Emerson was Thoreau's closest friend, played so dominant a role in his literary apprenticeship, and urged him to publish *A Week* at his own expense, assuring him he would be unlikely to lose financially by so doing, there can be little doubt that he is behind the often anguished passages on friendship from this period.

Thoreau's sense of injury over this criticism was probably only tangentially related to the change in his relationship with Emerson, however, for the roots of their estrangement lay deeper. It was clear that Thoreau did not and could not fulfill Emerson's expectations of him,[5] and for his part Thoreau could scarcely continue into his mid-thirties as a disciple of anyone, especially of the apostle of self-reliance. Even before this time he had been privately and publicly satirized for his apparent imitation of the older writer, and he must have been acutely self-conscious of his widely perceived position as Emerson's protégé.[6] Ironically, the book that everywhere testified to Emerson's influence was to be at least the apparent occasion of a breach between the two men that would never entirely be healed, although it would be patched over. Painful as it evidently was, the rift probably helped to propel Thoreau in the direction of what he came to view as his proper studies and lightened the pressures that he must have felt to live up to Emerson's expectations.

Another important change in Thoreau's social and domestic life about this time was in his relations with his family. Thoreau moved back to live with his parents and sisters after Emerson's return from Europe in the summer of 1848, and during the following year he helped to carry out extensive renovations in their new house on Main Street, into which the family settled permanently early in 1850.[7] He had lived at home for only about eighteen months during the previous eight years—in 1844 and the first half of 1845 while he was building his cabin at the pond—but now he settled back with the family for good, taking a hand as usual in the graphite business and working independently as a surveyor. He occupied the attic floor of the new house, a spacious finished area that gave him ample space for his belongings, his instruments, his writing desk and bookshelves, and his growing collections of natural history specimens.[8] The new house was near the river, and since Ellery Channing, his friend and frequent companion, now lived almost across the street in a house whose back yard sloped down to the bank, Thoreau had a convenient place to moor his boat for the river excursions that were almost as regular a habit as his walks. This domestic stability helped to shape Thoreau's literary habits and pursuits in the decade to come. His housing since college had been a series of makeshift and temporary arrangements, and now that his life had assumed more or less settled routines he could begin realistically to devote more time to the long-range projects that now increasingly interested him.

The most important of these new routines was the habit of daily walks that he began about this time, a habit that he would practice uninterruptedly all year round in all weathers until the onset of his final siege of tuberculosis. "Within a year," he wrote to H.G.O. Blake in November 1849, "my walks have extended themselves, and almost every afternoon, (I read, or write, or make pencils, in the forenoon, and by the last means I get a living for my body.) I visit some new hill or pond or wood many miles distant" (COR, 150–251). About the same time, in the Journal, he began to record and index "Places to Walk to," and gradually his settled practice when not engaged in a large surveying project became to spend the morning at some literary labor—whether working on a lecture or essay or writing up previous days' Journal entries from field notes—the afternoon in walking or boating, and the evening in reading. After narrating in the Journal a winter day's outdoor activities in December 1856, for example, Thoreau looked forward to a typical evening: "Now for a merry fire, some old poet's pages, or else serene philosophy, or even a healthy book of travels, to last far into the night, eked out perhaps with the walnuts which we gathered in November" (JL 9.173).

His daily walks were not primarily for exercise or recreation but for discipline. He was training himself to become a careful observer and recorder of natural phenomena, jotting on small sheets of paper details which would form the basis of journal passages that he would later write up in his study, sometimes composing several days' entries in one stint. It was about this time, too—1849 or 1850—that he began to study systematically botany and natural history in general. He describes, again in a Journal entry from December 1856, how "from year to year we look at Nature with new eyes" and how about a half-dozen years earlier he had begun to bring home plants in a "botany box" constructed inside the crown of his hat and busied himself "looking out the name of each one and remembering it" (JL 9.156–157).

As Thoreau's outward life and pursuits were becoming more regular and settled, and his literary projects grew more dependent upon reading and research, his access to important sources of books also improved. In September 1849 he petitioned Jared Sparks, president of Harvard College, for permission to withdraw books from the library, claiming—surely for the only time in his life—benefit of clergy. Normally, ordained ministers were the only nonresident alumni permitted to check out books. Thoreau, exercising a characteristic philological ingenuity turning on the fact that "clergy" and "clerk" (in the medieval sense of "scholar") were derived from the same root, argued that he should qualify *"because I have chosen letters for my profession, and so am one of the clergy embraced by the spirit at least of her rule"* (COR, 266–268). Whether or not Sparks found this line of reasoning compelling, he did grant the request, and thereafter Thoreau used the Harvard library regularly, especially for his researches in early American history and American Indian ethnology. The railroad, which had been completed out to Concord in 1844, made it possible to travel conveniently to Boston and return the same day. Thaddeus W. Harris, the librarian, was also an entomologist of note (he had been Thoreau's natural science instructor at Harvard), and Thoreau frequently improved his visits to the library by talking over scientific matters of mutual interest with Harris.

Other Boston libraries were also important to Thoreau's work. In 1850 he was elected a corresponding member of the Boston Society of Natural History, entitling him to charge books from the society's fine library, a privilege that proved to be of immense use to him as his study of natural history became more specialized and expert over the years.[9] The New England metropolis's other renowned library was in the Boston Athenaeum, and despite the fact that he was not a member, Thoreau made at least occasional use of its collections. Emerson had earlier introduced him as a guest and sometimes borrowed books for him on his charging privileges.[10] Non-members, especially if they were students or writers, could consult the catalogue and the collections, and Thoreau took advantage of this policy when he was beginning his extensive bibliographical survey of works on the

American Indians: One of his manuscript notebooks contains a lengthy list of books on the subject that is headed "At Athenaeum."[11]

He also added slowly and carefully to his personal library, buying mostly books on natural history, both ancient and modern, and planning each purchase as if it were a military campaign, for the expenditure represented no inconsiderable portion of his earnings. He paid fifteen dollars, for example, for Loudon's *Arboretum et Fruticetum Britannicum*, an eight-volume botanical encyclopedia that was also in the Town Library. According to Ellery Channing's memoir, Thoreau "prized 'Loudon's Arboretum,'" of which, after thinking of its purchase and saving up the money for years, he became a master."[12] When he was in Boston he generally visited Burnham's bookstore, where he would occasionally come across a bargain in old books, such as the three-volume edition of Pliny's natural history that he found in 1859. He jotted down the titles of used books that he found at Burnham's (with their prices) to carry back to Concord with him, obviously to meditate their purchase and plan for the outlay. His personal library never grew much in excess of four hundred volumes (not counting the seven hundred-odd volumes of *A Week* that he included when sardonically recounting the story of the publisher's return of unsold copies), but they were a carefully chosen and compact lot, selected to facilitate his literary and scientific work.

The availability of books in Concord also improved significantly about this time. In 1851 the Concord Town Library, which would become the Concord Free Public Library in 1873 (where many of the books in Thoreau's personal library are housed today), came into being as a public library, absorbing the collection of the old subscription Social Library and thereafter building its collections through regular acquisitions funded by tax revenue.[13] The librarian, Albert Stacy, also owned a stationer's store from which he operated a circulating library of books that could be borrowed for a small rental fee. The circulating library—a target of Thoreau's satire on "easy reading" in *Walden* (WA, 104)—tended to concentrate on popular current literature, especially fiction and travel books, and was the source of much of Thoreau's reading in the latter genre during the 1850s. The Town Library, on the other hand, tended to acquire (in a complementary way that suggests that being town librarian and owning his own circulating library did not constitute a conflict of interest for Stacy) more sober works of nonfiction in fields such as history, religion, and natural and applied science.[14] Its collections were quite important for Thoreau, who took an avid interest in the fledgling institution and even suggested acquisitions to the librarian (JL 5.41). No charging records from the early years of the Town Library have been discovered, but some acquisition records do survive, and they demonstrate that Thoreau frequently read books that came to the library almost as soon as they were accessioned.[15] Many of the books that the library acquired in the 1850s—especially documentary works such as the government surveys of the West and the *Collections* of the Massachusetts Historical Society—were invaluable to Thoreau's natural history and early American history projects. To a certain extent, his criticisms of the literary climate of Concord in *Walden*, the references to the "half-starved Lyceum ... and the puny beginning of the library" in "Reading," were met by a gradual improvement in the local collections during the decade (WA, 108).

Interestingly, Thoreau seems to have struck a bargain with Stacy to set up a sort of private subscription library that enabled him to read current books not otherwise available. James Spooner, a young man from Plymouth who met Thoreau in the early fifties and wrote fairly extensive accounts of conversations with him, noted on one of these occasions that Thoreau "asked me if we had convenient opportunity for obtaining books.... He said that he had made an arrangement with the Concord bookseller to furnish what books he might wish—there were some half dozen others who would read them too & at three or four cts. apiece he would get the price of the book and then sell it afterwards."[16]

Thoreau continued to borrow books from Emerson too, although he did most of his reading from this source in the early 1840s. He also relied on the libraries of other friends: Bronson Alcott had a collection especially rich in philosophy and religion, and Ellery Channing was an inveterate reader with an extensive collection of literary works. After 1855, Thoreau occasionally borrowed books from Franklin Benjamin Sanborn (later to be an editor and biographer of Thoreau), a young abolitionist schoolteacher boarding at the Thoreau house.[17]

He also read newspapers, more often and more regularly than the criticism of the popular press in *Walden* might lead one to expect. Probably because of his friendship with Horace Greeley, its publisher, he took a subscription to the weekly edition of the *New York Tribune* in 1852. Greeley was sympathetic to reform generally and to the temperance and abolitionist movements particularly, and was usually supportive of the Transcendentalists (he had provided jobs on his paper to both Margaret Fuller and the feckless Ellery Channing). The *Tribune's* editorial policy was thus more palatable to Thoreau than that of most other newspapers, even though it too had its share of lurid stories of crimes and disasters such as Thoreau alludes to in *Walden*. Greeley was moreover a sort of unofficial literary agent for Thoreau, and he saw to it that extracts from *Walden* appeared in his paper and that the book was prominently reviewed, perhaps by Greeley himself.

The *Tribune* was also issued in daily and semi-weekly editions, and Thoreau occasionally refers to articles in these as well as in the weekly edition that he took. As might be expected, most of his references to and clippings from the paper concern either natural history phenomena or the American Indian. But when an event gripped Thoreau, he read all the newspapers that he could get his hands on. Such was the case in the fall of 1859, when John Brown led his abortive raid on Harper's Ferry and was subsequently captured and hanged (JL 12.406ff.). At such a time Thoreau was more likely to become enraged by the timidity of editors than to learn much of value about the event. As had been his custom earlier, he read periodical literature regularly, with an eye especially for essays on developments in natural science or ethnology; the latest books were still not always easy to obtain, and the major monthly and quarterly magazines often provided essay reviews that apprised him of new works in these fields. During the 1850s he kept up with new and emerging American periodicals such as *Harper's*, the *Atlantic*, and *Putnam's* (the last two in which he published), and more intermittently with British magazines, from established journals such as the *Westminster Review* to more recent ventures such as Charles Dickens's *Household Words*.

As a consequence of his more settled habits, his wider and easier access to books, and his shifting literary interests, Thoreau began about this time to keep detailed records of his reading in a series of notebooks designed to facilitate his various literary and scientific projects. He was an almost compulsive note taker by now (Channing describes him as always reading "with pen in hand"),[18] and he quoted extensively from the books he read. The Journal is one of these repositories of information about his reading, although by no means the principal one. Thoreau tried as a rule to preserve the Journal for his own thoughts and his records of natural history observations, and not to use it for extensive extracts from books. Frequently, however, allusions to and quotations from his reading appear in the late Journal and provide a convenient way of dating his acquaintance with a particular work.

The later notebooks strictly devoted to extracts from his reading, all commencing around 1850, consist of the following: two commonplace books, one intended for "facts" and another originally for "poetry"; a notebook on reading related to the history and early exploration of Canada and Cape Cod; and eleven volumes of "Indian books," as he called them, of extracts on the history and culture of North American Indian tribes.[19] The two commonplace books are perhaps the most interesting of these volumes intrinsically, for they suggest that Thoreau at first tried to distinguish in his reading notes between "poetry" (in the broadest Transcendental sense of any literary material that contained some significant idea, expression, or insight), and "facts"—either striking or interesting phenomena that might be evidence of some process or law of nature, or the sort of data that might someday flower into truth in the manner of the story of the bug that hatched from the apple-tree table in the concluding chapter of *Walden*. Not surprisingly, however, he found it impossible to maintain this distinction, as he confessed in the Journal within a year or so of beginning the parallel notebooks: "I have a commonplace book for facts and another for poetry, but I find it difficult to preserve the vague distinction which I had in my mind, for the most interesting and beautiful facts are so much the more poetry and that is their success" (JL 3.311).

This remark was probably made with specific reference to the *Heimskringla*, historical and legendary accounts of Norse kings that Thoreau was currently reading and ambivalently making extracts from in both notebooks, but in any event he soon ceased to make "poetry" extracts at all, and he used the remaining leaves of the poetry commonplace book to continue his fact notebook when the latter was filled in 1857 or 1858. His professional interest in literary subjects was waning as his interest in history and natural science was waxing, although there is no indication that he considered these more factual disciplines fundamentally less poetic if rightly pursued. It needs to be borne in mind that Thoreau's extracts of "facts" from a particular work do not always register the nature of his interest in the book itself or indicate its significance to him. Oftentimes he noted oddities, colorful details or incidents, or even casual remarks that he might later work into or allude to in his own writing. In *Walden*, for example, when he describes having killed a woodchuck that had been ravaging his bean field, he observes casually that he "effect[ed] his transmigration, as a Tartar would say," and a Tartar does in fact say this in a passage from a travel book that he had copied into the "fact" book.[20] But on the other hand, the entries cannot be categorized as predominantly of this character: Some are clearly made for purposes of study, some express ideas that he found congenial, some offer theories or hypotheses about natural phenomena, and others merely describe phenomena that he was interested in. The scattered quotations that Thoreau typically extracted from a given work may thus be misleading, and anyone concerned with the influence of a particular book upon him would be on safe ground to assume that it may not have suited his purposes at the time of reading to quote the passages that ultimately most affected him.

The Canada notebook, whose contents and chronology have been described in detail by Lawrence Willson, had its origins in Thoreau's excursion to Montreal and Quebec in the fall of 1850.[21] He characteristically studied the geography and history of the places he visited, both to intensify the experience of his infrequent travels and to help him prepare to write about the journey and the locale, but his reading on Canada tended to an unusual extent to spill over and extend into other areas of interest. He began the notebook in November 1850, shortly after his return, and made a number of extracts from various works of history and cartography that were useful to him in preparing "An Excursion to Canada" between late 1850 and early 1852, when he sent the essay to Horace Greeley to try to find a publisher.[22]

Other extracts and notes in the volume, however, not all directly related to the Canada excursion, were made between 1850 and 1856 in a separate section. Although varied in nature, this second set of extracts mainly treats the early cartography of New England and Canada and the inadequacy of contemporary historians who failed to take into account (out of an Anglophilic bias, Thoreau implies) the earliest and most accurate French sources for the history and the mapping of the continent. He would treat this subject at great length in the last chapter of *Cape Cod*, "Provincetown," citing many of the sources in the Canada notebook, and the notebook most importantly reflects his growing fascination with the drama of early exploration and his excitement at the parallel discovery of the relatively unknown history of that exploration by nations—especially the French—other than the English.

The Indian notebooks make up Thoreau's largest single repository of extracts from his reading—eleven volumes containing nearly three thousand manuscript pages of text on all aspects of American aboriginal history, culture, and allied subjects. How (or even whether) he intended to employ these notes directly in his literary projects cannot be known with any certainty, but they do represent a monument to a major intellectual interest of the last dozen years of his life. The evolution of this specific interest will be taken up in the next chapter; suffice it to say for the present that the Indian books, like the other notebooks just described, appear to have their inception in the period following the publication of *A Week*. As Linck C. Johnson has argued, the first surviving Indian book appears to have been started (in a manner analogous to the Canada notebook) as a response to or in anticipation of Thoreau's first trip to Cape Cod in October 1849—so that it might with equal aptness be called the "Cape Cod notebook."[23] Thereafter its focus shifted toward the Indian, and its successors continued this emphasis.

In short, by 1850 Thoreau had begun to study in a fairly systematic fashion the three main interests of the second phase of his career—natural history, early American history, and the history of North American Indians before contact with Europeans—and had a series of notebooks and a regularly kept Journal in which he recorded his reading in these and ancillary fields during the remainder of his life. His pursuits were taking an increasingly scholarly and scientific direction, and if he sometimes voiced disappointment with what seemed a corresponding loss of emotional attachment to his inquiries, his intellectual curiosity remained undiminished. This faculty propelled him to work diligently and for the most part happily on these projects over the years, patiently adding information to his records and incorporating it into ongoing literary projects. His life had settled into patterns that normally permitted him to spend a portion of each day on his studies—both out of doors and within—and he had greatly improved access to libraries and to books in general.

The problem of getting a living was always more vexing philosophically and ethically than actually and practically to Thoreau. Countering the fact that he always could (and often did) make a comfortable living in the pencil business are a series of impassioned engagements (in his writing) with the idea of a man's proper calling: in his Harvard commencement address, in "The Service," in the first two chapters of *Walden*, in "Life Without Principle," and in many of his letters, especially to H.G.O. Blake. On a different sort of practical level, though, he shared the dilemma faced by most if not all American writers in the nineteenth century, and like them he had to make concessions to a culture that tended not to acknowledge or reward many of its most serious artists. His solution was characteristic and distinctive: Rather than work at a newspaper or take on editorial piece work, seek a government clerkship or customs house job, he trained himself to be a surveyor, an occupation that gave him some control over his day and permitted him to work outdoors, and he made his Journal the primary document of his imaginative life. But he remained at heart and in mind a literary man, a writer whose essential tools and stock in trade were books, and the last dozen years of his active life evince an increasing reliance upon them. "Decayed literature," he observed in an almost Jamesian mood while contemplating shelves of early Canadian history at Harvard in 1852, "makes the richest of all soils" (JL 3.353).

SHIFTING EMPHASES, 1850–1854

Since the surviving records of Thoreau's reading for the 1850s are more extensive than for the earlier decades, it will be best to treat the main areas topically in a separate chapter in order to suggest something of the outline and development of his principal interests. As I have already suggested, these interests involve varieties of history—natural history, the early history of North American discovery and exploration, and the history of American Indian tribes. None of these subjects was new to him, of course, but each assumed a significance in the early fifties that it had not had earlier. At the same time, a number of other interests, more or less related to these principal ones and carried over from the previous decades, need to be considered and briefly assessed as well.

From a literary standpoint, the early fifties culminate in the publication of *Walden* in 1854, and although that book incorporates Thoreau's reading less obtrusively and in more sophisticated ways than had *A Week*, it too is representative of a stage in Thoreau's intellectual maturation, a stage at which his mastery of familiar subjects (poetry, the classics, travel, Oriental scripture) is balanced against his growing absorption in natural history and history of other types as well: the history of New England, of Concord and Walden Pond, and ultimately of himself.

His interest in travel writing, for example, remained strong and in fact is often not to be distinguished from his more formally historical studies. A book such as William Bartram's *Travels* was not only a literary classic of the genre (it had inspired passages in Coleridge's "Kubla Khan" nearly fifty years before Thoreau read it) but also an important source of information about natural history and the customs of Indian tribes in the South. The account of the "busk" or ceremony of purification and renewal in "Economy" in *Walden* is derived from Bartram, and other early travel writers such as John Josselyn, William Wood, and Timothy Dwight provided similar information for Thoreau's investigations of New England natural and civil history.[24] Prominent scientists like Darwin, Lyell, and Humboldt published accounts of their travels that were rich in information about natural science, and accounts of Arctic and South American explorations furnished details about aboriginal life in those regions that were pertinent to Thoreau's own study of North American Indian cultures. It is typical, then, to find extracts from such travel works in his natural history commonplace books or Indian notebooks.

His interest in other subjects, however, notably Oriental philosophy and religion, diminished perceptibly during the decade. When Thoreau reestablished his borrowing privileges at Harvard in the fall of 1849, among his first withdrawals were a number of Oriental works, from which he made lengthy extracts in an early commonplace book which still had some blank pages. He even translated into English a French translation of "The Transmigration of the Seven Brahmins," a tale he found in *Harivansa, ou Histoire de la Famille de Hari*, an appendix to the Hindu epic the *Mahâbhârata*.[25] Since he had told President Sparks that he needed to consult the library for professional purposes, and since his other withdrawals in 1849 were of books that he needed for his Cape Cod lecture, it is possible that Thoreau may have contemplated some literary project on Oriental literature at this time. He had considered the subject for several years, had treated it briefly in *A Week*, and had read James Elliot Cabot's "The Philosophy of the Ancient Hindoos" in the inaugural issue of the *Massachusetts Quarterly Review* the previous year.[26] In November 1849 he told H.G.O. Blake, after quoting passages about the freedom of the yogin absorbed in contemplation and detached from the world, "To some extent, and at rare intervals, even I am a yogin" (COR, 251). This apparent renewal of interest in Eastern philosophy and religion may thus be related to his own adoption of a more settled mode of life and the beginning of the previously described regular rituals of walking, writing, and reading, of which Thoreau speaks in the same letter. It may also reflect an attempt on his part to explain and justify philosophically the retired life that he was to lead henceforth. Whatever the causes, his enthusiasm was relatively short-lived and led to no discernible literary results beyond the translation of the "Seven Brahmins" tale (which he never attempted to publish). In *Walden*, passages from the Eastern scriptures sharpen Thoreau's critique of his countrymen's modes of life and provide examples and analogues for his own more contemplative path. He does not tend to wield them, as he had done in *A Week*, as a stick with which to beat Christianity. The idea of the yogin's life is fully integrated into the perspective of the narrator, so that he can describe quite naturally in "The Pond in Winter" the interpenetration of East and West when "the pure Walden water is mingled with the sacred water of the Ganges" (p. 298). Significantly, the most resonant Eastern fable in *Walden*, the story of the artist of Kouroo, is apparently a product of Thoreau's own invention, demonstrating the extent to which he had internalized and absorbed this material.

By 1851, reading the *Harivansa* again, he could self-deprecatingly summarize the influence of such works on himself as essentially confirming tendencies already present: "Like some other preachers, I have added my texts—derived from the Chinese and Hindoo scriptures—long after my discourse was written" (JL 2.192). In 1854 he withdrew the *Bhăgvăt-Gêêtă* and *Vishńu-Puráńa*, both already familiar to him, from Harvard, but thereafter he seldom demonstrated an active interest in the subject—no further library withdrawals, infrequent and casual allusions in the Journal, and no extracts in the notebooks. When his English friend Thomas Cholmondeley sent him a magnificent gift of forty-four volumes of Oriental works in 1855 he responded warmly and gratefully, but he does not seem to have been inspired to read or reread the books themselves to any significant extent. Channing avers, with uncharacteristic plainness, "After he had ceased to read these works, he received a collection of them as a present, from England" (COR, 397–399).[27] Whether he ceased to read them or not, they certainly arrived after his discourse was written, at a time when he had become absorbed in other books and other interests.

Another field that he cultivated in a desultory fashion in the 1850s was "literary" nonfiction. (Fiction, of course, he read scarcely at all during his adult life, although he had had a fair acquaintance with Irving, Cooper, and Scott, as well as lesser novelists, during his college years. He apparently read no more of Melville after *Typee* [1846], and no more of Hawthorne after *Mosses from an Old Manse* [1846], which he mentions in a rather awkward poem in *A Week* [pp. 18–19]. He owned for a time a copy of *The Scarlet Letter*, probably a gift from the author, but crossed it off his library catalogue as either lost or given away.) He also appears not to have continued to read Carlyle avidly after his 1846 lecture and essay, perhaps because his own abolitionist convictions were growing stronger as Carlyle was expressing increasingly strident opinions on the other side, but he was quite strongly attracted during the fifties to both De Quincey and Ruskin.

De Quincey's works were being published for the first time in a uniform edition by Ticknor and Fields (the author having finally acquired the necessary leisure to collect his works after a lifetime of being jointly hounded by his creditors and his opium habit), and Thoreau kept up with and looked forward to new volumes as they appeared at something like yearly intervals. He read *Literary Reminiscences* (containing anecdotes about Wordsworth and Coleridge, among others) and *The Caesars* shortly after their publication in 1851, and *Historical and Critical Essays* and *Theological Essays*, which appeared in 1853 and 1854, respectively. It is probably to *Historical and Critical Essays* that he refers in a Journal entry in March 1853 that suggests his continuing interest in and critical concern with Concord libraries: "I told Stacy the other day that there was another volume of De Quincey's Essays (wanting to see it in his library). 'I know it,' says he, 'but I shan't buy any more of them, for nobody reads them.' I asked what book in his library was most read. He said 'The Wide, Wide World'" (JL 5.43).

He was critical of De Quincey as one of the contemporary writers (Dickens was another, he thought) who "express themselves with too great fullness and detail" and "lack moderation and sententiousness" (JL 2.418), but some quality obviously attracted him as well. Perhaps it was the high stature that De Quincey claimed for prose composition itself. In his essay on Herodotus, a passage from which Thoreau copied into one of his commonplace books, De Quincey makes claims for prose that Thoreau, then working through the latter stages of revision on *Walden*, may well have found congenial or even inspiring. Speaking of Herodotus as the original writer of prose, De Quincey argues: "If prose were simply the negation of verse ... indeed, it would be a slight nominal honour to have been the Father of Prose. But this is ignorance, though a pretty common ignorance. To walk well, it is not enough that a man abstain from dancing. Walking has rules of its own the more difficult to perceive or to practise as they are less broadly *prononcés*.... Numerous laws of transition, connection, preparation, are different for a writer in verse and a writer in prose. Each mode of composition is a great art; well executed, is the highest and most difficult of arts."[28]

In any event, it is perhaps mildly surprising to find that Thoreau should have preserved a regard for and a continuing interest in De Quincey, a writer known chiefly for *The Confessions of an English Opium Eater*. One doubts that Thoreau, who once told Alek Therien in his cups that he might as well go home and cut his throat, would have much sympathy for De Quincey's longstanding laudanum habit; nor did he approve of what he considered De Quincey's narrow-minded and merely orthodox defense of the English church (JL 4.486). All these objections aside, De Quincey was one of the most gifted and original prose writers of the century, and that is more than enough reason for Thoreau to have read him carefully. And, given all their differences, Thoreau may have been attracted also to De Quincey's methods of handling classical, scholarly, and arcane subject matter in ways that made it lively and readable.

Another unexpected enthusiasm he acquired was for Ruskin. In 1857 he asked H.G.O. Blake: "Have you ever read Ruskin's books? If not, I would recommend you to try the second and third volumes (not parts) of his 'Modern Painters.' I am now reading the fourth, and have read most of his other books lately. They are singularly good and encouraging, though not without crudeness and bigotry. The themes in the volumes referred to are Infinity, Beauty, Imagination, Love of Nature, etc.,—all treated in a very living manner. I am rather surprised by them. It is remarkable that these things should be said with reference to painting chiefly, rather than literature. The 'Seven Lamps of Architecture,' too, is made of good stuff; but, as I remember, there is too much about art in it for me and the Hottentots. We want to know about matters and things in general. Our house is yet a hut" (COR, 497).[29] Once again, as with De Quincey, one suspects that it was the "very living manner" in which Ruskin's subjects, especially nature, were treated that principally attracted Thoreau, for, as he suggests in the passage, he affected to be not much interested in art criticism as such.

The pose of cultural savage ("me and the Hottentots") is one he liked to assume in such circumstances, but if he was not much interested in painting he was very much interested in the artistic depiction of nature and in equipping himself generally with the vocabulary, sense of perspective, and if possible the eye of the painter and the art critic. He had read and written about Burke's ideas of the sublime and the beautiful in college, and early in the 1850s he read carefully several of William Gilpin's popular books on picturesque scenery, so it is appropriate that he should have read Ruskin. In addition to *Modern Painters* and *Seven Lamps of Architecture*, the books he mentions in the letter to Blake, Thoreau made extracts from *The Elements of Drawing* in one of his commonplace books, and his mention of having read "most of his other books lately" suggests that he probably knew Ruskin's most famous work, *The Stones of Venice* (1851–1853), although he does not specifically refer to it or to other of Ruskin's works. In the final analysis, although he found Ruskin "singularly good," he parted company with him as with so many other English writers for having failed (largely as a result of following conventional Christian orthodoxy, Thoreau thought) to carry his love of nature to its ultimate extension as a means to the worship of divinity. In a Journal entry of about the same time as the letter to Blake he says that Ruskin "expresses the common infidelity of his age and race.... The love of Nature and fullest perception of the revelation which she is to man is not compatible with the belief in the peculiar revelation of the Bible which Ruskin entertains" (JL 10.147). The Transcendentalists' persistent criticism of orthodox Christianity and established churches was that an insistence on "peculiar" or singular revelation such as Genesis or the gospels announced blinded humanity to the continuous and ever-present revelation that could be found through nature.

In sharp contrast to his interests and tastes in the previous decade, Thoreau's reading of poetry in the 1850s consisted almost exclusively of contemporary English and American verse. His taste was not wonderfully discriminating, by modern standards anyway, but along with Emerson he was among a very small number of his contemporaries who recognized and responded to the genius of Whitman's *Leaves of Grass* in 1855 and 1856. He gave a qualified approbation to Coventry Patmore's recently published *The Angel in the House* in a letter to Blake in 1856, saying, "Perhaps you will find it good for you" (COR, 422). Whether he found it good for himself or not, it is certainly curious to find this unsentimental bachelor celebrant of chastity recommending a poem that extols (albeit with Victorian delicacy and circumlocution) sexual love and marriage. Blake was married, though; perhaps Thoreau thought he might find it instructive. (He had earlier sent Blake copies of his own essays "Love" and "Chastity and Sensuality.") A useful shorthand index to the tone and subject of Patmore's poem, which is no longer widely read, might be his friend Edmund Gosse's praise of its author's handling of the central theme: "He dwells with chaste rapture on the joys which are the prelude to that mystery of immaculate indulgence."[30]

Thoreau also copied verse from William Allingham's *Poems* into one of his commonplace books and owned a copy of Allingham's *The Music Master ... And Two Series of Day and Night Songs*, whose title poem has been aptly characterized by a recent critic of Allingham as "appealing to the worst side of sentimental Victorian taste," telling as it does the story of two lovers whose exquisitely self-sacrificing reserve keeps them from ever declaring their love.[31] Both Allingham and Patmore were acquaintances of Emerson's (and Allingham had received a review copy of *A Week*), so it may be that their representation in the short list of contemporary poets Thoreau read is to be attributed as much to professional courtesy as to taste.[32]

A more significant volume of verse that he owned was Tennyson's *In Memoriam* (1850). He had some previous acquaintance with Tennyson's earlier work, for he had mentioned Tennyson in a Journal comment that was a part of his English poets project in the early 1840s (PJ I.436). If he read *In Memoriam*, however (no explicit mention of his having done so is extant), he might well have been attentive to the crisis in belief that Tennyson anatomizes there, for in the 1850s Thoreau's own reading in natural science (discussed in the next chapter) exposed him to the ideas and trends portrayed in *In Memoriam* that were pushing the consciousness of the literate public slowly but inexorably toward the disturbing implications of Darwin's *Origin of Species*.

Thoreau's principal and almost his only voiced enthusiasm for poetry during the decade, however, was for Walt Whitman, and though the circumstances of their acquaintance are well enough known, they are worth describing again as an example of the strengths and limitations of Thoreau's literary judgment.[33] He owned a copy of the 1855 first edition of *Leaves of Grass*, which had probably been recommended to him by Emerson, who had in turn received a copy from Whitman and had praised the book in his famous letter to the poet greeting him "at the beginning of a great career." Bronson Alcott was also enthusiastic about Whitman, and when Thoreau was surveying in Perth Amboy, New Jersey, in late 1856, Alcott, then living in New York City, took him out to Brooklyn to meet Whitman. There passed a wary but apparently not uncongenial interview, and Whitman gave Thoreau a copy of the 1856 second edition of *Leaves of Grass*. Thoreau's first response to the poet, jotted down in a letter to Blake shortly afterward, was to be "much interested and provoked," and he described Whitman as "apparently the greatest democrat the world has ever seen.... A remarkably strong though coarse nature, of a sweet disposition, and much prized by his friends. Though peculiar and rough in his exterior ... he is essentially a gentleman. I am still somewhat in a quandary about him" (COR, 441). A bit more than a week later, on December 7, Thoreau had had time to sort out his thoughts and to read the copy of the second edition that Whitman had given him, and he again wrote to Blake an assessment that needs to be quoted at some length:

> That Walt Whitman, of whom I wrote to you, is the most interesting fact to me at present. I have just read his 2nd edition (which he gave me) and it has done me more good than any reading for a long time. Perhaps I remember best the poem of Walt Whitman an American & the Sun Down Poem. There are 2 or 3 pieces in the book which are disagreeable to say the least, simply sensual. He does not celebrate love at all. It is as if the beasts spoke. I think that men have not been ashamed of themselves without reason. No doubt, there have always been

dens where such deeds were unblushingly recited, and it is no merit to compete with their inhabitants. But even on this side, he has spoken more truth than any American or modern that I know. I have found his poem exhilarating encouraging. As for its sensuality,—& it may turn out to be less sensual than it appeared—I do not so much wish that those parts were not written, as that men & women were so pure that they could read them without harm, that is, without understanding them. One woman told me that no woman could read it as if a man could read what a woman could not. Of course Walt Whitman can communicate to us no experience, and if we are shocked, whose experience is it that we are reminded of?

On the whole it sounds to me very brave & American after whatever deductions. I do not believe that all the sermons so called that have been preached in this land put together are equal to it for preaching—

We ought to rejoice greatly in him. He occasionally suggests something a little more than human. You cant confound him with the other inhabitants of Brooklyn or New York. How they must shudder when they read him! He is awfully good. (COR, 444–445)

Thoreau goes on to praise *Leaves of Grass* as "a great primitive poem" (an extremely approbative term for Thoreau, who persistently complained about the lack of wild or primitive vigor in English verse) and concludes by calling Whitman "a great fellow." In this letter Thoreau brought himself to focus more directly than in the earlier one on Whitman's poems themselves and less on the phenomenon of Whitman the person—the self-conscious advertisement or artifact of his vision. It is clear that Thoreau is still troubled by the "simply sensual" poems, but on the other hand, he allows that "it may turn out less sensual than it appeared," perhaps an inchoate acknowledgment of Whitman's ultimately symbolic and spiritualizing (while still earthy and, for the day, graphic) presentation of sexuality. The second edition did, in fact, contain a number of new poems explicitly treating sexual themes, such as "I Sing the Body Electric," "A Woman Waits for Me," and "Spontaneous Me." And it was a part of Whitman's self-proclaimed program for the second edition, as he told Emerson, to "celebrate in poems the eternal decency of the amativeness of Nature" and not to be one of the "bards of the fashionable delusion of the inherent nastiness of sex, and of the feeble and querulous modesty of deprivation."[34]

Thoreau's sense that the most memorable poems were "the poem of Walt Whitman an American & the Sun Down Poem" ("Song of Myself" and

"Crossing Brooklyn Ferry" in later editions) is a judgment certainly affirmed by most later readers. It is difficult to point to any particular effect that reading Whitman had on Thoreau's own work at this stage in his life, but tempting to speculate that Whitman might have exerted a far greater influence if Thoreau could have known *Leaves of Grass* when he was most interested in reading and writing poetry, in his early twenties. What is clear, however, is that Thoreau valued Whitman's poetry highly, despite the limitations imposed upon his taste by prevailing New England and Victorian cultural attitudes toward sex, and it is in some respects remarkable that he was able to see Whitman as clearly as he could since the new poet was in so many ways the opposite of himself: garrulous, urban, expansive, and self-promoting. Only one other contemporary figure stirred his imagination more vividly in this decade, and that was John Brown.

Thoreau, no less than his contemporaries, was always fascinated with the heroic personality—figures like Whitman or John Brown, who devoted themselves at great personal cost to some ideal—and this familiar nineteenth-century preoccupation led naturally enough to a fondness for biography and autobiography. Emerson's *Representative Men* and Carlyle's *Heroes and Hero-Worship* are representative documents of the age, as are Thoreau's own essays "The Service," "Sir Walter Raleigh," and "Thomas Carlyle and His Works." The "simple and sincere account of his own life" that Thoreau, in the opening passage of *Walden*, requires of every writer, reflects not only the rhetorical strategy of that book but also an active preference for biographical and autobiographical writing among literary genres. This strain in his reading is consistent, going back to his college years, although it never really becomes a major preoccupation.

Not surprisingly, Thoreau read literary biography and autobiography: In addition to De Quincey's *Literary Reminiscences*, already mentioned, he read Wordsworth's *Memoirs* and owned a copy of *The Prelude*, Wordsworth's autobiographical poem, published in 1850. Likewise, the lives of great naturalists attracted him, and he read both Humboldt's own *Personal Narrative* and Klencke's biography of that great German naturalist, as well as Stöver's life of Linneaus. He read a number of other more or less simple and sincere accounts of the lives of people in fields quite distant from his own interests: Benvenuto Cellini's autobiography, the classical historian B. G. Niebuhr's *Life and Letters*, Daniel Webster's *Private Correspondence*, the Italian dramatist Vittorio Alfieri's autobiography, and Henry Morley's life of Bernard Pallissy, a sixteenth-century potter who was also a self-taught natural scientist. Thoreau may have been attracted to Pallissy because he foresaw and wrote against the evils of deforestation and urged the careful management of forest lands. When Thoreau read Pallissy's life in 1859 he was deep in his own studies of plant dispersal and succession, and also concerned, in other late projects such as *The Maine Woods*, with the future of America's forests and the need to preserve wild land.

Most of the foregoing areas of inquiry, as well as Thoreau's developing interest in natural history and history, help to account for the richly allusive and yet concrete texture of *Walden*. *A Week* had been, among other things, a rather obvious compendium of Thoreau's early literary and intellectual interests, a kind of summary of his reading to date, but in *Walden* the relationship of reading to writing is more intricate and subtle. For one thing, in *Walden* Thoreau's reading is much more adroitly integrated into the text and subordinated to his central themes than it was in *A Week*. There are no separable essays on subjects derived from his reading, as in *A Week*, but instead a chapter called "Reading," which demonstrates both by argument and example the nourishing influence of a liberal classical education, and which at the same time contains a somewhat uncharacteristic plea for cooperation and communal action in building libraries and other cultural resources in New England. In his masterpiece, Thoreau confidently tells his audience not just what he has read but how to read.

The descriptive prose of *Walden* differs from that of *A Week* by virtue of its more copious allusion and illustration, the product of Thoreau's several years of careful revision and filling out of the book's structure during the 1850s, a process which involved not only adding to but integrating into his prose the results of his continuing study. This feature and this process are nowhere more evident than in the Conclusion to *Walden*, one of the last sections of the book to be written. The rhetorical and thematic high points of the chapter—the advice to live like a traveler at home and become "expert in home-cosmography," the fable of the artist of Kouroo, and the concluding exemplum of the "strong and beautiful bug which came out of the dry leaf of an old table of apple-tree wood"—are built and based upon his reading in travel literature, Eastern scriptures, and New England history, respectively. Yet each involves a quite different but equally subtle transformation of sources, from the sly humor of travel literature invoked on behalf of staying home, to the original fable of the artist of Kouroo, loosely modeled on Hindu mythology, to the metamorphosis of the story of the bug, in which Thoreau rescues a trivial incident from a "dry leaf" in the historical collections (a characteristic pun that emphasizes the sterility of both mind and nature unless transformed by spirit and imagination) to stand as a triumphant example of regeneration.

Walden's later chapters were generally written or significantly revised late in the book's genesis. Thus, "Economy" and "Where I Lived, and What I Lived For" were relatively complete in the first draft of 1846–1847, while most of "The Pond in Winter" and "Spring," and all of "Conclusion," for example, were written between 1851 and 1854.[35] The greater particularity of these later chapters, especially "The Pond in Winter" and "Spring," with regard to the description of natural phenomena and seasonal changes reflects Thoreau's growing absorption in the study of natural history during this period. His account of the ice on Walden Pond, for example, or the famous and climactic description of the thawing sand and clay foliage of "Spring" are both informed by his recently acquired habits of careful observation and description.

Likewise, the linking of language itself to natural phenomena, so evident in the sand foliage passage, where the shapes and sounds of various letters are posited to have some primordial meaning as basic as the meaning of the natural forms themselves, is also the product in part of a new development in his reading. From his early schooling onward, Thoreau had always been interested not only in languages but also in language itself, and as he matured his style grew increasingly to reflect his assimilation and extension of the Transcendentalists' language theory as sketched by Emerson in *Nature* and developed by him in greater detail in "The Poet": Like nature itself, language is a path back to spirit and to original unity; it is "fossil poetry" that reveals by its history and the etymology of particular words the original and primal significance of nature itself to mankind. Thoreau's contribution to this theory was to take it seriously and literally as a principle of his style, and consequently we find one of his most characteristic stylistic devices to be the often surprising reattachment of a word to its original sense, as when he describes the sand foliage in *Walden* as "a truly *grotesque* vegetation," calling attention to the original significance of "grotesque" (from the same root as "grotto") as coming from underground. He was assisted in this development— perhaps the key signature of his mature style—by his reading during the early 1850s of Richard Trench's *On the Study of Words* (1851) (itself indebted to Emerson's *Nature* and "The Poet") and especially by Charles Kraitsir's *The Significance of the Alphabet* (1846) and *Glossology* (1852). As the recent work of Michael West and Philip Gura has demonstrated, Thoreau was particularly indebted to Kraitsir for his belief in the primal intrinsic significance of human sounds, a belief manifested most explicitly in his glossological speculations in the "Spring" chapter of *Walden*. As Gura puts it, "What Thoreau offered as his most important 'lesson' from the worlds of matter and spirit was that words were not merely steps to a higher reality but themselves embodied and reflected the reality, a thought initially suggested to him by Kraitsir."[36] In his best work, Thoreau wrote painstakingly according to his fundamental principle of reading—"We must laboriously seek the meaning of each word and line, conjecturing a larger sense than common use permits out of what wisdom and valor and generosity we have"—and much of the perennial vigor of Walden is due to Thoreau's theory and practice of recovering the primeval significance of language, of "re-membering" words and of speaking "without bounds."

NOTES

1. The most authoritative case for Thoreau's "decline" is that made by Sherman Paul in *The Shores of America*, who says that during the 1850s "the sources of [Thoreau's] life began to dry up" and that "nature had become barren, and the method which Thoreau now adopted in order to find her meaning ... did not bear any significant crop of inspiration" (pp. 272, 274). This view, the culmination of a strain in Thoreau criticism that goes back to Emerson's funeral address, has been challenged recently by the work of scholars more sympathetic to Thoreau's aims as a naturalist and writer. See Sayre, *Thoreau and the American Indians*, p. 101; William L. Howarth, *The Book of Concord* (New York: Viking Press, 1982), pp. 190–208; and John Hildebidle, *Thoreau: A Naturalist's Liberty* (Cambridge: Harvard University Press, 1983), pp. 69–96.

2. See WE, "Historical Introduction," p. 469.

3. Emerson, *Letters*, 4.460.

4. MS Journal for 1849 (HM 13182); quoted in WE, "Historical Introduction," p. 478.

5. Emerson's charge, leveled in his funeral address, that Thoreau lacked ambition and failed to accomplish tangible results from all his studies, had been expressed as early as 1842, when he described to Margaret Fuller Thoreau's "perennial threatening attitude" (*Letters*, 3.75) that led to no significant output; and in 1844 he predicted in his Journal that Thoreau would "never be a writer," for he was "as active as a shoemaker" (JMN 9.45).

6. Harding, *Days*, pp. 65–66, 299–300.

7. Ibid. p. 263.

8. Howarth, *The Book of Concord*, pp. 4–5.

9. Kenneth Walter Cameron, "Emerson, Thoreau, and the Society of Natural History," *American Literature* 24 (March 1952): 21–30.

10. Harding, *Days*, p. 130.

11. Indian book 4 (NNPM MA 598).

12. *Thoreau: The Poet-Naturalist* (Boston: Roberts, 1873), p. 26.

13. Allen French, T. Morris Longstreth, and David B. Little, *A History of the Concord Free Public Library*, pamphlet printed for the centennial of the library by the Library Corporation (Concord: Concord Press Corp., 1973).

14. See the catalogue of the Town Library, reprinted by Kenneth Walter Cameron in *The Transcendentalists and Minerva*, 2.818–828.

15. Acquisition records of Concord Free Public Library. Darwin's *Origin of Species*, for example, was acquired by the library on January 23, 1860, and Thoreau made extracts from it in one of his "fact books" before extracts from a book that he borrowed from Harvard on February 6.

16. Francis B. Dedmond, "Thoreau as Seen by an Admiring Friend: A New View," *American Literature* 56 (October 1984): 335–336.

17. Harding, *Days*, pp. 352–355. Thoreau noted, for example, in Indian book 12 (NNPM MA 606) that his source for Henry Youle Hind's report on a Canadian exploring expedition was Sanborn's library.

18. *Thoreau: The Poet-Naturalist*, p. 40.

19. See the list of abbreviations in this volume, pp. 114–115, for a description of these manuscript notebooks.

20. The source of the Tartar's remark is Évariste Régis Huc's *Recollections of a Journey through Tartary, Thibet, and China* (see Bibliographical Catalogue).

21. "Thoreau's Canadian Notebook," *Huntington Library Quarterly* 22 (May 1959): 179–200.

22. Harding, *Days*, p. 282.

23. "Into History: Thoreau's Earliest 'Indian Book' and His First Trip to Cape Cod," *Emerson Society Quarterly* 28 (2 Qtr. 1982): 75–88. See also Sayre, *Thoreau and the American Indians*, p. 108, who suggests that the first Indian notebooks may have been begun somewhat earlier when Thoreau was at Walden.

24. WA, 68; see Philip F. Gura, "Thoreau and John Josselyn," *New England Quarterly* 48 (December 1975): 505–518, for a suggestive examination of Thoreau's reading of early travel and exploration accounts.

25. See Arthur F. Christy, *The Orient in American Transcendentalism* (New York: Columbia University Press, 1932), pp. 217–279; Thoreau's translation of "The Transmigration of the Seven Brahmins" may be found in *Translations*, ed. Kevin P. Van Anglen (Princeton: Princeton University Press, 1986), pp. 135–142.

26. "Hindoo Scripture" appears on a list of possible topics that Thoreau drew up in the early 1840s; see WE, "Historical Introduction," p. 437. Thoreau made extracts from Cabot's article in his DLC "Literary Notebook."

27. *Thoreau, The Poet-Naturalist*, pp. 40–41.

28. De Quincey, *Collected Writings*, 14 vols. (Edinburgh: Adam and Charles Black, 1890), 6.100.

29. According to acquisition records, the Town Library acquired nine volumes of Ruskin's works in August 1857.

30. Edmund Gosse, *Coventry Patmore* (London: Hadden and Houghton, 1905), p. 98.

31. Alan Wainer, *William Allingham* (Lewisburg, Pa.: Bucknell University Press, 1975), p. 26.

32. Harding, *Days*, p. 252.

33. Ibid. pp. 372–376; see also Andrew Schiller, "Thoreau and Whitman: The Record of a Pilgrimage," *New England Quarterly* 28 (1955): 186–197, and Charles Metzger, *Thoreau and Whitman: A Study of Their Aesthetics* (Seattle: University of Washington Press, 1961). Whitman's comments on Thoreau are recorded by Horace Traubel in *With Walt Whitman in Camden*, 3 vols. (New York: Rowman and Littlefield, 1961), I.212 and passim.

34. Gay Wilson Allen, *The New Walt Whitman Handbook* (New York: New York University Press, 1975), p. 83.

35. See J. Lyndon Shanley, *The Making of Walden* (Chicago: University of Chicago Press, 1957); Ronald L. Clapper, "The Development of *Walden*: A Genetic Text," Ph.D. diss., UCLA, 1967; and Donald A. Ross and Stephen Adams, "The Endings of *Walden* and Stages of Composition," *Bulletin of Research in the Humanities* 84 (Winter 1981): 451–469.

36. Michael West, "Charles Kraitsir's Influence upon Thoreau's Theory of Language," *Emerson Society Quarterly* 19 (4 Qtr. 1973): 262–274; Philip F. Gura, *The Wisdom of Words: Language, Theology, and Literature in the New England Renaissance* (Middletown, Conn.: Wesleyan University Press, 1981), p. 134.

GORDON V. BOUDREAU

Springs to Remember

Shall not a man have his spring as well as the plants?
J, II, 34

Remember thy Creator in the days of thy youth!
J, II, 330

In his *Divine Comedy*, Dante Alighieri placed himself imaginatively at midpoint in man's allotted threescore and ten, in the dark wood, about to pass beneath an arch that proclaimed the loss of hope to all who entered, but that instead gave entry to a passage ultimately leading to a heavenly vision of redemption. Thoreau left the woods of Walden shortly after his thirtieth birthday, having caught glimpses of his inner self in a landscape less sullen and forbidding than that in Dante's poem, and glimpses of an arch that proclaimed the discovery of hope, not its abandonment. He had not yet found himself: further reflection, speculation, and a struggle to articulate what he saw would be his means of doing so. On the threshold of his thirty-fifth year he sensed such an "interval between my ideal and the actual ... that I may say I am unborn" (J, II, 316), for his life seemed "in the germ" only, "almost wholly unexpanded." But as the "year of observation" came to a close, it seemed to Thoreau, now "in the fulness of life," that nature "rushes to make her report. To the full heart she is all but a figure of speech" (J, IV, 174). Having hitherto

From *The Roots of* Walden *and the Tree of Life*, pp. 89–104. © 1990 by Gordon V. Boudreau.

felt "differently timed" (J, II, 316) than the seasons, on the brink of spring 1852, he seemed full of expectations: "I go forth to make new demands on life.... I pray that the life of this spring and summer may ever lie fair in my memory" (J, III, 351). By April the incongruity between the cycles of the seasons and of his own life had so far diminished that he could write: "For the first time I perceive this spring that the year is a circle. I see distinctly the spring arc thus far" (J, III, 438). And his passage beneath this arc is attended by a radical reshaping of the *Walden* manuscript, a process beginning in late January 1852, as critics generally agree.[1]

A month before this creative renewal, Thoreau, on Christmas Day, 1851, seems to have been haunted by the warning of Ecclesiastes in writing,

> Remember your Creator in the days of your youth and justify His ways to man, that the end of life may not be its amusement, speak—though your thought presupposes the non-existence of your hearers—thoughts that transcend life and death. (J, III, 157–58)[2]

And as he began a major reshaping of *Walden* as an organic work, he linked authorial self to a mythic spring by means of radical imagery:

> If thou art a writer, write as if thy time were short, for it is indeed short at the longest. Improve each occasion when thy soul is reached. Drain the cup of inspiration to its last dregs. Fear no intemperance in that, for the years will come when otherwise thou wilt regret opportunities unimproved. The spring will not last forever. These fertile and expanding seasons of thy life, when the rain reaches thy root, when thy vigor shoots, when thy flower is budding, shall be fewer and farther between. Again I say, Remember thy Creator in the days of thy youth. (J, III, 221–22)

At the beginning of the period of such "rememberings," Thoreau's journal discloses a genesis of several important meanings of "spring" that will inform *Walden*: (1) a season of the year (and of the day), (2) a welling up of waters, and (3) a rapid growth, a leap—all of which shape *Walden* as a spring of springs.

* * *

Standing vigil over the workings of Thaw on the frost in the Deep Cut, Thoreau in 1852 remarked that "the element of water prevails" (J, III, 437), thereby suggesting an aqueous "spring of the year." On the last day of 1851 he had found a low mist suffusing the woods, making an "exhibition of lichens at Forest Hall," and wrote approvingly: "True, as Thales said, the world was made out of water. That is the principle of all things" (J, III, 167). Some fifteen years earlier he had entertained an etymological basis for Thales' true principle by copying into his first notebook a passage from "Gebelin—blonde Primitif—Dictionnaire Etymol. Francoise":

> From the primitive word, Ver, signifying water ... is derived the word verite; for as water, by reason of its transparency and limpidness, is the mirror of bodies—of physical etres, so also is truth equally the mirror of ideas—of intellectual etres, representing them in a manner as faithful and and [sic] clear, as the water does a physical body.[3]

Thus in Thoreau's mind "Ver" seemed at once significant of Spring, the vernal season, and of water, the "true" element that mirrored and reflected nature.

To be sure the watery element had long prevailed in Thoreau's imagination, at least from the time he journalized in 1838 under the heading "Resource" that while some were "constantly dinging in my ears their fair theories and plausible solutions of the universe," he would "return again to my shoreless—islandless ocean, and fathom unceasingly for a bottom that will hold an anchor, that it may not drag" (PJ, I, 51; J, I, 54). During expeditions to Cape Cod in 1849 and 1850, Thoreau not only visited "Ocean," but attempted to interpret the powerfully voiced expression of Thales' element, which seemed the utterance of a "Reverend Polyphloisboios Thalassa," as he phonetically sounded the Greek for this "loud-roaring" and "infinite smiling" ocean (CC, 51–52).

His ear was better attuned to fluvial preachments—those of the Concord (and its branches, the Sudbury and Assabet), of the Merrimack, and of the turbulent rivers of the Maine woods. But even after publication of *A Week*, he had not yet put the foot of his mind into the true element so as to be influenced by it, to flow with it. In the summer of 1851, he felt he could not "get wet through," even with repeated bathing in the river. So when he came to a river in his walks, he would remove his clothes, carrying them on his head. "I would fain take rivers in my walks endwise" (J, II, 335). So compulsive did his immersive tendencies become that the next summer he did indeed begin such "endwise" walks, on July 10 making "quite an excursion up and down [the Assabet] in the water, a fluvial, a water, walk. It seemed the properest highway for this weather" (J, IV, 212). Two days later he took another fluvial walk, and a fortnight thereafter, on a day too cool for such a pilgrimage, wrote at length about the virtues of such holy exercises (J, IV, 220, 260). When he came across Richard Chenevix Trench's *On the Study of Words* early in 1853, he found, in a discussion of "rivals," philological support for radical, if paradoxical, meanings in the Concord River:

> Trench says that "'rivals,' in the primary sense of the word, are those who dwell on the banks of the same stream" or "on opposite banks," but as he says, in many words, since the use of water-rights is a fruitful source of contention between such neighbors, the word has acquired this secondary sense. My friends are my rivals on the Concord, in the primitive sense of the word. There is no strife between us respecting the use of the stream. The Concord offers many privileges, but none to quarrel about. It is a peaceful, not a brawling, stream. It has not made rivals out of neighbors that lived on its banks, but friends. My friends are my rivals; we dwell on opposite banks of the stream, but that stream is the Concord, which flows without a ripple or a murmur, without a rapid or a brawl, and offers no petty privileges to quarrel about. (J, IV, 467–68)

Such fluvial and etymological saunterings show the degree to which Thoreau, situated on the banks of the Concord, was influenced to think of himself as a hydrostatic paradox. Moreover, he interiorized, almost surely with a pun on his name, his preference to be "a channel or *through*fare ... of the mountain springs, and not the town sewers,—the Parnassian streams" (J, II, 289–90; emphasis added).

But the essential factor in his etymological interiorizing and radicalizing was not stasis, but movement, a sense of flowing. A river was "superior to a lake in its liberating influence," he would write in 1858, for it has "motion and indefinite length. A river touching the back of a town is like a wing.... With its rapid current it is a slightly fluttering wing. River towns are winged towns" (J, XI, 4–5). In 1850 he wrote in sympathy with a river on the rise: "The life in us is like the water in the river; it may rise this year higher than ever it was known to before and flood the uplands—even this may be the eventful year ..." (J, II, 33). A few days later he queried, "Does not the stream still rise to its fountain-head in you?" (J, II, 44). On the very eve of his thirty-fifth birthday, with the Concord River running low, he commented that "the shrunken stream of life overflows its banks, makes and fertilizes broad intervals," and these flooded and fecund "intervals" are enough to sustain generations. "If we have not dissipated the vital, the divine, fluids, there is, then, a circulation of vitality beyond our bodies" (J, IV, 219).

When the stream in the prevailing figure shifts from shrunken and static to boisterous and living, its "circulation of vitality" is attributed to the elevation of its source or wellspring above any other point on the river's course. When the stream's inclination is most emphatic and pronounced, the plane of its movement tending from the horizontal to the vertical, its utterance is most lavish, vocal, gleeful. Thoreau sensed "something more than association at the bottom of the excitement which the roar of a cataract produces." There seemed to be a boisterous stream in the veins as well:

> We have a waterfall which corresponds even to Niagara somewhere within us. It is astonishing what a rush and tumult a slight inclination will produce in a swollen brook. How it proclaims its glee, its boisterousness, rushing headlong in its prodigal course as if it would exhaust itself in half an hour!

Then, bending his ear, he seemed to catch what the flowing water expressed: "I would say to the orator and poet, Flow freely and *lavishly* as a brook that is full,—without stint. Perchance I have stumbled upon the origin of the word 'lavish'" (J, II, 155–56).[4]

In 1851, his "watershed year" according to Lewis Leary, the flow of his thought seemed without stint, his journal a lavish, loving concordance. And in 1857, another year of high water, he wrote of an autumnal "rise of the waters [that] must affect every thought and deed in the town. It qualifies my sentence and life." He hoped there might be some perceptible influence in his journal, "some flow, some gradual filling of the springs and raising of the streams, that the accumulating grists may be ground" (J, X, 126). In learning to "express adequately only the thought which I *love* to express" (J, II, 291), Thoreau suggests a lavish confluence of outer and inner streams in an expression of truth, *verite*, especially pronounced in Spring (*Ver*).

But it was to Walden Pond that Thoreau turned in 1845–47 for an expression of spring. He found its surface a continual fascination, a "field of water [which] betrays the spirit that is in the air" (J, II, 57). Here was a "pool of Bethsaida [*sic*] which must be stilled and become smooth before we can enter to be healed" (J, V, 454). When subject and object shared a reflective mood, the still surface of this water became a tabula rasa upon which the aerial spirit breathed a sentence that on land could be discerned only by the most sensitive brow. Perhaps Walden Pond presented such a brow, a temple sur-face better able than the brow of man to sense the least movement of spirit. In the late spring of 1854, a few months before the publication of *Walden*, Thoreau wrote in his journal of how dead the earth would appear if it were not for these water surfaces! We are slow to realize water,—the beauty and magic of it. It is interestingly strange to us forever. Immortal water, alive even in the superficies, restlessly heaving now and tossing me and my boat, and sparkling with life! I look round with a thrill on this bright fluctuating surface on which no man can walk, whereon is no trace of footstep.... (J, VI, 246)

But Walden Pond presented a reflecting mirror of deeper realities as well. Gazing into the "bottomless" pond was like looking to the backing of a magic mirror wherein one could not only see a reflection of the animal (or animated) self, but also catch a glimpse of an image or shadow divine, a similitude of the "ungraspable phantom of life" Melville's Ishmael sought in his watery reflections. And this glimpsed if ungraspable reflection becomes a kind of revelation uniting man and pond in a universal, aqueous expression. As he gazes upon its reflecting surface, Thoreau seems to merge his personality with that of the pond, just as the pond—returning his gaze from an "iris" (Wa, 176) deep in "earth's eye" (Wa, 186)—assumes a personality and even "licks its chaps" (Wa, 181) as if about to speak. The water seems to be lapping its lips, its shoreline, boundary of the literal, from which its beard, its trees, have been "*shorn*" (Wa, 181). Except for John Field's well, and perhaps Flint's Pond, the bodies of water that figure in the pages of *Walden* serve as vital links with the springs below. For Thoreau the very sight of a spring seemed an expression of the divine. Going out of his way to pass Boiling Spring, he exclaimed: "What a treasure is such a spring! Who *divined* it?" (J, IV, 104). And in *Walden* he would complain that the "devilish Iron Horse ... has muddied the Boiling Spring with his foot" (Wa, 192). For him the sealing up of a well was a funereal ceremony forestalling the pilgrimage of water from its radical springs to its celestial destination, and if we would "go in search of the springs of life," Thoreau believed, we would "get exercise enough" (J, II, 472).[5]

Walden Pond was such a spring, having no inlet except from springs below, no outlet except to the overarching heavens. In a journal poem of 1838, Thoreau had provokingly suggested a dialogue with the ebullient spring, even as he discounted that literal possibility:

True, our converse a stranger is to speech;
Only the practiced ear can catch the surging words
That break and die upon thy pebbled lips.
Thy flow of thought is noiseless as the lapse of thy own waters,
Wafted as is the morning mist up from thy surface,

So that the passive Soul doth breathe it in,
And is infected with the truth thou wouldst express.
(J, I, 50; PJ, I, 47)

By the early 1850s, Thoreau's ear had grown so practiced in listening to nature that in the living waters of Walden Pond his "passive Soul" could detect the articulations of a perennial "flow of thought." The "noiseless ... lapse" from "these lips of the lake, on which no beard grows"—had they become a littoral expression of a paradoxical "sound silence" he had come to hear? Might he now be able to express, from the shores of his Walden spring, the very silence over which *A Week* had closed?

But the deepest, as well as the most lavish, expressions of spring were subject to the stilling tyranny of nature's frost, which might seal to silence the deep springs of the text of Walden Pond. In 1853, as summer's flame began to gutter, Thoreau mused upon the names of those months for the period of frost's tyrannic grip. With kinesthetic extravagance he noted,

> September is at hand; the first month (after the summer heat) with a *burr* to it, month of early frosts; but December will be tenfold rougher. January relents for a season at the time of its thaw, and hence that liquid *r* in its name. (J, V, 400)

Of special pertinence in unfolding a sense in his remarks about these "ber" months is that Thoreau had a speech "defect" that gave a peculiar sort of "burr" sound to the letter *r*, thus the terminal syllable of each "-ber" month would elicit an equivalent shiver from him.[6] That winter, Thoreau enlarged on the relationship between the names of the months and the freezing and thawing they signified:

> But the last part of January and all February thus far have been alternate thaw and freeze and snow. It [February] has more thaws, even as the running 'r' (root of ῥέω) occurs twice in it and but once in January. I do not know but the more light and warmth plainly accounts for the difference.... We begin to have days precursors of spring. (J, VI, 127–28)

His verbal radicalism here suggests that the seasonal thaw converts a frozen (radical) *r* of the "-ber" months to a running liquid *r* in January, and as with a more intensive or repetitive thaw, to a double liquid *r* in February. If one could weather January, "the hardest month" for Thoreau, he would be "into the gulfstream of winter, nearer the shores of spring" (J, VI, 91).

In the spring of 1852, at a time when he was reading Sir John Richardson's account of a polar expedition, Thoreau had tried to dig some parsnip roots out of the half-frozen ground and wrote that "the Greek word ἔαρ [Spring] runs in my head in connection with the season and Richardson's Book" (J, III, 363; my brackets); but "though the frost is nearly out of the ground, the winter has not broken up in me".[7] Two days later he found in the thoughts and sentences of William Gilpin's *Forest Scenery* a frost-free expression, as if "some of the cool wind of the copses converted into grammatical and graceful sentences, without heat" (J, III, 370). That day he walked along the railroad causeway near the pond, where the laborers had "dug around the sleepers [railway ties] that the sun may thaw the ground and let them down" (J, III, 371). From this place of vantage he could see the "cheering," open waters of the Great Sudbury Meadows (J, III, 372). Still, and despite hearing the "*spring* note of the chickadee from over the ice" at Walden Pond, his thoughts went "back at once some weeks toward winter, and a chill comes over them" (J, III, 370). Flint's Pond, still nearly frozen over, seemed "that Icy Sea of which I have been reading in Sir J. Richardson's book" (J, III, 372), an "opaque dumb pond ... unexpectedly dumb and poor," a "dull, white ice" doubtless all Greek, a riddling, frost-encrusted blankness. But beneath the frost, as December gave way to January with one thaw, to February with two, Thoreau sensed an impending spring that would release the "living waters" in the stream of nature as in language, even as the burr in the first syllable of his last name, *Thor*, thawed to express -*eau*, water. By such radical expressions, Thoreau's verbal artistry paralleled that of the primal artist laboring in the Deep Cut near the shores of a woodland "spring." There Thoreau studied the tracing of leaves and fossil words in the thawing bankside, and there the fluid, lapsing sounds of running water filled the ear of one now practiced to "catch the surging words / That break and die upon [Walden's] pebbled lips" (J, I, 50; PJ, I, 47).

In a moving journal entry for February 7, 1841, Thoreau had anticipated frost's subsiding to the breath of spring and the flow of waters, capturing in sibilants and liquids the affecting results of a midwinter thaw:

> The eaves are running on the south side of the house; the titmouse lisps in the poplar; the bells are ringing for church; while the sun presides over all and makes his simple warmth more obvious than all else. What shall I do with this hour, so like time and yet so fit for eternity? Where in me are these russet patches of ground, and scattered logs and chips in the yard? I do not feel cluttered. I have some notion what the John's-wort and life-everlasting may be thinking about when the sun shines on me as on them and turns

my prompt thought into just such a seething shimmer. I lie out indistinct as a heath at noonday. I am evaporating and ascending into the sun. (J, I, 203–4; PJ, I, 256)

Though he might not know what to do with the hour in 1841, he would store it in his journal for the day in which he might fulfill his injunction of July 21, 1851, at the threshold of his thirty-fifth year, to "remember thy Creator in the days of thy youth; *i.e.*, lay up a store of natural influences. Sing while you may, before the evil days come. He that hath ears, let him hear" (J, II, 330). And when he came to sing of Walden Pond as his spring of natural influences, he found that "A thousand rills which have their rise in the sources of thought burst forth and fertilize my brain" (J, II, 405). He had stopped short of such sources in *A Week*; now he was prepared to go on.

* * *

What inspired Thoreau's wonder about the thoughts of the "John's-wort" and "life-everlasting" four years before taking up residence at Walden Pond, thirteen years before the publication of *Walden*? Was he merely attempting to drive a wedge into *sainte terre* by cheap wordplay? upon the Gospel of St. John (John's "wort") and the promise of immortality (life-everlasting) in St. Paul? Or was he so elementally soiled that he likewise anticipated a lavish, liquid call to life, engendered by the vernal sun, by which the germs and radicals that endured the winter would spring into life? One sign of the latter is the emergence of "spring" as a verbal in the pages of his journal, as when he speculates that "perhaps after the thawing of the trees their buds universally swell before they can be said to spring" (J, III, 366). Pulling up a lily by the roots that summer, he closely considered "how it sends its buds upward to the light and air to expand and flower in another element. How interesting the bud's progress from the water to the air!" (J, IV, 162). The next spring, looking for signs of the vitalizing fluid in plants, he reported on March 13 that "no sap flows yet from my hole in the white maple by the bridge" (J, V, 19); a week later, however, he "rejoiced to see the sap falling in large, clear drops from the wound" (J, V, 31). The flow of sap running in vertical rivers in the cambium layer or liber of trees prophesied leaf, flower, and fruit; and the sight of a load of rock maples transported from the north country on the Fitchburg Railroad on May 8, 1852, prompted him to write that "their buds have not yet started, while ours are leaved out.... A tree, with all its roots, which has not felt the influence of spring is a most startling evidence of winter ..." (J, IV, 38). The next spring it was still more evident that Thoreau conceived vegetation as an organic consequence of the flow of living waters through a root system:

"Now, when the sap of the trees is probably beginning to flow, the sap of the earth, the river, overflows and bursts its icy fetters" (J, V, 11). Within plant systems, rivers flowed vertically to become lavish expressions, flowed into flowers and leaves, even as Thoreau's interior stream flowed into "flowers of thought, and ... leaves of thought; most of our thoughts [being] merely leaves, to which the thread of thought is the stem" (J, II, 441).[8]

Thoreau had witnessed a dry run of the bud's progress from the water to the air in 1842 by watching corn popping on his hearth, which he considered "a more rapid blossoming of the seed" that nonetheless observed the same "law by which flowers unfold their petals." In the rapid, dry "blossoming" of the popcorn into white flowers, not only was the element of water, the law of currents, absent; but the "blossom," an expression of the law of vegetation, was merely fanciful: "By my warm hearth sprang these cerealious blossoms ..." (J, I, 311–12; PJ, I, 357). A somewhat less rapid patterning of vegetation was the frost on his window, which Thoreau had witnessed in 1837 as another formulation of nature's springing. A few months before the publication of *Walden*, he again reflected upon the formation of ice foliage, this time outside his window: "I saw some crystals beginning to shoot on the pools between the tussocks, shaped like feathers or fan-coral,—the most delicate I ever saw." So, too, did the ice begin "with crystal leaves, and birds' feathers and wings are leaves, and trees and rivers with intervening earth are vast leaves" (J, VI, 154).

* * *

With fire effecting a similitude of rapid blossoming in popcorn, and the formation of ice a swift and delicate growth of vegetation, the influence of an actual spring was only somewhat less urgent in advancing the bud's progress. As Thoreau wrote in May, 1853: "How rapidly the young twigs shoot ... as if they had acquired a head by being repressed so long.... Many do most of their growing for the year in a week or two at this season. They *shoot*—they *spring* ..." (J, V, 189). His excited passage—the emphasis is his—only finds relief from an intense struggle for expression in the verb "spring." And when *Walden* was all but complete, Thoreau, sitting on a rail over a brook in which there was "the least possible springing yet," caught sight of "a little yellow lily in the ditch and sweet flag *starting* in the brook" (J, VI, 182; again Thoreau's emphasis), whereupon he heard "something which reminded me of the song of the robin in rainy days in past springs. Why is it that not the note itself," he mused, "but something which reminds me of it, should affect me most?—the ideal instead of the actual" (J, VI, 182). And to this outward sound of spring he started, for it seemed a confirmation of spring—sweet flag, robin, and

Thoreau springing in consort with the yellow lily in the ditch. And it seemed a remembrance as well—of a dreamlike vision on a day in his youth when he had first visited the pond that would become his own spring of springs.

Finally, Thoreau's style of writing, no less than his vision, has a spring to it. Like the mythic Antaeus, his expression, never "long absent from the ground," found its basis on "the spring floor of our life." His were sentences with "little resiliencies" of meaning, having "a distinct fruit and kernel ..., springing from terra firma" (J, III, 107). In a cattail he examined in the spring of 1853, he found a natural exemplar of such sentences: "Apparently there is a spring to the fine elastic threads which compose the down, which, after having been so closely packed, on being the least relieved at the base, spring open apace into the form of parachutes to convey the seed afar" (J, V, 44). His own manner of walking was of a kind: his Harvard classmates noticed a kind of Indian elasticity in his gait, and his friend Channing once "kept up an incessant strain of wit, banter, about my legs, which were so springy and unweariable," declaring "I had got my double legs on ... not cork but steel" (J, III, 96).

Thoreau's manner of walking provided the physiological base for a writing style that has been called walked; moreover, he confounded walking and writing in brilliantly characterizing Bronson Alcott's poetic style as "sublimo slip-shod" (J, III, 118). To Emerson, Thoreau's style seemed somewhat military; Thoreau himself wrote of there being

> a true march to the sentence, as if a man or a body of men were actually making progress there step by step, and these are not the mere *disjecta membra*, the dispersed and mutilated members though it were of heroes, which can no longer walk and join themselves to their comrades. They are not perfect nor liberated pieces of art for the galleries, yet they stand on the natural and broad pedestal of the living rock, but have a principle of life and growth in them still, as has that human nature from which they spring. (J, I, 480; PJ, II, 118–19)

By cultivating beans at Walden Pond, Thoreau ran the risk of the money farmer, who soon "lost his elasticity" (J, II, 160), became stiff-jointed, and could neither run nor jump. He sensed that "at a very early age the mind of man, perhaps at the same time with his body, ceases to be elastic...." No longer expansive in his thinking, as in "his growing days," one's movements would contract and harden. "What was flexible sap hardens into heart-wood, and there is no further change" (J, III, 903). In youth one's spring came without thought, he could then "run and leap; he has not learned exactly how far, he knows no limits" (J, III, 204). With some notable exceptions, however, Thoreau would maintain his spring walk throughout life, sometime with extravagant bounding, in a way to sympathize with the plant's aspirations to spring.[9] In his approach for the spring, however, Thoreau had his eye not so much on the height to which he aspired as on the ground from which he would spring. In his downward thrust for the leap, he compared himself to the leaves that fall "at the first earnest touch of autumn's wand. They stoop to rise, to mount higher in coming years ..." (J, V, 444). Unlike most of the Transcendentalists—and especially Emerson, who found promise in many a youth, only to be disappointed later—he was wary of the premature spring that was warned of in the parable of the sower (Wa, 297), a spring that would quickly exhaust the resources of the root system and conclude in a fruitless fall, hope unfulfilled.[10] What counted was the harvest, not early growth merely; so he checked the impulse to leap before his roots were planted:

> When introduced to high life I cannot help perceiving how it is as a thing jumped at, and I find that I do not get on in my enjoyment of the fine arts which adorn it, because my attention is wholly occupied with the jump, remembering that the greatest genuine leap on record, due to human muscles alone, is that of certain wandering Arabs who cleared twenty-five feet on level ground. The first question which I am tempted to put to the proprietor of such great impropriety is, "Who boosts you?" (J, II, 230)

While his testy friend Channing would not "stoop to rise" (J, III, 108), Thoreau, because the only real booster was the "spring floor of life," relished delving to a sound base for his leap:

> Better dive like a muskrat into the mud, and pile up a few weeds to sit on during the floods, a foundation of your own laying, a house of your own building, however cold and cheerless.
>   Methinks the hawk that soars so loftily and circles so steadily and apparently without effort has earned this power by faithfully creeping on the ground as a reptile in a former state of existence. You must creep before you can run; you must run before you can fly. Better one effective bound upward with elastic limbs from the valley than a jumping from the mountain-tops in the attempt to fly. The observatories are not built high but deep; the foundation is equal to the superstructure. It is more important to a distinct vision that it be steady than that it be from an elevated point of view. (J, III, 108)

Thoreau once questioned Alex Therien, that finest expression of mere animal vitality in the pages of *Walden*, to find out "if he was satisfied with himself. I was trying to get a point d'appui within him, a shelf to spring an arch from, to suggest some employment and aim for life" (J, VI, 35–36). The implied architectural image, another form of "springing," is explicit in Thoreau's noting that the mason requires "but a narrow shelf to spring his brick from; man requires only an infinitely narrower one to spring the arch of faith from." He then remarks that "the only ledge I can spring the arch of friendship from is the ground of infinite faith" (J, III, 259). Sometimes the spring "arch of faith" was in the form of the rainbow, a "faint vision of God's face" (J, IV, 128) transcendentally suggesting an "infinite faith." His claim to have once stood in the light at the end of the rainbow arch has been disputed earnestly by critics whose concern for objective truth is frustrated by Thoreau's willfully extravagant, fabulous truth. What he may have meant was that he was standing on *sainte terre*, a sacred point d'appui from which every "arch of faith" must be sprung, especially the arch of faith that is the sign of the covenant sprung in the heavens by the divine architect, perhaps Thoreau's ideal friend. On the spring floor of that arch Thoreau basked in the "faint vision of God's face," and "lived like a dolphin" (Wa, 202) in a light that, refracted, made a rainbow arch.[11]

But it was in vegetation, chiefly, that Thoreau found his spring "arch of faith." At Flint's Pond in late summer 1851, he found in the swamp loosestrife, a "willow-like" formulation:

> It grows up two feet from a large woody horizontal root, and droops over to the sand again, meeting which, it puts out a myriad rootlets from the side of its stem, fastens itself, and curves upward again to the air, thus spanning or looping itself along. The bark just above the ground thickens into a singular cellular or spongy substance, which at length appears to crack nearer the earth, giving that part of the plant a winged and somewhat four-sided appearance. (J, II, 501–2)

Many of the spring arches come together in Thoreau's observation of "the firm earth mingled with the sky, like the spray of the sea tossed up." In such an arch, as he saw it, is there not always "a latent reference to its beauty? The arch supports itself, like the stars, by gravity,—by always falling never falls (*semper cadendo nunquam cadit*)" (J, IV, 152). The most nearly perfect expression of such arches, however, was in poetry. "Methinks there are few specimens of architecture so perfect as a verse of poetry," Thoreau wrote. "Architectural remains are beautiful not intrinsically and absolutely, but from association" (J, IV, 153). And the poet, "he who generates poems," was affected by his work so that "by continence he rises to creation on a higher level, a supernatural level" (J, III, 191).[12]

The level to which Thoreau rose was proportional to the resilience of his "understanding." In the early spring of 1853, he wrote of his open-soled communion with the earth, which struck him

> as a wonderful piece of chemistry, that the very grass we trample on and esteem so cheap should be thus wonderfully nourished, that this spring greenness was not produced by coarse and cheap means, but in sod, out of sight, the most delicate and magical processes are going on. The half is not shown. The very sod is replete with mechanism far finer than that of a watch, and yet it is cast under our feet to be trampled on. (J, V, 69)

He thought the process that goes on "in the sod and the dark, about the minute fibres of the grass,—the chemistry and the mechanics,—before a single green blade can appear above the withered herbage," if adequately described, "would supplant all other revelations." And he went on to suggest his brief contact with the fine organization on the other side of nature's sentence: "We are acquainted with but one side of the sod. I brought home some tufts of the grass in my pocket, but when I took it out I could not at first find those pearly white fibres and thought that they were lost, for they were shrunk to dry brown threads"; and when he examined the "still finer gossamer ... with few exceptions they were absolutely undiscoverable,—they no longer stood out around the core,—so fine and delicate was their organization" (J, V, 69).

The apex of the spring arc is implicit in Thoreau's lengthy description of the flight of the hawk in paragraph 22 of "Spring" ("On the 29th of April ..."), which had appeared, almost verbatim, in the first version of *Walden* in 1847.[13] A number of journal analogues point up the impression made upon Thoreau by such stirring flights, though no single journal source survives. On March 27, 1842, Thoreau was observing two little hawks overhead when suddenly a new bird, flying in over Fairhaven Cliffs, joined them with stunning abruptness. It was "probably an eagle, quite above me, laboring with the wind not more than forty rods off." The "largest bird of the falcon kind" he had ever seen, he "was never so impressed by any flight" (J, I, 351; PJ, I, 393–94). Four days later he was still fascinated by "the majesty of that bird at the Cliff.... It was a great presence, as of the master of river and forest" (J, I, 356; PJ, I, 398). On December 20, 1851, he was impressed by the flight of what appeared to be a large hawk, rising above him and circling, and showing with beautiful distinctness its wings against the sky,—primaries and secondaries, and the rich tracery of the outline of the latter (?), its inner wings, or wing-linings, within the outer,—like a great moth seen against the sky. A will-o'-the-wind. Following its path, as it were through the vortices of the air. The poetry of motion. (J, III, 143)

And after a journal aside, Thoreau underscored his awe: "What made the hawk mount? Did you perceive the manoeuvre? Did he fill himself with air? Before you were aware of it, he had mounted by his spiral path into the heavens" (J, III, 145). With his own heart "on the mount" (J, IV, 467) in sympathetic aspiration, Thoreau was answering his complaint of 1850 that "we hug the earth. How rarely we mount! ... Shall not a man have his spring as well as the plants?" (J, II, 34). And when he related the flight of the bird to the spring of the plant, he drew himself into a pattern of natural spring arches that he stood within, understood. In *Walden*. he would work these impressions into "sentences in which there is no strain," sentences without "a fluttering and inconstant and *quasi* inspiration, and ever memorable Icarian fall, in which your helpless wings are expanded merely by your swift descent into the *pelagos* beneath" (J, III, 108).

"What made the hawk mount?" It was a question he posed in the first version of *Walden*: "Where was the parent that hatched it [the bird], its kindred, and its father in the heavens?"[14] As Thoreau pushed the cause of its mounting back from leaf, to bud, to radicals, and finally to the spring floor of life, the answer was emerging as nature's revelation. In a journal entry for April 2, 1852, Thoreau described how, a few weeks before the birds actually returned to Concord,

there came to my mind in the night the twittering sound of birds in the early dawn of a spring morning, a semiprophecy of it, and last night I attended mentally as if I heard the spray-like dreaming sound of the midsummer frog and realized how glorious and full of revelations it was. Expectation may amount to prophecy. (J, III, 377)

By summer he had mentally reversed the "bud's progress from the water to the air," seeing in the lily root, which "sends its buds, upward in the light and air to expand and flower in another element," a rudimentary expression of the same principle. In his search for the radical cause of the bud's progress, his eye was turning to the Deep Cut, where nature seemed to be tracing its vernal fable—in Greek (ἔαρ), in Latin (*Ver, Verite*), and finally, in Thoreau's native tongue—*Spring*.

* * *

In his classic mid-life pilgrimage, Dante begins in a wooded maze of the spirit to pass beneath the arch of despair and the Fall; in his pilgrimage to his classic, Thoreau, recovering from the dashed hopes or lapsing dreams of *A Week*, passes beneath the arch of hope and spring in his thirty-fifth year. Like Dante, he may have been on his way to a fabulous "mountain in the easterly part of our town (where no high hill actually is) which once or twice I had ascended, and often allowed my thoughts alone to climb" (J, X, 141). But if his "way up used to lie through a dark and unfrequented wood at its base," as he reports in 1857, he paid little attention to the wood, and soon "lost [himself] quite in the upper air and clouds." Even this late the thoughts Thoreau entertains about these mountains are in a formative stage, as the phrasings and interlineations suggest:

> It chances, now I think of it, that it [the mountain] rises in my mind where lies the Burying-Hill. You might go through its gate to enter the dark wood, but that hill and its grave are so concealed and obliterated by the awful mountain that I never thought of them as underlying it. (J, X, 142–43)

For Thoreau, who had a positive phobia about graveyards, the Dantean passageway through the arch of death in order to ascend the mountain seems rarely to have entered his mind:

> There are ever two ways up: one is through the dark wood, the other through the sunny pasture. That is, I reach and discover the mountain only through the dark wood, but I see to my surprise, when I look off between the mists from its summit, how it is ever adjacent to my native fields, nay, imminent over them, and accessible through a sunny pasture. Why is it that in the lives of men we hear more of the dark wood than of the sunny pasture?[15]

In *Walden* he would briefly attend to such dark wood sounds, singling out the call of the hooting owl as "the most melancholy sound in Nature ... some poor weak relic of mortality ... yet with human sobs, on entering the dark valley..." (Wa, 125). Without a Virgil—as a fellow saunterer Channing filled the bill only peevishly and inconstantly—a solitary Thoreau would reject the Dantean note of despair, as exemplified in the hooting owl, to recover a lapsed hope beneath a spring arch. Emerging in an upland "sunny pasture," Thoreau pushed aside the medicinal cup of Hygeia and communed with the laws of currents and vegetation by drinking deeply from the cup of Hebe (Spring), "cupbearer to Jupiter, who was the daughter of Juno and wild lettuce, and who had the power of restoring gods and men to the vigor of youth." And he continued with what is again almost surely a pun on his own name: "She was probably the only *thoroughly* sound-conditioned, healthy, and robust young lady that ever walked the globe, and wherever she came it was spring" (Wa, 139; emphasis added). Indeed, she was its personification, a spring to remember. But a spring to re-member as well, and make of a two-year sojourn at Walden Pond a fitting, organic response to the admonition "Remember thy Creator in the days of thy youth" (J, II, 330), a response that was a spring of springs.

Notes

1. J. Lyndon Shanley, *The Making of* Walden (Chicago: Univ. of Chicago Press, 1957), p. 31, dates the beginning of the process of the creative reshaping of *Walden* as January 17, 1852; Ronald Clapper, "The Development of *Walden*: A Genetic Text" (Ph. D. diss., Univ. of California at Los Angeles, 1967), p. 22, proposes January 22, 1852. For a broader view of the period, see Lewis Leary, "'Now I Adventured': 1851 as a Watershed Year in Thoreau's Career," *ESQ: A Journal of the American Renaissance* 19 (1973): 141–48.

2. On July 21, 1851, Thoreau had written: "Remember thy Creator in the days of thy youth; *i.e.*, lay up a store of natural influences. Sing while you may, before the evil days come. He that hath ears, let him hear. See, hear, smell, taste, etc., while these senses are fresh and pure" (J, II, 330); and in *Walden*, "Remember thy Creator in the days of thy youth. Rise free from care before the dawn, and seek adventures" (Wa, 207). The passage paraphrases Ecclesiastes 12:1:

Remember now thy Creator in the days of thy youth,
While the evil days come not,
Nor the years draw nigh, when thou shalt say,
I have no pleasure in them.

The twelfth verse of this chapter is, "And further, by these, my son, be admonished: of making many books there is no end; and much study is a weariness of the flesh." To this passage Thoreau took exception: "Much study a weariness of the flesh, eh? But did not they intend that we should read and ponder, who covered the whole earth with alphabets—primers or bibles—coarse or fine print?" (J, VI, 132). See Gordon V. Boudreau, "'Remember Thy Creator': Thoreau and St. Augustine," *ESQ: A Journal of the American Renaissance* 19 (1973): 149–60.

3. Paul, *Shores*, p. 335; MA 594, the Pierpont Morgan Library. "Ver" is also the name of the spring goddess.

4. On his Minnesota journey in 1861, Thoreau wrote with obvious pleasure that "all water falls, in the Dakota tongue, are called Ha-ha, never Minnehaha [as Longfellow has it]. The 'h' has a strong gutteral sound. The word is applied because of the curling of the waters. The verb I-ha-ha primarily means to curl; secondarily to laugh because of the curling motion of the mouth in laughter." "Notes on the Journey West," in *Thoreau's Minnesota Journey: Two Documents*, ed. Walter Harding, Thoreau Society Booklet no. 16 (Geneseo, N.Y., 1962), p. 12. The comment in brackets is Thoreau's.

5. In the concluding paragraph of *Cape Cod*, Thoreau wrote: "What are springs and waterfalls? Here is the spring of springs, the waterfall of waterfalls" (CC, 215); and in "Civil Disobedience": "They who know of no purer sources of truth, who have traced up its streams no higher, stand, and wisely stand, by the Bible and the Constitution, and drink at it there with reverence and humility; but they who behold where it comes trickling into this lake or that pool, gird up their loins once more, and continue their pilgrimage toward its fountainhead" (W, IV, 385–86).

6. Harding, *Days*, p. 346, mentions Thoreau's speech "defect," citing William Ellery Channing, *Thoreau, the Poet-Naturalist* (Boston, 1873), p. 2.

7. In 1860 Thoreau wrote that "February may be called *earine* (springlike)" (J, XIII, 129).

8. Thoreau regarded Chaucer as "almost ... a personification of spring" (Wk, 368), and often quoted or paraphrased Milton's "Lycidas" in his journal, a poem that may have supplied much of the rich suggestiveness in Thoreau's "laves" by the line "With nectar pure his [Lycidas's] oozy locks he [Christ] laves" (l. 175).

9. Harding, *Days*, pp. 357–63, gives an account of Thoreau's being afflicted with weak legs in 1855. Raymond Gozzi, "Tropes and Figures," p. 141, gives a Freudian interpretation that his weak legs were "the response of his unconscious to the success of *Walden*."

10. "I say that sometimes by their fruits ye shall know them" (J, IV, 306), Thoreau's paraphrase of Matthew 7:16, the parable of the sower.

11. Charles Anderson, *The Magic Circle of Walden* (New York: Holt, Rinehart & Winston, 1968), pp. 136–37, believes that Thoreau did stand in the end of a rainbow: "The incident he reports in *Walden* is not fabulous, though the rainbow itself is central to several fables." Walter Harding, *The Variorum Walden* (New York: Washington Square Press, 1968), p. 279, denies this possibility, advanced earlier by Charles D. Steward, "A Word for Thoreau," *Atlantic Monthly* 116 (1935): 110–16.

12. Cf. John Ruskin, "The Lamp of Memory," in *The Seven Lamps of Architecture* (New York: Longmans, Green, 1909), p. 324: "There are but two strong conquerors of the forgetfulness of men, Poetry and Architecture; and the latter in some sort includes the former, and is mightier in its reality: it is well to have not only what men have thought and felt, but what their hands have handled, and their strength wrought, and their eyes beheld, all the days of their life." Cf. Thoreau, June 20, 1840: "If we only see clearly enough how mean our lives are, they will be splendid enough. Let us remember not to strive upwards too long, but sometimes drop plumb down the other way, and wallow in meanness. From the deepest pit we may see the stars, if not the sun. Let us have presence of mind enough to sink when we can't swim. At any rate, a carcass had better lie on the bottom than float an offense to all nostrils. It will not be falling, for we shall ride wide of the earth's gravity as a star, and always be drawn upward still,—*semper cadendo nunquam cadit*,—and so, by yielding to universal gravity, at length become fixed stars" (J, I, 146). Thoreau read Ruskin in the fall of 1857; see Richardson, "Autumnal Tints, John Ruskin, and the Innocent Eye," in *HT: Life*, pp. 357–62.

13. Shanley, p. 104. See also Clapper, pp. 837–39.

14. Shanley, p. 207.

15. In "Walking," Thoreau wrote, "When I would recreate myself, I seek the darkest wood ..."; and in the same essay of how in surveying a line through a swamp that might appear the "entrance to the infernal regions,—'Leave all hope, ye that enter'"—he was cheered as if he were entering "a sacred place,—a *sanctum sanctorum*" (W, V, 228, 230).

LANCE NEWMAN

"Patron of the World": Henry Thoreau as Wordsworthian Poet

Though men return to servitude as fast
As the tide ebbs, to ignominy and shame,
By nations, sink together, we shall still
Find solace—knowing what we have learnt
    to know....
Prophets of Nature, we to them will
    speak
A lasting inspiration, sanctified
By reason, blest by faith: what we have loved,
Others will love, and we will teach them how;
Instruct them how the mind of man becomes
A thousand times more beautiful than the earth
On which he dwells....
    —Wordsworth, *Prelude*, XIV, lines 435–50

Early in his long relationship with Henry David Thoreau, Ralph Waldo Emerson wrote to Thomas Carlyle, telling him, "I have a young poet in this village named Thoreau, who writes the truest verses" (*Correspondence*, 246). Thoreau's poetry was "the purest strain, the loftiest ... that has yet pealed from this unpoetic American forest" (*Journals* 7:230–231). Later, Emerson would include the poems in his disappointed final assessment of his

From *The Concord Saunterer*, vol. 11 (2003), pp. 155–172. © 2003 by The Thoreau Society.

protégé's unfulfilled potential, claiming that Thoreau "wanted a lyric facility and technical skill," but still insisting that he "had the source of poetry in his spiritual perception ..." (*Works* 10:442). The distinction here, between making musical verse and the far more important ability to see and speak truly, was central to the Transcendentalists' thinking about poetry and poets. As Emerson put it in his most sustained statement on the subject, "it is not metres, but a metre-making argument, that makes a poem ..." (*Works* 3:15). Poetry was not a genre or form, it was the ability to harness the "universality of the symbolic language" (*Works* 3:21). By virtue of this ability, "the poet is representative. He stands among partial men for the complete man, and apprises us not of his wealth, but of the commonwealth" (*Works* 3:11). We sometimes forget about this Romantic idea that "poet" is the name of a social and political role, an "office," to use Emerson's term—and it is because we do that we have not appreciated Thoreau's poems fully. They are exploratory and miscellaneous, and they do not show the same kind of absolutely confident and single-minded formal invention that marks the work of Whitman or Dickinson. So we have not fit them into the standard tale of the American poetic revolution, in which twin innovators threw off the oppressive yoke of the Fireside Poets and began to sing the natural music of democracy. However, reading Thoreau's verse in an altered transatlantic context—as selectively appropriating and extending rather than simply rejecting the practice of his predecessors—reveals his poetry, in all its diversity, to be unified, along with the rest of his writing, by his lifelong dedication to the Wordsworthian model of the poet as public intellectual ministering to the moral health of a natural republic.

WORDSWORTH IN MASSACHUSETTS

During the first three decades of the nineteenth century, William Wordsworth's books sold slowly in the United States. However, American appreciation for the poems grew steadily during this period in ways that we have only recently begun to appreciate (Pace, "Gems" and "Wordsworth"). The modest American distribution of Wordsworth's books was supplemented by

the hundreds of times that passages from *The Excursion* were reprinted in Unitarian anthologies and the thousands of times Wordsworth's verse appeared in magazines, journals, papers, and miscellanies. American reprints of one school reader containing Wordsworth, C. L. Murray's *The English Reader*, sold through thousands and thousands of copies. Also, an anthology,

The American First Class Book, edited by the Unitarian John Pierpont, was, according to law, issued to every schoolchild in Massachusetts.... (Pace, Letter)

After this period of gestation, there came a culminating moment in the late 1830s, a rush of enthusiasm for Wordsworth. In 1835, James Munroe, the Boston publisher who would bring out Ralph Waldo Emerson's *Nature* the following year, published *Yarrow Revisited and Other Poems*. The book met with a storm of praise from reviewers for American magazines (Newton). Two years later, James Kay of Philadelphia published Wordsworth's *Complete Works* in an edition that was received as a national triumph and was widely reprinted for the rest of the century. By 1840, Emerson was able to declare that "the fame of Wordsworth is a leading fact in modern literature" ("Thoughts," 150).

Emerson went on to say that "more than any other poet [Wordsworth's] success has not been his own, but that of the idea which he shared with his coevals, and which he has rarely succeeded in adequately expressing" (150). The "idea" in question is a complex of attitudes and responses which Emerson glosses in his next few sentences: "The Excursion awakened in every lover of nature the right feeling. We saw stars shine, we felt the awe of mountains, we heard the rustle of the wind in the grass, and knew again the ineffable secret of solitude. It was a great joy. It was nearer to nature than anything we had before" (150). For the New England Transcendentalists, William Wordsworth was, above all, the Prophet of Nature. Now, Percy Bysshe Shelley had declared, infamously, that by turning to nature Wordsworth had abdicated his duties as the Poet of Democracy. Since then it has been difficult to see that many readers saw these two roles as cognate. The fact is that many of New England's intellectuals felt that the turn to nature they made with Wordsworth's help *was* a turn to the people. And it is no accident that they made this turn when they did. They discovered nature in the midst of a period of sustained ideological experimentation in response to the continuing domination of electoral politics by brawling Jacksonians, as well as to the intense misery and class polarization brought on by the depression of 1837–1845. For these readers Wordsworth's rustic persona, the Bard of Rydal Mount, seemed to embody an especially benign version of the democratic impulse, one that helped them reimagine the grounds of their legitimacy as, to use Henry David Thoreau's phrase, America's "natural aristocracy" (Newman, "Wordsworth").

Emerson's journal provides a sketch of this history. His library included a copy of the 1824 Boston *Poetical Works* (Harding 305–306). And it was not long after this book's appearance that he began to quote and allude to its contents from time to time. He also began to mention Wordsworth in his obsessive lists of important contemporaries. But his comments on Wordsworth remain relatively sparse and hesitant until after the appearance of Munroe's 1835 *Yarrow Revisited*, which he also owned and probably purchased and read at its release. Following his encounter with this text, his tone shifts. In July of that year, he writes that "some divine savage like Webster, Wordsworth, & Reed whom neither the town nor the college ever made shall say that [which] we shall all believe. How we thirst for a natural thinker" (*Journals* 5:60). This passage is diagnostic, focusing as it does on the persona rather than the poetry, and emphasizing Wordsworth's rootedness in a nature sacralized as an alternative to both the amorality of the new urban bourgeoisie and the scholasticism of college-bred clergy. Emerson records his first extended appreciation of the poet in May 1836:

> It is strange how simple a thing it is to be a great man, so simple that almost all fail by overdoing. There is nothing vulgar in Wordsworth's idea of Man. To believe your own thought, that is Genius. To believe that a man intended to produce the emotion we feel before his work is the highest praise, so high that we ever hesitate to give it. (*Journals* 5:163)

Again, the focus is on the persona, Wordsworth the great man, the genius, whose greatness inheres in the plainness, the naturalness, and by implication, the apparent democracy of his sentiments. At a time of intense anti-elitism, Wordsworth provided a perfect model of the ways of thinking appropriate to a liberalizing elite. As Emerson put it in August 1837, "Wordsworth now act[s] out of England on us ..." (*Journals* 5:370).

WORDSWORTH AND THOREAU

The central focus of scholarship on the relation between Wordsworth and Thoreau has always been on their habits of thought about the relationship between humans and nature. For decades, debate centered on whether Wordsworth saw Imagination (or Mind or Man) as shaping Nature or vice versa, and on whether Thoreau maintained the same position.[1] In the last twenty years, the terms of the debate have shifted somewhat, especially with the rise of ecocriticism. Ecocritics, giving an environmentalist edge to the question, ask whether Wordsworth and Thoreau were homocentric or biocentric. James McKusick's *Green Writing: Romanticism and Ecology* provides the culminating statement of this avenue of research, arguing that the English Romantics inaugurated a tradition of organicist, localist, ecocentric writing that the American Transcendentalists cultivated and extended.[2] In any case, it has never been seriously questioned that there are extensive ideological parallels between Wordsworth and Thoreau, and sequence has been taken rightly to imply a strong vector of influence. The question has then become this: what was the tone of this relationship? Grudging, indifferent, unconscious, reverential?[3] In the context of recently increasing interest in Romanticism as a transatlantic phenomenon, this relationship has come to operate as a central case study, bearing the weight of generalizations about the overall relation between British and American national literatures. In his *Atlantic Double-Cross* (1986), Robert Weisbuch (following Harold Bloom) argues that Wordsworth's influence was not only strong, but strongly resented, and that Thoreau had to reject it in order to claim his own voice (133–150). This psychologistic reading individualizes, somewhat mechanically, what had long been understood as the necessary anxiety of Boston's provincial literary society with respect to London, the English-speaking world's cultural center. More recently, Richard Gravil, in his *Romantic Dialogues* (2000), argues compellingly that retrospective cultural nationalism has led to exaggeration of nineteenth–century intellectuals' desire for literary independence, and shows that *Walden* manifests an "astonishing openness to the living Wordsworth" and that Thoreau's attitude towards the elder poet was one of "profound identification" (103–104).

Thoreau began to train himself seriously as a poet during the year before his 1837 graduation from Harvard. His most ambitious and compelling project was an intensive study of the history of poetry in English. He consumed two massive anthologies, including Alexander Chalmers's twenty-one-volume collection of the British poets, which he claims in *Walden* to have read through "without skipping" (259). And during the ensuing ten years, he wrote hundreds of poems and filled several commonplace books with extracts of poetry (Sattelmeyer 3–24). Indeed, it is not too much to say that for this first formative decade of his adult life he thought of himself mainly as a practicing poet (Witherell, "Thoreau as Poet," 57–70). During this time, his primary model, the main poet he emulated, was Wordsworth. His personal library included a copy of the 1837 edition of the *Complete Works* (Sattelmeyer 294). Wordsworth appears consistently in Thoreau's early essays in literary criticism as a benchmark of poetic excellence. He is always described, either explicitly or implicitly, as one of the most important of English poets, though Thoreau's praise is always mixed. For instance, in a passage from the early essay, "Aulus Persius Flaccus," Thoreau simultaneously pays homage to Wordsworth by placing him in the first rank of English poets and dismisses him in a gesture of youthful bravado: "Homer, and Shakespeare, and Milton, and Marvell, and Wordsworth, are but the rustling of leaves and crackling of twigs in the forest, and not yet the sound of any bird" (*Early Essays* 122). Of course, the implication is that Thoreau himself will burst into bird-like song at any moment, silencing his rustling, but necessary, forebears.

Like Emerson and the rest of his contemporaries, Thoreau read Wordsworth's poems through the lens of a deep interest in the poet's life and public persona:

> To live to a good old age such as the ancients reached—serene and contented—dignifying the life of man—in these days of confusion and turmoil—That is what Wordsworth has done—Retaining the tastes and the innocence of his youth—There is more wonderful talent—but nothing so cheering and world famous as this. (Thoreau, *Journal* 2:200–01)

The center of interest here is Wordsworth's role as a public intellectual, as the first, best inspiration for Shelley's idea that "poets are the unacknowledged legislators of the World" (7:140). In fact, and again like Emerson, Thoreau often complains that the poetry does not match the stature of the public man:

> Wordsworth with very feeble talent has not so great and admirable as persevering genius
> heroism—heroism—is his word—his thing.
> He would realize a brave & adequate human life. & die hopefully at last. (*Journal* 2:223)

Wordsworth operated on his Transcendentalist readers not through the medium of printed matter but through the shared cultural text of the life. His poetic achievement was inseparable from, only one part of, the complete picture of his historical and cultural importance (Weisbuch 143). In the early essay "Homer. Ossian. Chaucer." Thoreau specifies the terms of his admiration: Wordsworth embodies "a simple pathos and feminine gentleness" (*Early Essays* 169). This is not, though, a genteel or trivial emotionalism: the essay stresses the radicalism of Wordsworth's preference for "his homely but vigorous Saxon tongue, when it was neglected by the court, and had not yet attained to the dignity of a literature ..." (165). In other words, Thoreau valued Wordsworth on the poet's own terms, as expressed in the preface to the *Lyrical Ballads*: he appreciated the democratic implications of the decision to write in "a selection of language really used by men" (59), a decision that reflected a poet's "rational sympathy" for "the great and universal passions of men" (79).

And, crucially, Thoreau saw such democratic sentiments, not as opposed to, but as a necessary corollary of, a close relationship with nature. In the early essay, "Thomas Carlyle and His Works," he describes the Scottish intellectual's early moral education in "Annan, on the shore of Selway Frith":

> From this place, they say, you can see Wordsworth's country. Here first [Carlyle] may have become acquainted with Nature, with woods, such as are there, and rivers and brooks ... and the last lapses of Atlantic billows. (*Early Essays* 219)

After taking the impress of this decidedly natural place, Carlyle produced books that Thoreau describes this way:

> When we remember how these volumes came over to us ... and what commotion they created in many private breasts, we wonder that the country did not ring from shore to shore ... with its greeting; and the Boones and Crocketts of the West make haste to hail him, whose wide humanity embraces them too. (222)

Carlyle, like Wordsworth, learned his "wide humanity," his ability to embrace the experience and win the sympathy of proud commoners, from the rugged border country in which he was raised. Moreover, such democratic sympathies are a key measure of natural vigor, as opposed to degeneracy. While making a final comparative assessment, Thoreau states that "Carlyle has not the simple Homeric health of Wordsworth" (248). While Carlyle may not measure up entirely, still he and Wordsworth occupy one end of a spectrum whose implied other is marked by the hyper-civilized and unnatural personae of Coleridge the Morose Scholar, Byron the Dissipated Rake, Shelley the Radical Atheist, and others (Weisbuch 137–142). During "days of confusion and turmoil," when the health of the nation and of the body politic was the object of great concern, Wordsworth's "sanative poetry," as Christopher Pearse Cranch put it in a late retrospective of the period, seemed to offer an "antidote" to "the morbid Byronism and Werterism ... the stagnant scum of the malarial waters which infected those days!" (251).

Thoreau generalized from this understanding of Wordsworth's cultural significance to develop his initial sense of the ideal social and political function of poetry and the poet. First, poetry is a vehicle for the weightiest and most urgent human truths: "There is no doubt that the loftiest written wisdom is either rhymed, or in some way musically measured,—is, in form as well as substance, poetry" (*A Week* 91). The ability to create such music is not the reward of study, not the produce of culture: "Yet poetry, though the last and finest result, is a natural fruit. As naturally as the oak bears an acorn, and the vine a gourd, man bears a poem, either spoken or done" (91). It is not just that poetry is the organic language of humanity, but more, that when people produce poetry, nature is working directly and immediately through them: "The poet sings how the blood flows in his veins. He performs the functions, and is so well that he needs such stimulus to sing only as plants to put forth leaves and blossoms.... It is as if nature spoke" (91–92). Just as poetry is the language of nature, it is also definitively wholesome, even hygienic: "Good poetry seems so simple and natural a thing that when we meet it we wonder that all men are not always poets. Poetry is nothing but healthy speech" (*Journal* 1:338). During diseased times, when most people have lost contact with nature, the poet must protect himself by maintaining a safe distance:

> We are often prompted to speak our thoughts to our neighbors or the single travelers we meet, but poetry is a communication addressed to all mankind, and may therefore as well be written at home and in solitude, as uttered abroad in society. (*Journal* 2:44)

The poet's solitude should not be mistaken for aloofness, though. Instead, detachment from particulars allows a more general engagement, a clear focus on matters that the rest of humanity has lost sight of: "Though the speech of the poet goes to the heart of things, yet he is that one especially who speaks civilly to Nature as a second person, and in some sense is the patron of the world" (*Journal* 1:338). This last phrase renders with exquisite accuracy Thoreau's developed sense of the cultural role of the poet in degenerate times—"patron of the world." The poet serves as a beacon of natural health and wholesome democratic sentiments to a world diseased by the rising tide of urbanization, industrialization, and class conflict under capitalism.[4]

THOREAU AS POET

The understanding of poetry and the role of the poet that Thoreau appropriated from Wordsworth provided a base of operations, a working model that closely informed his work, but from which he regularly and increasingly departed as time went on. He produced a remarkably various body of poetry, at first writing reverential imitations and later experimenting, searching for ways to embody in verse ideas and stances that extended and developed the tradition he had entered.[5]

Perhaps his clearest attempts to emulate his predecessor come in poems that, like Wordsworth's great odes, take "a fact out of nature into spirit" (*Journal* 1:69), mounting extravagant sallies of speculative thought in response to common events or conventional scenes (Gravil 108). For instance, the deceptively simple poem "The Bluebirds" begins with the building of a nest-box "in the midst of the poplar that stands by our door." Thoreau lovingly narrates the arrival of a breeding pair, their mating rituals, nesting, and eventual migration. Only when this preparatory work is complete does he go on to describe a moment of self-transcendence triggered by contemplation of the spectacular perfection of the natural world:

> I dreamed that I was an waking thought—
> A something I hardly knew—
> Not a solid piece, nor an empty nought,
> But a drop of morning dew. (*Collected Essays and Poems*, 514)

In this kind of romantic lyricism, the premium is on the immaterial, the spiritual revelation or emotional response stimulated by encounters with physical phenomena that are only indistinctly particular. In many poems the stimulus is even left unstated so that we read only the revelation, stripped of its triggering context, as in the following quatrain that Thoreau composed for *A Week*:

> True kindness is a pure divine affinity,
> Not founded on human consanguinity.
> It is a spirit, not a blood relation,
> Superior to family and station. (577)

This is a kind of abstract poetry that we are no longer trained to appreciate. However, it has a recoverable coherence, based on the idea that the poet's special ability is to distill the universal from the particular, to mine the truth from experience, refine it, and deliver it pure. Thoreau explains in *A Week*: "There are two kinds of writing, both great and rare; one that of genius, or the inspired, the other of intellect and taste, in the intervals of inspiration. The former is above criticism, always correct, giving the law to criticism. It vibrates and pulsates with life forever. It is sacred, and to be read with reverence, as the works of nature are studied" (375). Thoreau approached the discipline of poetry with the kind of high seriousness reflected here, striving in his early work to achieve just such inspiration, to breathe directly the atmosphere of the ideal.

However, as his poetic decade progressed, his practice began to shift. He moved increasingly in the direction of particularity, isolating and focusing on the moment of generative stimulus. By doing so, he began to develop his own distinctive practice, informed by the idea that the poet should speak directly about his immediate experience to an audience of his actual peers (Williams, "Thoreau's Growth," 189–198):

> I seek the Present Time,
> No other clime,
> Life in to-day....
> What are deeds done
> Away from home?
> What the best essay
> On the Ruins of Rome? (608)

His initial response to this imperative was to compose loco-descriptive poems that at first were only weakly local: "On Ponkawtasset" and "Assabet" use eastern Massachusetts place names but operate in the generic space of highly conventional pastoral. On the other hand, poems like "The Old Marlborough Road" sustain a high level of detailed engagement with quite particular places:

> Where they once dug for money,
> But never found any;
> Where sometimes Martial Miles
> Singly files,
> And Elijah Wood,
> I fear for no good;
> No other man
> Save Elisha Dugan,—
> O man of wild habits,
> Partridges and rabbits,
> Who hast no cares
> Only to set snares,
> Who liv'st all alone,
> Close to the bone,
> And where life is sweetest
> Constantly eatest. (626)

Thoreau's emphasis on the specifics of a place and its peculiar inhabitants was at least partially validated by Wordsworth's practice in the many pieces of occasional and travel verse titled simply with dates or place names. Moreover, the choice of subject matter here constituted an extension of Wordsworth's theoretical focus on "incidents and situations from common life," for Thoreau particularized the common: Elisha

Dugan is an actual local, not an idealized commoner like Wordsworth's "Simon Lee."[6]

Similarly, one of Thoreau's most successful poetic innovations was his attempt to complete Wordsworth's decision to write in the "real language of men"—in this case, real Yankees. Many of the published poems are marked by the kind of elevated diction that was felt to reflect the universality of the ideal:

> Thou dusky spirit of the wood,
> Bird of an ancient brood,
> Flitting thy lonely way,
> A meteor in the summer's day. (579)

But at the same time that he was working this vein, he was also experimenting with pithy and local language like the following:

> Conscience is instinct bred in the house,
> Feeling and thinking propagate the sin
> By an unnatural breeding in and in.
> I say, Turn it out doors,
> Into the moors.
> I love a life whose plot is simple,
> And does not thicken with every pimple,
> A soul so sound no sickly conscience binds it,
> That makes the universe no worse than't finds it. (615)

Colloquialisms like "bred in the house" and "turn it out doors" give a familiarity to the diction that is new in Thoreau's writing, and in Romantic poetry generally, as is the decision to abandon iambs for a more spontaneous, unmetered verse. Moreover, Thoreau rounds out the localism of the voice with his comical and deflationary rhyme on "simple," giving real weight and authenticity to the homely philosophy of the final couplet. This decision to recreate New England vernacular speech reaches its peak in verse that never saw print in Thoreau's lifetime, much of which has only quite recently become available. At its best, Thoreau's poetry in this mode is vibrantly alive:

> I have seen some frozenfaced Connecticut
> Or Down east man in his crack coaster
> With tort sail, with folded arms standing
> Beside his galley with his dog & man
> While his cock crowed aboard, scud thro the surf

> By some fast anchored Staten island farm,
> But just outside the vast and stirring line
> Where the astonished Dutchman digs his clams
> Or but half ploughs his cabbage garden plot
> With unbroken steeds & ropy harness—
> And some squat bantam whom the shore wind drownd
> Feebly responded there for all reply,
> While the triumphant Yankee's farm swept by. (614)

Not only is this resolutely anchored in the physical specifics of New England, but the clotted, spondaic rhythms combine with the insistent alliteration and the arresting vernacular to produce a poetry that is quite new and powerful. Had Thoreau produced a large and consistent body of work in this mode, he might well be ranked with Whitman and Dickinson as one of the inaugurators of modern American poetry (Wells 99–114).

Part of what drove Thoreau to innovate was the pressure of historical events on his working model of poetry: there was an inherent conflict between the urgency of the period's social and political debates and the genteel lyricism apparently required by the genre. Early on Thoreau had attempted to address political questions but was unable to break free of a kind of contemplative abstraction:

> In the busy streets, domains of trade,
> Man is a surly porter, or a vain and hectoring bully,
> Who can claim no nearer kindredship with me
> Than brotherhood by law. (517)

The depression of 1837–1844, the movement to abolish slavery, Polk's invasion of Mexico—these all demanded passionate and particular response. And Thoreau responded, writing several poems that directly addressed the most urgent questions of the mid-1840s. His earlier efforts are often quite conventional, as in this address to the people of the North, which draws a parallel between southern chattel slavery and the slavery to convention and money of the north:

> Wait not till slaves pronounce the word
>   To set the captive free,
> Be free yourselves, be not deferred,
>   And farewell slavery. (577)

At a time when the abolition movement had become an immovable fact of daily life, this poem is so uniformly abstract that it is quite possible to forget that it makes an argument against slavery. It is almost as though Romantic metaphoricity caricatures itself here: Thoreau deliteralizes, dematerializes the brutal oppression of millions, using it to figure the rather less urgent bondage of his fellow townspeople. More successful is Thoreau's meditation on the woman question, a poem that enacts the kind of essentialist beliefs that were typical even of the feminists within his milieu:

> Ive seen ye, sisters, on the mountain side
> When your green mantles fluttered in the wind
> Ive seen your foot-prints on the lakes smooth shore
> Lesser than man's, a more ethereal trace,
> Ive heard of ye as some far-famed race—
>
> Daughters of god whom I should one day meet—
> Or mothers I might say of all our race. (604)

Still, this remains cast in elevated and artificial language that almost lampoons the spirituality it ascribes to its implied female audience. It wasn't until Thoreau deployed the vernacular that his political verse became truly compelling. For instance, in his journal for November 28, 1850, he transcribed the following Blakean monologue:

> I am the little Irish boy
>   That lives in the shanty
> I am four years old today
>   And shall soon be one and twenty
> I shall grow up and be a great man
>   And shovel all day
>   As hard as I can...
>
>   Down in the deep cut
>   Where the men lived
>   Who made the Rail road. (631)

The absolute simplicity of Thoreau's language gives real power to this sketch of the stark poverty afflicting hundreds of thousands of Irish immigrants. Overall, then, Thoreau's poems became increasingly forceful as he followed through on the implications of his mentor's ideas about how to write poetry. He did so in fact more consistently than Wordsworth himself, abandoning accentual-syllabic meter and closed verse forms for more flexible, organic structures, and focusing his work directly on the vocabulary and experience

of Concord's common inhabitants, rather than limiting that material to the
subordinate function of stimulating conventional idealisms.

There is no shortage of speculation about why Thoreau began to shift
his attention increasingly from poetry to prose in the mid-1840s. The most
practical reason is that once the *Dial* folded in 1844 he was left without a
venue for his poems. But it has been usual, even among the most dedicated
admirers of his verse, to intuit a narrative of failure. Emerson started this
tale in motion with his assessment that Thoreau's "verses are often rude and
defective. The gold does not yet run pure, is drossy and crude. The thyme and
marjoram are not yet honey. But if he want lyric fineness and technical merits,
if he have not the poetic temperament, he never lacks the causal thought,
showing that his genius was better than his talent" (*Works* 10:443). Robert O.
Evans writes that "Thoreau knew his gift for poetry was running out ..." (43).
Arthur L. Ford maintains that Thoreau failed to "become Emerson's poet
[because] he lacked the courage to throw off all conventions and create a new
expression" (21). And Elizabeth Hall Witherell makes this final assessment:
"In aspiring to write poetry Thoreau set higher standards than he could reach
in that medium: his efforts survive as relics of the apprenticeship of a master
of poetic prose" ("Thoreau's Watershed Season," 62). But did Thoreau in
fact abandon the medium? Certainly the rhythms and melodies of the prose
bear witness to his lifelong dedication to the music of language. One widely
quoted quatrain suggests an alternative reading of this speculative tale:

> Each more melodious note I hear
> Brings this reproach to me,
> That I alone afford the ear,
> Who would the music be. (530)

In other words, it is not that Thoreau was unable to compose regular verse
and so dropped the genre, but rather he recognized that the essence of poetry
was not accentual-syllabic meter and regular form. As he puts it elsewhere:
"My life has been the poem I would have writ, / But I could not both live
and utter it" (*Week* 343). Does Thoreau mean here that he was unable to
maintain simultaneously the poet's heightened receptivity to experience and
the discipline of poetic composition? Probably not. After all he never quit
writing intensively composed material; he just quit writing formal verse.
Instead, Thoreau may have meant to record his recognition that the stance or
voice of the poet is more culturally important than meter or rhyme (Williams,
"Inspiration," 466–472). Indeed, the narrative persona he adopts throughout
Walden corresponds closely to his exalted notion of the poet as great man.
He establishes himself as one whose total immersion in nature authorizes an

admonitory relationship, based on democratic sympathies, to a degenerate society badly in need of liberation from debilitating conventions. Moreover, these changes in his writerly practice mirrored the overall direction of his intellectual development during the 1840s: he moved away from Emersonian idealism, toward increasingly particular engagement with the material world (McIntosh 17–48). So the larger truth must certainly be that he turned to prose because to do so was the culmination of the trends that had developed in his poetic experimentation, to do so allowed him to directly engage the particular natural and social landscape before him, in language wrought into organic structures rich in local music.

In fact, Thoreau refreshed his connection to his old mentor at a critical time during the composition of his most unmistakably poetic piece of prose. He acquired a copy of the *Prelude* not long after it was published in 1850. And while we cannot fix the date that he read it absolutely, his journal suggests that he did so sometime in late 1851 (Fergenson, "Was Thoreau Reading," 20–23): the volume for August 1851 through April 1852 is littered with references to Wordsworth, poets, and poetry. Then, energized by this new encounter, Thoreau began the most intensive period of rewriting *Walden* (Gravil 104). From early 1852 to 1854, he amplified the manuscript's account of his retreat into nature, with its central critique of alienation under capitalism, added a much more full account of the texture of his life at the pond, and finally added the chapter "Conclusion" (Shanley 18–33, 55–73). The rewritten book amounts to an aestheticist manifesto, an extravagantly confident paean to the power of the creative, self-reliant individual to inspire organic, wholesale social change (Newman, "Thoreau"). This manifesto begins by laying a foundation of particularity, with the long passage about sand flowing out of the bank in the railroad cut:

> As it flows it takes the forms of sappy leaves or vines, making heaps of pulpy sprays a foot or more in depth, and resembling, as you look down on them, the laciniated, lobed, and imbricated thalluses of some lichens; or you are reminded of coral, of leopard's paws or birds' feet, of brains or lungs or bowels, and excrements of all kinds. (305)

Thoreau builds from this lovingly rendered concrete image of renewal toward the claim that even "a man [is] but a mass of thawing clay," and from here to the assertion that not only the earth, "but the institutions upon it are plastic like clay in the hands of the potter" (309). Throughout the two concluding chapters of *Walden*, Thoreau speaks in the voice of a "patron of the world," a seer, a poet rooted in nature, who can see "the character of that morrow which mere lapse of time can never make to dawn," and who can guide a blind world to the truth that "There is more day to dawn. The sun is but a morning star" (333). In other words, the book recapitulates the structure of a Wordsworthian lyric poem, building from a recollected experience to a crescendo of wisdom, but that wisdom and the voice that speaks it remain deeply rooted, more deeply than anything that had gone before, in the particulars of an actual place. In other words, were it not for Thoreau's apprenticeship to Wordsworth, rather than becoming one of the nineteenth century's most powerful long poems, *Walden* might well have remained the story of a field of beans.

NOTES

1. The best summaries of those conversations are Dennis, "Correspondence" and Fergenson's dissertation, "Wordsworth and Thoreau: A Study of the Relationship between Man and Nature," which she later condensed into an article.

2. Garrard sees a more antagonistic relationship, arguing that Thoreau appropriates Wordsworth's tentative early biocentrism and then radicalizes it in an act of agonistic rejection.

3. Miller and Smith offer valuable overviews of Thoreau's place in the international tradition of Romanticism. McIntosh maps out ideological parallels between Thoreau and Wordsworth. Garber describes the importance of Wordsworth as Thoreau's exemplar of both the strengths and weaknesses of Anglo-European Romanticism. Joy first suggests and Moldenhauer exhaustively documents the influence of Wordsworth's *Guide to the District of the Lakes* on Thoreau's general ideas about landscape, as well as specifically on *Walden*. Kalinevitch documents *Walden*'s many allusions to the great odes.

4. Thoreau shared many of his habits of thought about poetry and the poet with the rest of the Transcendentalist circle. Hennessy and Myerson survey these ideas in the context of histories of the central Transcendentalist organ, *The Dial*.

5. Thoreau's poetry has been re-edited in a new collected edition by Elizabeth Hall Witherell, superseding Carl Bode's edition, which had been the standard for several decades. Witherell has also condensed the results of her textual and historical scholarship into two articles, one a survey of his poetic decade, the second a reading of what she regards as Thoreau's crowning poetic achievement, a sequence of five related poems exploring "the place of man in nature." Ford mounts the most extensive close reading of the verse, focusing on Thoreau's desire to capture in poetry the experience of self-transcendence through total immersion in nature. Ford also provides a very useful annotated bibliography of sources on Thoreau's poetry through 1970. Since then, critical work on the subject has been quite sparse and was mostly produced in a burst of activity during the early 1970s. Colquitt provides a sensitive and concise survey of Thoreau's theories of poetry. Evans argues that Thoreau's poems are destroyed when removed from the context of the prose narratives within which many were originally published. Several articles explore particular tropes or image clusters: Kaiser surveys the symbolism of celestial bodies; Silverman explores Thoreau's unfulfilled desire for energy and heroic action; Mazzini describes two poems that center on epiphanic experiences; and Williams documents the centrality of the concept of inspiration to Thoreau's poetics.

6. I am indebted to the reviewer of this article who, in addition to helping me improve it in many other ways, pointed out that Elisha Dugan "is a real person, born to

Thomas and Jenny Dugan on June 17, 1807, according to *Concord, Massachusetts Births, Marriages, and Deaths* (1894)."

WORKS CITED

Colquitt, Betsy Feagan. "Thoreau's Poetics." *ATQ* 11 (1971): 74–81.

Cranch, Christopher Pearse. "Wordsworth." *Atlantic Monthly* 45 (1880): 241–252.

Dennis, Carl. "Correspondence in Thoreau's Nature Poetry." *ESQ: A Journal of the American Renaissance* 58 (1970): 101–109.

Emerson, Ralph Waldo. *The Journals and Miscellaneous Notebooks of Ralph Waldo Emerson*. William Gilman, et al. eds. Cambridge: The Belknap Press of Harvard UP, 1965.

———. "Thoughts on Modern Literature." *Dial* 1 (1840): 137–158.

———. *Works*. Ed. Edward W. Emerson. 14 vols. Boston: Houghton, Mifflin, 1883.

Emerson, Ralph Waldo and Thomas Carlyle. *The Correspondence of Emerson and Carlyle*. Ed. Joseph Slater. New York: Columbia UP, 1964.

Evans, Robert O. "Thoreau's Poetry and the Prose Works." *ESQ: A Journal of the American Renaissance* 56 (1969): 40–52.

Fergenson, Laraine. "Was Thoreau Re-Reading Wordsworth in 1851?" *Thoreau Journal Quarterly* 5.3 (1973): 20–23.

———. "Wordsworth and Thoreau: A Study of the Relationship between Man and Nature." Unpublished Ph.D. Dissertation. Columbia University, 1971.

———. "Wordsworth and Thoreau: The Relationship between Man and Nature." *Thoreau Journal Quarterly* 11.2 (1979): 3–10.

Ford, Arthur L. "The Poetry of Henry David Thoreau." *ESQ: A Journal of the American Renaissance* 61 (1970): 1–26.

Garber, Frederick. "Thoreau and Anglo-European Romanticism." Ed. Richard J. Schneider. *Approaches to Teaching Thoreau's Walden and Other Works*. New York: Modern Language Association, 1996. 39–47.

Garrard, Greg. "Wordsworth and Thoreau: Two Versions of Pastoral." Ed. Richard J. Schneider. *Thoreau's Sense of Place: Essays in American Environmental Writing*. Iowa City: U of Iowa P, 2000. 194–206.

Gravil, Richard. *Romantic Dialogues: Anglo-American Continuities, 1776–1862*. New York: St. Martin's Press, 2000.

Harding, Walter. *Emerson's Library*. Charlottesville: U of Virginia P, 1967.

Hennessy, Helen. "*The Dial*: Its Poetry." *New England Quarterly* 31 (1958): 66–87.

Joy, Neill. "Two Possible Analogues for 'The Ponds' in *Walden*: Jonathon Carver and Wordsworth." *ESQ: A Journal of the American Renaissance* 24 (1978): 197–205.

Kaiser, Mary I. "'Conversing with the Sky': The Imagery of Celestial Bodies in Thoreau's Poetry." *Thoreau Journal Quarterly* 9.3 (1977): 15–28.

Kalinevitch, Karen. "Apparelled in Celestial Light/Bathed in So Pure a Light: Verbal Echoes in Wordsworth's and Thoreau's Works." *Thoreau Journal Quarterly* 12.2 (1980): 27–30.

Mazzini, Carla. "Epiphany in Two Poems by Thoreau." *Thoreau Journal Quarterly* 5.2 (1973): 23–25.

McCusick, James C. *Green Writing: Romanticism and Ecology*. New York: St. Martin's Press, 2000.

McIntosh, James: *Thoreau as Romantic Naturalist: His Shifting Stance Toward Nature*. Ithaca: Cornell UP, 1974.

Miller, Perry. "Thoreau in the Context of International Romanticism." *New England Quarterly* 34 (June 1961): 147–59.

Moldenhauer, Joseph J. "*Walden* and Wordsworth's *Guide to the English Lake District.*" Studies in the American Renaissance (1990), 261–292.

Murray, [C.] Lindley. *The English Reader; or, Pieces in Prose and Poetry Selected from the Best Writers.* York: Longman and Rees, 1799.

Myerson, Joel. *New England Transcendentalism and The Dial.* Rutherford, NJ: Fairleigh Dickinson UP, 1980.

Newman, Lance. "Thoreau's Natural Community and Utopian Socialism." *American Literature.* 75.3 (September 2003): 515–544.

———. "Wordsworth in America and the Nature of Democracy." *New England Quarterly* 72.4 (December 1999): 517–538.

Newton, Annabel. *Wordsworth in Early American Criticism.* Chicago: U of Chicago P, 1928.

Pace, Joel. "'Gems of a soft and permanent lustre': The Reception and Influence of the Lyrical Ballads in America." *Romanticism on the Net* 9 (February 1998). Accessed 8 August, 2002. <http://users.ox.ac.uk/-scat0385/americanLB.html>

———. Letter to the Author. April 1, 2002.

———. "Wordsworth, the Lyrical Ballads, and Literary and Social Reform in Nineteenth-Century America." Marcy L. Tanter, ed. "*The Honourable Characteristic of Poetry*": *Two Hundred Years of Lyrical Ballads.* Romantic Circles Praxis Series (November 1999) 8 August 2002. <http://www.rc.umd.edu/praxis/lyrical/pace/wordsworth.html>

Sattelmeyer, Robert. *Thoreau's Reading: A Study in Intellectual History.* Princeton: Princeton UP, 1988.

Shanley, J. Lyndon. *The Making of Walden.* Chicago: U of Chicago P, 1957.

Shelley, Percy Bysshe. *Complete Works.* Ed. Roger Ingpen and Walter E. Peck. 10 vols. New York: Gordian Press, 1965.

Silverman, Kenneth. "The Sluggard Knight in Thoreau's Poetry." *Thoreau Journal Quarterly* 5.2 (1973): 6–9.

Smith, Lorrie. "'Walking' from England to America: Re-Viewing Thoreau's Romanticism." *New England Quarterly* 58.2 (June 1985): 221–241.

Thoreau, Henry D. *Collected Essays and Poems.* Ed. Elizabeth Hall Witherell. New York: Library of America, 2001.

———. *Collected Poems.* Ed. Carl Bode. Baltimore: Johns Hopkins UP, 1964.

———. *Early Essays and Miscellanies.* Ed. Joseph J. Moldenhauer and Edwin Moser. Princeton: Princeton UP, 1975.

———. *Journal 1: 1837–1844.* Ed. Elizabeth Hall Witherell, et al. Princeton: Princeton UP, 1981.

———. *Journal 2: 1842–1848.* Ed. Robert Sattelmeyer. Princeton: Princeton UP, 1984.

———. *Walden, or Life in the Woods.* J. Lyndon Shanley, ed. Princeton UP, 1971.

———. *A Week on the Concord and Merrimack Rivers.* Ed. Carl F. Hovde, et al. Princeton: Princeton UP, 1980.

Weisbuch, Robert. *Atlantic Double-Cross: American Literature and British Influence in the Age of Emerson.* Chicago: U of Chicago P, 1986.

Wells, Henry W. "An Evaluation of Thoreau's Poetry." *American Literature* 16 (May 1944): 99–114.

Williams, Paul O. "The Concept of Inspiration in Thoreau's Poetry." *PMLA* 79 (1964): 466–472.

————. "Thoreau's Growth as a Transcendentalist Poet." *ESQ: A Journal of the American Renaissance* 19 (1973): 189–198.

Witherell, Elizabeth Hall. "Thoreau as Poet." *The Cambridge Companion to Henry David Thoreau*. Ed. Joel Myerson. Cambridge: Cambridge UP, 1995. 57–70.

————. "Thoreau's Watershed Season as a Poet: The Hidden Fruits of the Summer and Fall of 1841." *Studies in the American Renaissance* (1990): 49–106.

Wordsworth, William. *The Complete Poetical Works of William Wordsworth, together with a Description of the Country of the Lakes in the North of England*. Philadelphia: James Kay, 1837.

————. *Lyrical Ballads*. Ed. Michael Mason. London: Longman, 1992.

————. *Yarrow Revisited and Other Poems*. Boston: James Munroe, 1835.

DAVID M. ROBINSON

Living Poetry

THE BLOOM OF THE PRESENT MOMENT

The blistering critique of conventional life and artificial values that opens *Walden* is extended by implication in "The Beanfield" and other chapters in which we see Thoreau enacting a new way of living in the natural world. This new way of life is grounded in a meticulous and discerning awareness of the particularities of nature, which includes the human body and the operations of consciousness and perception as part of an interrelated, constantly interactive whole.

Life at Walden provided much but by no means all of the impetus and fabric for this representation of a new experience. The text of *Walden* evolved through an extended process of composition, enlargement, and revision—seven versions in all. It therefore reflects both Thoreau's immediate experience at the pond and his later recollection, interpretation, and shaping of that experience in the seven-year period, 1847–54, between his leaving Walden and his publication of the book. Those years were pivotal in his development, providing the perspective that allowed him both to expand and complete *Walden* and to begin a new phase of his work that has only recently begun to come into full appreciation.

Building on the earlier work on the *Walden* manuscripts by J. Lyndon Shanley, Robert Sattelmeyer explains that the book evolved through two major

From *Natural Life: Thoreau's Worldly Transcendentalism*, pp. 100–124. © 2004 by Cornell University Press.

phases of composition, an initial set of four versions written while Thoreau was at the pond and in the years immediately following his leaving, and a later series of three revisions (1852–54). The later revisions provided the seasonal shape and "organic form" that brought *Walden* recognition as a literary masterpiece in the mid-twentieth century.[1] The most important changes in these years were Thoreau's return from Walden in 1847, his family's move in August 1850 to the larger "yellow house" on Concord's Main Street, and his resolution to make a serious and detailed study of plant characteristics and classification in the early 1850s. Thoreau occupied an attic room in the new house which was more private, and also spacious enough to accommodate his books and various botanical and artifact collections.[2] Although he was no longer at Walden Pond, he now had in some ways more freedom and opportunity to explore the countryside and study the natural world through his pattern of afternoon walks. He began to use his Journal as an extension of these walks, compiling both observations and interpretive insights there, and gradually transforming it into a rich compendium of information about the climate, seasonal cycles, and ecosystems of the Concord area.

Thoreau's new pattern of life after Walden, especially his deepening engagement with field observation and natural history, generated an intellectual tension that is evident both in the Journal and in *Walden*. A fact collector, fascinated with the working details of the natural world, Thoreau also wanted to understand the larger patterns that gave meaning and connection to these facts. He remained a believer in nature's unity even as he noted its disparate details. His study of Hindu scriptures in the late 1840s reinforced the holistic perspective he had absorbed from Brownson, Emerson, and others, as did his continuing commitment to a Transcendentalist idea of a higher law that informed human conduct. That principle was becoming increasingly prominent in his thinking as the slavery crisis intensified in the late 1840s and early 1850s.

Walden thus evolved through its several revisions as a work in which Thoreau attempts to depict his life as a thing of the moment and of the eternal simultaneously. His burden is to maintain the recognition that every object and every perception bears an enormous weight of significance. *Walden* thus urges a new way of comprehending nature and also a new way of living in nature. Each of these emphases informs and reinforces the other.

In rejecting the life of "quiet desperation" that so many of his contemporaries were living, Thoreau resolved to "live deliberately," assuming a new responsibility for the decisions that constituted the quality of daily life. "Every man is tasked to make his life, even in its details, worthy of the contemplation of his most elevated and critical hour" (Wa 90). The patterns of the day became the artist's medium at Walden, demanding the same balance, economy of means, detailed craft, and sense of purpose that the canvas or the blank page demanded. It also required a constantly renewed effort to see the world afresh. To live a natural life, one must shed the inherited categories of perception and refuse to take appearances as truths. "I perceive that we inhabitants in New England live this mean life that we do because our vision does not penetrate the surface of things. We think that that *is* which *appears* to be" (Wa 96).

Thoreau's wish to live deliberately, artistically shaping the experience of each successive day, entailed a demanding commitment to literature, both as a reader and as a writer. His Walden sojourn was in part a writer's sabbatical, and while he makes almost no mention of his literary projects in the text of *Walden*, he does devote an early chapter to the centrality of disciplined "Reading" as the first of his enterprises at the pond. Reading is thus the first call of the natural life. In "The American Scholar" Emerson described a fundamental tension between books and nature, arguing that reading posed a certain danger to the formation and cultivation of the intellect, and was capable of transforming "Man Thinking" into "the bookworm": "The sacredness which attaches to the act of creation,—the act of thought,—is instantly transferred to the record. The poet chanting, was felt to be a divine man. Henceforth the chant is divine also. The writer was a just and wise spirit. Henceforward it is settled, the book is perfect; as love of the hero corrupts into worship of his statue. Instantly, the book becomes noxious. The guide is a tyrant" (CW 1:56). Although he shared Emerson's suspicions of the artificiality and potential corruption of reading that was a substitute for original thought, Thoreau works to defuse the inherent tension between reading and natural experience by portraying reading as a natural and essential act, a means by which the individual can become part of an expansive and liberating dialogue that spans ages and cultures.[3]

"My residence was more favorable, not only to thought, but to serious reading, than a university" (Wa 99), he remarks, beginning a series of observations through which he transforms reading from an artificial activity associated with social norms and institutions into an organic one, connate with the self and its continuing development. Living deliberately, returning to a freedom beyond any set of imposed social expectations, will inevitably incline us toward reading and study. "With a little more deliberation in the choice of their pursuits, all men would perhaps become essentially students and observers, for certainly their nature and destiny are interesting to all alike" (Wa 99). The problem, of course, is achieving that degree of deliberation in our choice of pursuits. The sort of reading he demands of himself requires an openness and freedom, and also a disciplined commitment. He insists that reading is neither an emotional escape nor a means of mental or physical relaxation; it is a difficult achievement, one that engages and challenges all the resources of the self.

Admitting these demands, and confessing even his own failures to meet them, is one of the most important achievements of Thoreau's chapter on his reading. "I kept Homer's Iliad on my table through the summer," he reports, "though I looked at his page only now and then" (Wa 99). Thoreau's open Homer is the symbol of so many well-intended but never-completed reading projects—the ever-growing list that we always carry mentally, waiting for that magical summer of absolute freedom. But Thoreau had to postpone this obligation. "Incessant labor with my hands, at first, for I had my house to finish and my beans to hoe at the same time, made more study impossible" (Wa 99–100). This is a frank but not a rueful admission, because of the sense of ultimate priorities that his house-building embodied. "Yet I sustained myself," he tells us, "by the prospect of such reading in the future" (Wa 100). He made his open book a kind of promise, the reminder of a commitment that predated his work on the house and in the field and made it meaningful. Homer had been postponed, but not postponed indefinitely. Thoreau knows himself to be creating the conditions within which he can sustain the sort of reading necessary to his reformed living. That "prospect" was implicit in Homer's narrative of the heroic search for one's rightful place.

Thoreau's reading was primarily a morning exercise, the kind of intensive activity that required a depth of attention available only to what he called an awakening mind. His praise of the morning comes with the related observation that few individuals are fully awake as they experience the world. "Every morning was a cheerful invitation to make my life of equal simplicity, and I may say innocence, with Nature herself" (Wa 88). This repeated invitation, triggered by the rhythms of nature, signified the possibility of a fresh access to the buried powers of thought and observation that were the necessary constituents for the reformulation of life. "That man who does not believe that each day contains an earlier, more sacred, and auroral hour than he has yet profaned, has despaired of life, and is pursuing a descending and darkening way" (Wa 89). The realm of dreams, like the realm of fable or poetry, signified a larger life of varied, metamorphic identity. One awoke with this newly enlarged sense of possibility, which amplified the significance of the natural world and added acuity and discernment to reading.

Thoreau's proposition that "morning brings back the heroic ages" (Wa 88) is thus echoed in his conception of his morning work with the classics. "The student may read Homer or Aeschylus in the Greek without danger of dissipation or luxuriousness, for it implies that he in some measure emulate their heroes, and consecrate morning hours to their pages" (Wa 100). The mind, fresh in the morning from its immersion in dreams, is capable of meeting the conceptual and imaginative demands of literature and more effective in responding to the voice of the text with its own inner voice.

Although it is engendered by the natural rhythms of the night and morning, and is part of the process by which the self is remade in the mold of nature, such reading is nevertheless an act of will and discipline, demanding an unusual dedication and tenacity. Such labor "will task the reader more than any exercise which the customs of the day esteem," Thoreau warns. "It requires a training such as the athletes underwent, the steady intention almost of the whole life to this object" (Wa 101). Again he links the act of reading to that definitive word "deliberate," placing reading on the same plane of importance as the highest decisions of life: "Books must be read as deliberately and reservedly as they were written" (Wa 101). The complex and sometimes painful work of choosing words, building intellectual structures out of them, and revising and refining a growing text is a mirror of the process of reading, in which each word is weighed as it contributes to the emerging patterns of the text. In Stanley Cavell's apt explication, "reading is not merely the other side of writing, its eventual fate; it is another metaphor of writing itself."[4]

Reading of this kind is a determined and skeptical scrutiny of a work, breaking it into its constituent parts and rewriting it as if one were its author. We thus become the author in the highest acts of reading. But the strain and severity of this conception belies the element of passion in reading, the keen desire that finds fulfillment in it. In the deepest acts of reading, something compels us; we are pulled into the text and through the pages almost will-lessly. Although both formulations of the act of reading help us to understand the intensity and all-consuming nature of "deliberate" reading, their difference also suggests the tension that Thoreau continued to wrestle with, one akin to the dichotomy between grace and works in the explanation of religious experience. The text is a gift, an offering of "the treasured wealth of the world" from authors who constitute "a natural and irresistible aristocracy in every society" (Wa 102, 103). But it is also an earned attainment, available only to those who have paid the cost of devotion and discipline required for its acceptance.

Thoreau expands his analysis of the nature of reading in "Sounds," integrating the internal voices of books with the myriad voices of the natural world.[5] Reading must be seen, he argues, as one aspect of a much larger process of listening, translating, and decoding that includes our entire experience of the natural world. Confinement to books, even "the most select and classic," may cause us to forget "the language which all things and events speak without metaphor" (Wa 111). Thoreau's move from the written world to the natural world is important, not because it signals any abandonment of language as a crucial medium of the understanding, but because it synthesizes reading and writing with other acts of perception and self-expression.

He laid the groundwork for that synthesis in "Reading" by maintaining that the written word "is something at once more intimate with us and more universal than any other work of art. It is the work of art nearest to life itself" (Wa 102). Reading as he had depicted it was a complete absorption of the words of another, an internalization of the very processes of thought and feeling that are the necessary prerequisites of authorship. In taking the thoughts of another within us and reconstituting the grounds on which the words took the form they did, we reanimate the record of human experience. The written word may "not only be read but actually breathed from all human lips; not be represented on canvas or in marble only, but be carved out of the breath of life itself. The symbol of an ancient man's thought becomes a modern man's speech" (Wa 102).

If the written word can bring the past into a living present, the sounds of the natural world are the constant reminder of the "now" in which we are immersed. An essential step in Thoreau's recovery of a "natural life" is to reawaken and expand his awareness of the present moment, in the sense not only of "knowing" more of the world around him but also of entering into it fully. Thoreau hoped to give himself over to his senses, finding a fulfillment in his own attentive presence at the pond and the surrounding hills. "Much is published, but little printed" (Wa 111), he observed, comparing the vast text of nature with the more limited books written by men. If books made certain thoughts and expressions permanent, the expressions of nature were confined to their moment, and were in a sense all the more valuable because of their transience. Such events, however, were not necessarily laden with a meaning that somehow transcended their present manifestation. Thoreau warned against "forgetting the language which all things and events speak without metaphor," a language wholly contained within itself and within the moment in which it comes into being. An event as seemingly incidental as the cast of the light within a room has a call on our attention. "The rays which stream through the shutter will be no longer remembered when the shutter is wholly removed." These rays do not necessarily point beyond themselves, or "mean" anything, but they are part of the fabric of reality that constitutes our experience. Thoreau was attempting to learn to understand himself, his body, his senses, his thoughts, as part of that fabric, to realize the "necessity of being forever on the alert" (Wa 111).

Immersion in the present is antithetical to the conventional rules of daily scheduling and the usual clock-oriented methods of timekeeping. "I love a broad margin to my life" (Wa 111), Thoreau declared, and one of the pleasures of life at Walden was his liberation from artificial measurements of time. But the chapter on "Sounds" is in fact a description of the passage of the day, marked by the characteristic sounds that set its pattern. Thoreau's immersion in the present is not, then, an erasure of time, as he shows, but a more complete and effectual recognition of time's movements and cycles.

These markers of the day are, for the most part, the sounds of the creatures who inhabit the pond and its environs, the background sounds of nature that Thoreau teaches himself to bring to the foreground. "Regularly at half past seven ... the whippoorwills chanted their vespers for half an hour" (Wa 123), the screech owls ushered in nightfall with "their wailing, their doleful responses" (Wa 124), and the bullfrogs passed the night with their drunken-sounding bellows of "*tr-r-r-oonk*" (Wa 126). Attention to sound meant attention to the varied life around the pond, making Thoreau a member of a new community.

Complicating this easy absorption into his surroundings, however, was the most dominant sound in the area, that of the Fitchburg Railroad, whose tracks ran past the pond some five hundred yards from Thoreau's cabin. "I watch the passage of the morning cars," he says, "with the same feeling that I do the rising of the sun, which is hardly more regular" (Wa 116). There is irony in this association of the locomotive with the morning, that sacred time of full awakening that Thoreau had consecrated to meditation and study. The train's presence dramatizes the limits of his idyllic setting, constantly reminding him of the presence of the commercial world that he is to some extent hoping to escape. "I usually go to the village along its causeway," he tells us, "and am, as it were, related to society by this link" (Wa 115). While he would no doubt have preferred not to have the train's intrusion, he also recognized that its presence was an important test of his ability to maintain his focus on recovering a natural life in the face of technological modernity and the expansion of commerce.

In describing his reaction to the train (Wa 115–22; see also JP 2:358–59), Thoreau acknowledges the admirable qualities of those who operate it, and of commerce in general, but he cannot dismiss the flawed and limited ends to which their skills are put: "If the enterprise were as innocent as it is early ... as heroic and commanding as it is protracted and unwearied!" (Wa 117). The challenge of living with this new technology is one of discrimination, of learning to formulate and follow one's own sense of purpose despite the false opportunity that such technological advance seems to offer. "We do not ride on the railroad; it rides upon us" (Wa 92), an inversion of ends and means that Thoreau deplores. The rails, he writes mordantly, are laid over the human "sleepers," laborers who have sacrificed themselves through their extraordinary toil to build it. Their sacrifice seems pointlessly tragic. "They are sound sleepers, I assure you" (Wa 92).

He extends this consideration of technology with his punning admonition to "keep on your own track." While we may feel compelled "to do things 'railroad fashion,'" keeping schedules not of our own making and moving without fail to predetermined destinations, Thoreau argues that we should instead adopt the "enterprise and bravery" (Wa 118) of commerce for our own work of self-development. Finding commerce to be "unexpectedly confident and serene, alert, adventurous, and unwearied" and "very natural in its methods" (Wa 119), he responds by seeing in it the promise of accomplishment that can be translated to the work of self-formation.

Although the railroad is at first an alien and threatening presence, a "travelling demigod" and "cloud-compeller," or an "iron horse" with a "snort like thunder, shaking the earth with his feet, and breathing fire and smoke from his nostrils" (Wa 116), Thoreau revises this initial impression to argue that however alien or non-human the railroad may seem, it is in fact the most human of inventions because of its central role in human commerce. By offering a detailed description of its amazingly varied cargo—palm leaves, rusty nails, torn sails, lumber, Spanish hides, cattle (Wa 119–22; see also JP 2:237–38)—he links it to all forms of human economic activity, and shows it to be a force that was created, and can be controlled, by human decisions. This is a subtle reminder of the potentially enslaving nature of the economics of consumption, and a declaration that, noise and smoke notwithstanding, no one need necessarily be the captive of this new technological invention. "What's the railroad to me?" he asks in a verse that summarizes his sense of freedom from its demands. "I never go to see / Where it ends" (Wa 122).

Absorbed into the larger rhythm of the natural world, the train cannot alter Thoreau's sense of the pace of his life. He is too far immersed in the pattern of the natural day to be disturbed by this artificial interruption. The train becomes instead another of the creatures to whose habits he is able to adapt as he learns a new way to make each day. He does, however, remark on the absence of one creature usually closely associated with time: "I am not sure that I ever heard the sound of cock-crowing from my clearing" (Wa 127). Thoreau praises the song of "this once wild Indian pheasant" and imagines "a winter morning in a wood where these birds abounded, their native woods," their calls "clear and shrill for miles over the resounding earth ... think of it! It would put nations on the alert" (Wa 127). But even in its domestic state, the still resonant call of the bird is a forceful symbol. "All climates agree with brave Chanticleer. He is more indigenous even than the natives. His health is good, his lungs are sound, his spirits never flag" (Wa 127). Like Chanticleer, Thoreau has been domesticated, but his experiment at the pond returns him to a natural home, and makes him again an essential part of it.

FACE TO FACE TO A FACT

To insist that written words are living utterances and that the sounds of nature are a language was a crucial step in Thoreau's attempt to make his literary endeavors part of a larger quest for enlightenment and personal reform at Walden. Reading and writing became an essential part of a spiritual practice, woven into the daily texture of activity of an awakened, fully conscious self.[6] Exploratory walking ("sauntering," as he would later label it in "Walking"), work in the field or on the house, detailed observation of the parts and processes of the natural world, meditative thought, and even daydream and reverie were also strands of this new fabric of experience. This life could be most easily distinguished for its growing process of awareness, of being fully "awake."

Thoreau's principal vehicle for representing this achievement of perception is an event in which he experiences ("observes" is too limited a word) some aspect of the natural world as an instance of a more comprehensive, even infinitely expanding pattern of interconnections. I have already noted one such interpretive encounter, his hoeing of the beans, which expands into a portrait of the varied and abundant life and the layers of time and culture in his one small field of endeavor. Several other significant moments offer a similar pattern of narrated activity layered with observation and expansive interpretation.

These interpretive encounters include most prominently the personification of Walden in "The Ponds" and its measurement in "The Pond in Winter," the account of animal life in "Brute Neighbors," and the sand foliage passage in "Spring." They are marked by Thoreau's keen observational eye and his usually vivid account of the process by which he comes into fuller recognition of the world around him, a world to which, he implies, we should all be more attentive. But they display not only an arresting sense of detail but also a concomitant desire to reach for a more comprehensive category of explanation for the particular phenomenon. Thoreau consistently tries to see a particular fact or event not as a random or unique occurrence but as indicative of a more comprehensive idea or law. "Men esteem truth remote," he writes, "in the outskirts of the system, behind the farthest star, before Adam and after the last man. In eternity there is indeed something true and sublime. But all these times and places and occasions are now and here. God himself culminates in the present moment, and will never be more divine in the lapse of all the ages" (Wa 96–97).

Such a conception neither denigrates nor subordinates "facts" and their study, nor does it refuse the intellectual task of categorization, generalization, and system building. The intellectual ferment of *Walden*, the element that communicates so vividly a sense of philosophical breakthrough, is Thoreau's growing recognition that "fact" and "theory" are inextricably fused, that the observation or close reading of detail is the entry point of comprehensive and ordered knowledge. A "fact" is always a bundle of relations, the product of a convergence of many entities and events. To "know" a particular fact, he saw with increasing clarity and excitement, is to be given a glimpse into a much wider array of processes and circumstances, an event that is revelatory in every sense.

"If you stand right fronting and face to face to a fact, you will see the sun glimmer on both of its surfaces, as if it were a cimeter, and feel its sweet edge dividing you through the heart and marrow, so you will happily conclude your mortal career" (Wa 98). Thoreau's strange celebration of death by fact suggests the dual quality of such moments of insight. The "fact" is the dividing edge, on either side of which we see the sun, here the representation of both illumination and power. Those two surfaces, coordinate aspects of the same fact or object, are the particular detail and the inclusive law that constitute such revelations. We are indeed "divided" by this edge, asked to look in two directions simultaneously, toward the unique specificity of things and to the larger frames of reference that make them discernible. We are permitted to achieve this seemingly impossible feat in that single moment when fact opens itself to us, or, as Thoreau would have it, opens *us* in its presence.

In light of the recent critical emphasis on Thoreau's increasing engagement with the fact-gathering processes of empirical studies of plant and animal life, it is crucial to see Thoreau's praise of "fact" and his increasing attention to the concrete detail of the material world of nature as one side of a complex attempt to move toward larger projects of categorization and explanatory theorizing about the unifying laws and structures of the universe. He struggled to keep his empirical studies within a larger purposive framework that included philosophical speculation and the search for a unifying theory of the nature and structure of the universe. "Facts should only be as the frame to my pictures," he wrote in 1851. "They should be material to the mythology which I am writing" (JP 4:170).

Thoreau's skill and dedication in empirical study, signaled by his closely observed field notes and his collecting of botanical and even zoological specimens, set him apart from Emerson temperamentally, and most readers of Emerson and Thoreau have recognized Thoreau as a more "physical" or embodied thinker, closer in a practical way to the natural world than Emerson, and somewhat less ethereal in his imagination and forms of expression. The year after Thoreau's death, Emerson praised, with a touch of envy, his gift for concrete metaphor and vivid description, attributing it to "the vigor of his constitution."

That oaken strength which I noted whenever he walked or worked or surveyed wood lots, the same unhesitating hand with which a field-laborer accosts a piece of work which I should shun as a waste of strength, Henry shows in his literary task. He has muscle, & ventures on & performs feats which I am forced to decline. In reading him, I find the same thought, the same spirit that is in me, but he takes a step beyond, & illustrates by excellent images that which I should have conveyed in a sleepy generality. (JMN 15:352–53)

Robert Kuhn McGregor has described this difference as more than a question of temperament or style, identifying Emerson's philosophical idealism as a major point of distinction between them, and a significant obstruction to Thoreau's intellectual development.[7] In developing a portrait of Thoreau as one of the first ecologists, McGregor depicts Emerson's idealism as a subordination of the material world, a theory that reduced "Nature to the point of possible nonexistence" and also devalued Thoreau's real scientific expertise: "By devaluing the importance of the facts of natural history, Emerson reduced to a mere symbol a portion of the world where Henry possessed some real knowledge." For McGregor, Thoreau's development was a struggle to throw off Emersonian idealism in order to become a naturalist.[8]

At issue here is the complex question of Emerson's influence (and Thoreau's "originality"), an influence that is unquestionably significant but very hard to measure and assess. There was a deep bond between the two men and a shared vision and sense of purpose, but also, as we have come to see more clearly, a tension and a growing sense of betrayal and failed intimacy in their relationship. But McGregor also raises a question that is vital to our understanding of the motives and methods with which Thoreau perceived the natural world. In what ways, and with what impact, did Emerson's idealistic theorizing affect the impressionable and intellectually hungry Thoreau? Did an idealism that seemed to subordinate the material world philosophically become a cumbersome hindrance to Thoreau's perceptual engagement with nature?

Emerson's "noble doubt ... whether nature outwardly exists" (CW 1:29) is one of the more striking and controversial aspects of *Nature*. But his vivid account of idealism was not a novel or unique philosophical theory for Thoreau but rather one articulation among several of the problem of reconciling the singularity of things with their equally compelling similarities and relations. Emerson's seemingly ethereal dismissal of nature seems strange and even somewhat sinister to many readers today, who react to it as a dismissal of the reality of bodily experience. Those same readers are likely to feel an ardent sense of kinship with Thoreau because of his compelling descriptions of his experience in the natural world and his implicit advocacy of the preservation of the wild. Emerson's idealism thus strikes the modern reader as alien to Thoreau's central message and purpose.

Thoreau, however, found in *Nature* less a denial of the reality and specificity of the material world than a theory that gave facts significance because of their interrelations. Thoreau brought to his reading of *Nature* an already well-developed sense of the Platonic tradition, of eighteenth-century idealism, and of the emerging philosophies that were attempting to synthesize idealism and empiricism. As I noted earlier, both *Nature* and Brownson's *New Views* were published during Thoreau's senior year at Harvard, and we have every reason to believe that he found in them a new and liberating philosophy of experience. His earlier tutelage under Brownson, with whom he shared an interest in German idealism and Victor Cousin's philosophical "eclecticism," had shown him that philosophy and religious thought were on the verge of a major shift. Idealism had to be transcribed into a larger philosophical synthesis, an "eclectic" philosophy that would preserve the values of both empiricism and idealism. This discourse, coming at a moment when he was formulating his own sense of an intellectual mission, taught Thoreau that the task of philosophy is both to observe and to speculate, to collect facts and synthesize them into larger categories and explanatory systems.

Thoreau's interest in idealism was thus more than a deferential imitation of Emerson. He shared Emerson's concern with a set of questions that idealist philosophy was attempting to answer: How can we understand the many particulars of experience as constituting coherent patterns or categories, or of providing discernible similarities among themselves? How can we think of the things of the world as related, or of our own relation to the world? How can the mind comprehend matter? These are among the oldest of philosophical questions, but they posed a fresh challenge to Thoreau, who was introspective, inclined to philosophical speculation, and keenly observant of the natural world. In the last issue of the *Dial* in 1844, James E. Cabot wrote an essay that emphasized how idealism had framed the epistemological basis of modern thought: "Modern speculation, therefore, has returned to the fundamental problem of human science; and asks, first of all, 'Can we know anything?'"[9] *Nature* had been Emerson's attempt to address this question, and his conclusion—that a particular fact can be known completely only as one part of a much larger web of relations and interconnections—proved to be a dynamic and energizing principle for Thoreau. Idealism remained at the center of the continuing discourse among the Transcendentalists, who kept these issues alive for him through the 1840s and 1850s as he was becoming more committed to his field studies in natural history.

A close examination of Emerson's discussion of idealism in *Nature*, moreover, suggests another reason for its appeal to Thoreau, one that continued well into his Walden experiment and beyond. Emerson was proposing not an idealism that made nature disappear, but an idealism that made nature dynamic. He presented idealism as a theory that undermined the common view of matter as inert, and of nature as fixed or static. Idealism was for Emerson, as it was for Thoreau, a way to confirm the ever-mutating energy of the material world. Thoreau was an attentive reader who would not have missed Emerson's nuanced discussion of the paradox of disappearing nature.

To begin with, Emerson rejected the naive idea that idealism should alter our behavior in relation to material things. Most telling is the ironic humor of Emerson's guilty confession that there is "something ungrateful" about his theorizing, and his resulting declaration of his innocent devotion to nature. "I have no hostility to nature but a child's love to it. I expand and live in the warm day like corn and melons. Let us speak her fair. I do not wish to fling stones at my beautiful mother, nor soil my gentle nest" (CW 1:35–36). This disarming rhetoric responds to our instinctive mistrust of idealism by allowing Emerson to explain how idealism is both misperceived and unacknowledged in daily life, a part of the fabric of our ordinary experience even while we reject it on the grounds of common sense. Our capacity to interact with and use the material world, and our obligation to respect its laws and operations, are not open to question or alteration. "Whether nature enjoy a substantial existence without, or is only in the apocalypse of the mind," he argued, "it is alike useful and alike venerable to me" (CW 1:29). The "permanence of laws" remained inviolable whatever the ontological constitution of nature, and only "the frivolous make themselves merry with the Ideal theory, as if its consequences were burlesque" (CW 1:29).

This quality of permanence did not mean that the material world was dead or inert, or that there was no essential relation between it and our consciousness. One of Emerson's most amusing illustrations of the theory of idealism is his recommendation that we view the world through our legs, one of several examples of optical distortions that serve to undermine the settled familiarity and solidity of the world. "Turn the eyes upside down, by looking at the landscape through your legs, and how agreeable is the picture, though you have seen it any time these twenty years!" (CW 1:31). The appeal is that the familiar is made new, the fixed is made indeterminate. Our sense of the variety and richness of things is reconfirmed, and the possibilities of experience are vastly expanded.[10]

The fundamental perceptual shift that he describes as idealism is to replace a static world with a dynamic one, a detached or isolated world with one that shares with us a fundamental identity. Thus, even when he refers to nature as "an accident and an effect," his actual purpose is to reinvest it with a significance that will pull us into closer relation. "It is the uniform effect of culture on the human mind, not to shake our faith in the stability of particular phenomena, as of heat, water, azote; but to lead us to regard nature as a phenomenon, not a substance to attribute necessary existence to spirit; to esteem nature as an accident and an effect" (CW 1:30). The distinction between "substance" and "phenomenon" is critical, the first indicating a fixed and inert entity, and the second a convergence of energies or forces. A phenomenon is both in process and in relation, and represents nature's openness and mutability, and the affinity of all its constituent parts. As H. Daniel Peck has observed, "the term that Thoreau most often uses to reconcile the power of the creative eye with the independent status of the world is 'phenomenon.'"[11]

Emerson speaks of idealism less in terms of its absolute truth than of its relative advantage, its pragmatic effect on the human ability to respond to and reshape experience. "It is essential to a true theory of nature and of man, that it contain somewhat progressive" (CW 1:36), he argued. The phenomenal quality of nature implies its mobile and pliant quality as well, and suggests a progressive dynamism that mirrors human nature. "Nature is not fixed but fluid. Spirit alters, moulds, makes it" (CW 1:44). To understand the fluidity of nature is to recognize a correspondent energy within that is the basis of constructive and purposive action. "Know then, that the world exists for you. For you is the phenomenon perfect" (CW 1:44). This is less a justification for the subordination of nature, as many modern readers might at first suspect, than a declaration of the unperceived harmony between nature and the soul, making men and women an essential component of the "phenomenon" of nature that Emerson has been describing. This recognition begins "when the fact is seen under the light of an idea," making us understand that "a fact is true poetry, and the most beautiful of fables" (CW 144).

The recognition of nature as a changing, multifarious "phenomenon" of manifold relations takes us more deeply and securely into the world of facts rather than divorcing us from that world. "The invariable mark of wisdom is to see the miraculous in the common," Emerson wrote. "What is a day? What is a year? What is summer? What is woman? What is a child? What is sleep?" (CW 1:44). These questions about the nature of ordinary experience are the most profound, and open the interconnected fabric of phenomena that we call nature. To face a fact, then, is to face the world, to see the particular thing or event clearly and directly, but not in isolation, The most crucial lessons of *Walden* are Thoreau's repeated enactments of the intimate connection between observation and synthesis. The larger identities and relationships of things, their ideal qualities, yield the specific, factual identities to Thoreau, just as the specific identities of things and events inevitably suggest their relationships and their partaking of larger categories of identity.

THE SHADOW OF THE WHOLE

Thoreau's celebration of "fact" and his demonstration of the fruits of detailed observation in *Walden*, however insightful and philosophically significant, betray a growing self-doubt about the course of his intellectual development and the state of his philosophical and speculative powers. At times he felt himself to be drying up intellectually, and though drawn temperamentally toward more intensive projects of field observation and data collection, he distrusted his own tendency to become a collector of information. In August 1851, after his stay at Walden but before he had finally revised and reshaped his manuscript, he confessed his struggle to rein in the increasingly dominant empirical side of his personality: "I fear that the character of my knowledge is from year to year becoming more distinct & scientific—That in exchange for views as wide as heaven's cope I am being narrowed down to the field of the microscope—I see details not wholes nor the shadow of the whole. I count some parts, & say 'I know'. The cricket's chirp now fills the air in dry fields near pine woods" (JP 3:380). Thoreau senses a certain dishonesty in claiming to "know" when that knowledge excludes the larger frame of reference which invests details with their significance. But this worried self-analysis leads to an observation of the "cricket's chirp," the kind of detail that he has just labeled problematic. While Thoreau's fascination with the details of the natural world grows, he continues to doubt that such details can in themselves be fulfilling. He fears that he is gaining the particulars of the world but losing his soul.

This tension between the close observation of the particular and the more expansive pursuit of the whole sharpened for Thoreau in the late 1840s and early 1850s, as he was drawn more directly into the growth of scientific study at Harvard. In 1847 Louis Agassiz began a major effort to build Harvard's presence in science. Committed to a theory of the "special creation" of particular species, as opposed to a developmental theory that would later be articulated by Darwin, Agassiz began an extensive effort to gather and preserve large numbers of animal specimens and developed a network of field naturalists to collect them. Thoreau was one of his cooperating colleagues in this endeavor, enlisted by Agassiz's assistant, and *Dial* contributor, James E. Cabot. Laura Dassow Walls has noted that Thoreau devoted a month or more to such hunting and capturing in 1847, his second spring at Walden, a detail that he does not include in his narrative of his life at the pond. "What are we to make," Walls asks, "of a Thoreau who so cheerfully trapped, packed, and shipped so many of his Walden 'friends' and neighbors to Harvard's halls of science?" Although he "seems to have lost interest quickly" in such collection, and returned to his more literary projects while at the pond, the experience had a definite impact on him. Even though Agassiz's scientific theories had at best a limited appeal to Thoreau, participating in such collecting provided him with the opportunity to observe and participate in the systematic fieldwork of scientific observation and collection. Even though his misgivings about the activity surfaced quickly, the work had, as Walls argues, reinforced his penchant for vigilant alertness and observational acuity in the field as well as what he felt were his growing tendencies to move "away from a grand and abstract transcendentalism toward a detailed observation of the specifics of nature, in all its unaccountable diversity."[12]

That Thoreau excelled in this work of field observation, data collection and recording, and specimen gathering is unquestionable, but his continuing uneasiness about the ends of such work is suggested in his reaction to a questionnaire sent him by the Association for the Advancement of Science asking him "to fill the blanks against certain questions—among which the most important one was—what branch of science I was specially interested in." Unable to answer the questions as he felt he should—"I felt that it would be to make myself the laughing stock of the scientific community"—he was "obliged to speak to their condition and describe to them that poor part of me which alone they can understand." The questionnaire could not get at the vital truth about him. "The fact is I am a mystic—a transcendentalist—& a natural philosopher to boot. Now I think—of it—I should have told them at once I was a transcendentalist—that would have been the shortest way of telling them that they would not understand my explanations" (JP 5:469–70). Thoreau's insistence on his dual identity as a "transcendentalist" and a "natural philosopher" and his derisive discomfort with the narrow categories that the fields of "science" offered him are important reminders of a tension that sharpened for him through the 1850s, years that were marked by his struggle to balance, and finally to reconcile, this seemingly dual identity.

Even as his interest in gathering the facts that now dominated the study of "natural history" was growing, it is perhaps somewhat surprising to find that his interest in Hinduism was rekindled by an 1848 article by James E. Cabot, an essay that, as Robert D. Richardson Jr. argues, "gave Thoreau an added impetus to explore Hinduism as a powerful independent corroboration of the central concept of Idealism," and initiated an extensive reading project on Hinduism. The impact of Thoreau's immersion in Hinduism can be seen in *Walden*, with its extensive network of allusions to Hindu texts.[13]

Cabot's article was less an essay than a compilation of passages from recent translations of the Vishnu Purana, the Bhagavad Gita, and other Hindu texts, providing a brief anthology of Hindu wisdom and philosophical precepts. Cabot explained that he had gathered "fragments of a speculative character" from "the theogonies and myths of the Hindoos." These fragments did not "properly [amount] to a system," but they did represent "an attempt to theorize on the Universe." Although Cabot kept his own explication and theorizing to a minimum, the selection and arrangement of his compilation did have a controlling thesis, one of particular relevance to Thoreau's own philosophical concerns in the late 1840s and early 1850s. Cabot describes the development of "three very distinct epochs" in Hindu literature, beginning with "the age of the Vedas," which shows "little trace of reflection, or of intense religious consciousness." The succeeding era, "the age of the Puranas and the Bhagavat Gita, is a meditative, mystical period, during which speculation among the Hindoos reached its highest point." That high point has been followed by a long "age of commentators, of subtile distinctions, and of polemics," a "Scholastic Age" secondary to the creative age that preceded it.[14] Cabot argued that the meditative and mystical era of the Bhagavad Gita, "the essence of the Hindoo metaphysics," could be expressed in one fundamental precept: "the reduction of all Reality to pure, abstract Thought." Although this idea cannot be illustrated by "a methodical arrangement of propositions," it is nevertheless a "constant theme," expressed metaphorically in "often sublime imagery." "The main principle of Hindoo Idealism—that Reality is equivalent to pure abstract Soul or Thought, unexistent, and thus simple and unformed; in a word, pure Negation,—is presented especially under the aspect of the unity and identity of all things in the Deity."[15]

Thoreau read Cabot's essay with care, copying out a number of quotations, including this passage from the Vishnu Purana:

> Liberation, which is the object to be effected, being accomplished, discriminative knowledge ceases. When endowed with the apprehension of the nature of the object of inquiry, then there is no difference between it and supreme spirit; difference is the consequence of the absence of true knowledge. When that ignorance which is the cause of the difference between individual and universal spirit is destroyed, finally and for ever, who shall make that distinction between them which does not exist?[16]

Perception is described here as a process of unification, in which the isolated part is reunited with its original whole through the act of perception.

"Difference," the result of an initial act of discriminating perception, is the condition that complete knowledge hopes eventually to overcome.

The idea that "difference is the consequence of the absence of true knowledge" had important implications for Thoreau's conception of his work as a naturalist, especially as he took up the more detailed activities of data and specimen collection. The empirical accumulation of facts could be justified only as one stage of a process that ultimately aimed at an explanation of the inclusive whole of nature. Thoreau's immersion in the world of "fact" in the late 1840s and early 1850s was accompanied, then, by a continuing, indeed renewed, interest in idealism, significantly reinforced by his interest in Hinduism.

It seems clear from this seemingly incongruent pattern of study and reading that the intensity with which Thoreau engaged in empirical science in the late 1840s and early 1850s did not undermine his interest in and broad adherence to idealism, if we give that term the comprehensive characterization that Thoreau did. One view of Thoreau's intellectual development, based largely on the increasingly factual character of his journal entries through the 1850s, is that for better or worse, he increasingly surrendered to his passion for fact and detail, and became progressively distanced from the kind of philosophical speculation that Emerson had shown him. But Thoreau's persistent efforts in *Walden* and beyond to push specific observations toward more encompassing theories were a response to his fear of losing his capacity to see "wholes." This fear is also related to a worried sense of personal declension and inadequacy that haunted him in the early 1850s as he revised and augmented the *Walden* manuscript.[17]

Thoreau's struggle to reconcile the particularized empiricism of Agassiz and others with the quest for unified wholes that were represented by the traditions of both Western idealism and Hindu mythology was intensified by a more personal crisis of confidence in his own perceptual capabilities. On July 16, 1851, Thoreau confessed, "Methinks my present experience is nothing my past experience is all in all." He fears the fading of his perceptual power, of a present whose intensity is dwarfed by a remembered past. "I think that no experience which I have today comes up to or is comparable with the experiences of my boyhood—And not only this is true—but as far back as I can remember I have unconsciously referred to the experience of a previous state of experience. 'Our life is a forgetting' &c" (JP 3:305). Underlying this Wordsworthian lament is a wish for a liminal experience in which the boundaries of self and nature evaporate, and we experience an unusual sense of both harmony and elevation. "Formerly methought nature developed as I developed and grew up with me. My life was extacy. In youth before I lost any of my senses—I can remember that I was all alive—and inhabited my body with inexpressible satisfaction, both its weariness & its refreshment were sweet to me. This earth was the most glorious musical instrument, and I was audience to its strains" (JP 3:305–6). Thoreau associates the health and vigor of youth with a bond with the natural world, and expresses some alarm at the progressive diminishment of that bond.[18]

But what of Thoreau's project both to live and describe the "natural life" under these conditions? The "simple and sincere account of his own life" (Wa 3) that he had set out to provide had become deeply problematic. Thoreau's ultimate completion of *Walden*, made possible around 1852 by a breakthrough in his sense of the work's structure and a corresponding recovery of purpose and vision, was in part a response to this sense of intellectual and experiential slippage. Shaping an account of his experience in *Walden* thus became one part of Thoreau's answer to a disappearing capacity to envision enlarged and unifying categories. The *Walden* manuscript, beginning with his journal entries and lectures while he was living at the pond, and evolving through its seven stages of composition in the late 1840s and early 1850s, became the repository of his struggle to maintain his capacity for philosophical reflection on the natural world and the place of the self within it.[19]

Thoreau's chapter "The Ponds," which includes his intricate analysis of the richly symbolic identity of Walden Pond, is indicative of his strategy of portraying perception as factual and sensuous yet also productive of ever-enlarging frames of reference.[20] Walden is a character who is absolutely pure and "perennially young" (Wa 193). Thoreau attributes such human characteristics as eyelids and lips to Walden, and dramatizes his relationship with the pond as that of friendship. Such tactics infuse an imaginative life into material nature and contribute to Thoreau's attempt to re-mythologize the natural world. The humanization of the pond helps to quicken and vitalize it, and stands as the culmination of a series of depictions of an animated natural world which include the besotted, "aldermanic" bullfrogs who "*tr-r-r-oonk*" (Wa 126) at the pond shore in the evening in "Sounds," and the visits from the "old settler and original proprietor, who is reported to have dug Walden Pond," and the "ruddy and lusty old dame, who delights in all weathers and seasons" (Wa 137–38).

Personification is the most easily recognizable strategy through which Thoreau attempts to use the pond and its landscape to enlarge our commonplace perception. It is supplemented by the more extensive passages of description in which Thoreau strives to produce a mental image of the scenery of Walden, which, though "on a humble scale" (Wa 175), becomes impressive through his careful verbal reconstructions. His close observations of the pond's shoreline and the shifting color of its water help us to locate ourselves and begin to see the world with him. But perhaps the most subtle and telling of these passages, rich in descriptive power and resonant with suggestiveness about the pond's unifying qualities, is his observation of the pond's still surface, the very blankness of which is shown to be its secret of association.

Thoreau describes the unusual optical impression of the pond surface on "a calm September afternoon, when a slight haze makes the opposite shoreline indistinct." In a comment that recalls Emerson's looking through his legs at the world in "Idealism," Thoreau writes, "When you invert your head, it looks like a thread of finest gossamer stretched across the valley, separating one stratum of the atmosphere from another." Whereas Emerson altered his usual perspective to make the solid world seem unfixed and malleable, Thoreau likes to think of the surface of the pond as solid, a perfectly integrated extension of the shoreline. "You would think that you could walk dry under it to the opposite hills, and that the swallows which skim over might perch on it" (Wa 186). This shift in perspective discloses the pond as the point of union among the disparate elements of nature, connecting land, water, and sky to suggest that each of these is a version of all the others, and that each part or aspect of nature contains all of nature if seen completely.

Thoreau's descriptive argument extends to his portrait of the remarkable power of the pond's surface to record all the life and energy around it, its even, smooth plane a medium that can disclose the smallest presence and the finest movements above and below it.

> It is literally as smooth as glass, except where the skater insects, at equal intervals scattered over its whole extent, by their motions in the sun produce the finest imaginable sparkle on it, or, perchance, a duck plumes itself, or, as I have said, a swallow skims so low as to touch it. It may be that in the distance a fish describes an arc of three or four feet in the air, and there is one bright flash where it emerges, and another where it strikes the water; sometimes the whole silvery arc is revealed; or here and there, perhaps, is a thistle-down floating on its surface, which the fishes dart at and so dimple it again. (Wa 186–87)

This closely observed and poetically expressive prose is of course one of Thoreau's great achievements in *Walden*, but aside from the compelling visual image that he creates, the description re-creates the pond surface as a medium of cognition, an ideal analogue for the completely perceptive mind. The line of demarcation between two different realms, water and sky, the surface is also the place where these realms meet and merge, recording and thus comprehending each such event. Perception, as represented by Thoreau through the perfectly impressionable pond surface, is thus a process of merger or unification.

Thoreau confirms the metaphoric reach of his description of the pond's surface by concluding that "a field of water betrays the spirit that is in the air. It is continually receiving new life and motion from above" (Wa 188). The spirit above the lake's surface is of course the wind, but Thoreau's choice of words here is significant. "*Spirit* primarily means *wind*," Emerson had written in *Nature*, using this etymological connection as one of his illustrations of how language reveals the connection between the ideal and material realms. "Every word which is used to express a moral or intellectual fact, if traced to its root, is found to be borrowed from some material appearance" (CW 1:18). Thoreau uses "spirit" with this same sense of the identity of the material and the ideal, suggesting that the act of perception unifies the material and the ideal, that the physical discernment of a phenomenon in nature suggests more intangible "moral or intellectual" facts.

Thoreau's account of his return to the frozen surface of the pond in "The Pond in Winter" adds new emphasis on the pond as an embodiment of an enlarged perception that encompasses both material and ideal, fact and law.[21] His morning work of cutting through the ice to obtain fresh water, one of the most memorable lyric moments in the narrative, confirms the eternal presence and inevitable return of the pond's natural life, and also represents the importance and availability of the inner life, perhaps buried or not immediately apparent, but always available. He cuts through the ice and looks down "into the quiet parlor of the fishes, pervaded by a soft light as through a window of ground glass, with its bright sanded floor the same as in summer." The "perennial waveless serenity" of the scene, the inner possession of the pond and of every individual who can delve deeply enough within, leads Thoreau to declare that "heaven is under our feet as well as over our heads" (Wa 283). The pond reveals a further lesson when Thoreau sets about measuring it, intending both to satisfy his curiosity and to dispel the lore that it is bottomless. He finds and records its depth, using measurable fact to counter superstition, but also concludes that fact will open into law if fully examined.

Discovering "that the line of greatest length intersected the line of greatest breadth *exactly* at the point of greatest depth" (Wa 289), Thoreau believed that he may have discovered a law for determining the deepest point in any lake.[22] Although such is not, in fact, the case, the immediacy of Thoreau's reach for the larger implications of his experiment, his eagerness to make Walden a representative entity, is indicative of his need to see his work of observation as a search for more inclusive categories. In this sense, detail can become transformative insight. "If we knew all the laws of Nature, we should need only one fact, or the description of one actual phenomenon, to infer all the particular results at that point" (Wa 290). This is an assertion about the nature of knowledge but also, perhaps more significantly, about the unity of what the mind perceives:

> Our notions of law and harmony are commonly confined to those instances which we detect; but the harmony which results from a far greater number of seemingly conflicting, but really concurring, laws, which we have not detected, is still more wonderful. The particular laws are as our points of view, as, to the traveller, a mountain outline varies with every step, and it has an infinite number of profiles, though absolutely but one form. (Wa 290–91)

This faith that no matter how various it may seem, nature is "absolutely but one form" was Thoreau's justification for his attention to the particulars of nature, an assurance that no act of observation or recognition ended in itself.

The most dramatic and far-reaching of these incidents of observation is the well-known description of the "sand foliage," in which Thoreau recognizes that the forms of melting sand and clay manifest the workings of the laws that control and shape all natural processes of growth and change, including those of the body. One small and seemingly insignificant occurrence becomes revelatory of the entire system of nature. Generally recognized as the climactic scene of *Walden*, the passage has been accorded both intense scrutiny and illuminating explication in recent criticism. Gordon V. Boudreau has shown in impressive detail that the sand foliage passage was a culminating statement of a "resurrection myth" toward which Thoreau had striven in *A Week* and his Journal, in which the thawing of the earth becomes an act of both birth and utterance. Thoreau's observation and description of it links mental perception and linguistic expression to this archetypal moment in the creative process. Robert D. Richardson Jr. calls attention to Thoreau's exclamation that "there is nothing inorganic" (Wa 308) as the recognition that the unifying processes of law invigorate and explain all physical phenomena. Noting that the expansion of the sand foliage description was the most important revision in the final drafts of the *Walden* manuscript, Richardson connects this late expansion with Thoreau's sighting of the thawing sand flow on February 2, 1854, a signal to him of the end of winter. This climactic insight of the triumph of life is part of Thoreau's own emergence from a period of disorientation and despondency in the early 1850s in which his emotional resiliency was keyed to seasonal change. The completion of the

Walden manuscript, after its long postponement and repeated revision, thus seems to have represented a personal and spiritual achievement as well as a literary one. As Richardson writes, "The 'Spring' chapter of *Walden*, with its exhilarating description of the flowing clay bank at its center, is finally an affirmation of foliage over fossil, natural fact over historical relic, life over death."[23]

Thoreau's detailed and intricate description of the sand foliage phenomenon, coupled with the reach of his interpretive insight, make this one of the most telling examples of the "reading" that was the cornerstone of his natural life at Walden. Confessing the "delight" (Wa 304) that the sand foliage gave him, the loving detail with which he unfolds his description and interpretation dramatizes his enraptured witness to life's origin. The earth's "living poetry" (Wa 309) was a vivid expression of the merging of fact with law, a process that required language as an essential element. The earth itself became a poem, and Thoreau its reader. His toil over Homer and his devotion to his journal were thus as natural and necessary as the seasonal cycle, and a part of that larger process. "You find thus in the very sands an anticipation of the vegetable leaf. No wonder that the earth expresses itself outwardly in leaves, it so labors with the idea inwardly. The atoms have already learned this law, and are pregnant by it" (Wa 306). Thoreau thus recognized his own efforts to understand and express the work of thinking and writing as consonant with the very process of creation itself. The natural life around him corresponded to the natural life within.

NOTES

1. Sattelmeyer, "The Remaking of *Walden*." F. O. Matthiessen presented the classic reading of *Walden* as a masterpiece of organic form in his chapter "The Organic Principle" (*American Renaissance*, 133–75). Charles R. Anderson's reading of *Walden* as an extended poem in *The Magic Circle of Walden* was also significant.

2. Harding, *The Days of Henry Thoreau*, 263–66.

3. See Robert Milder's discussion of Thoreau's conception of reading as "a spiritual calisthenics whose effect is to elevate the soul" (*Reimagining Thoreau*, 76).

4. Cavell, *Senses of Walden*, 28. See also Charles R. Anderson's discussion of Thoreau's reading as part of the new patterns of his activities (*The Magic Circle of Walden*, 39–47).

5. On the connection between "Reading" and "Sounds," see Matthiessen, *American Renaissance*, 168–69; and Anderson, *The Magic Circle of Walden*, 39–41.

6. See Cavell, *The Senses of Walden*, 26–35 and passim for a detailed and perceptive discussion of the activity and the motif of reading in *Walden*.

7. McGregor, *A Wider View of the Universe*, 33–86. McGregor also notes, however, the importance of Emerson's influence in encouraging Thoreau to begin his career as a writer. More subtle readings of the complexities of Thoreau's reception of idealism are offered by Charles R. Anderson (*The Magic Circle of Walden*, 93–130), H. Daniel Peck, and Laura Dassow Walls. Peck (*Thoreau's Morning Work*, 66–78) has depicted Thoreau's early

work, including *Walden*, as a test of idealism, a theory that Thoreau eventually rejected for a conception of experience that much more closely resembles the phenomenology of Heidegger. "Philosophical idealism was inevitably his legacy," Peck writes. "But what makes him so interesting to us is that he inherited idealism not as a faith but as a problem" (73). Walls (*Seeing New Worlds*, 53–93) describes Thoreau's principal direction of intellectual development as a rejection of "rational holism," one form of idealism that she terms the "dominant paradigm of romanticism" (54) propounded by Coleridge and Emerson, and a movement toward a more fact-oriented "empirical holism" characteristic of the scientific method of Humboldt.

8. McGregor, *A Wider View of the Universe*, 40, 44. Recent critical discourse on two related issues, the history of science and "ecocriticism," have helped to frame this issue. Both seek to present Thoreau as a "naturalist," as opposed to a literary or philosophical figure, and concentrate on his later journal and the natural history projects of his later career. In addition to the work of Peck, Walls, and McGregor, see also Howarth, *The Book of Concord*; Buell, *The Environmental Imagination*; Rossi, "Education in the Field" and "Thoreau's Transcendental Ecocentrism"; and Berger, *Thoreau's Late Career and "The Dispersion of Seeds."* Also of importance is the recent editorial work on late Thoreau manuscripts by Bradley P. Dean: *Faith in a Seed* (1993) and *Wild Fruits* (2000).

9. Cabot, "Immanuel Kant," 409.

10. See Anderson, *The Magic Circle of Walden*, 112–30, and Dieter Schulz (*Amerikanischer Tranzendentalismus*, 110–45) for further discussion of Emerson's and Thoreau's discussions of the eye and its significance.

11. Peck, *Thoreau's Morning Work*, 67–68.

12. Walls, *Seeing New Worlds*, 113–16, quote from 115. As Robert Sattelmeyer (*Thoreau's Reading*, 82–86) and Robert D. Richardson Jr. (*Henry Thoreau*, 362–68) have shown, Thoreau also read Louis Agassiz and A.A. Gould's *Principles of Zoology* (1848; revised edition 1851) and Agassiz's "Essay on Classification" (1857), learning much from them even as he moved away from Agassiz's larger conception of special creation of each species. For an informative reading of Thoreau's developing reaction to pre-Darwinian ideas of evolution, see Rossi, "Thoreau's Transcendental Ecocentrism."

13. Richardson, *Henry Thoreau*, 205. On the impact of Hindu writings on Thoreau, see Hodder, "'Ex Oriente Lux'" and *Thoreau's Ecstatic Witness*, 139–59.

14. Cabot, "The Philosophy of the Ancient Hindoos," 400–401.

15. Ibid., 403.

16. Ibid., 417; see also Richardson, *Henry Thoreau*, 206–7; Cameron, *Transcendental Apprenticeship*, 222.

17. In *The Senses of Walden* (110), Stanley Cavell has remarked on the problematic quality of "the depth of the book's depressions and the height of its elevations" and "the absence of reconciliation between them." These gaps can be taken as the signs of Thoreau's attempt to use his literary task in *Walden* to address his inner conflicts and fears of slippage and deterioration. Of pertinence on this issue is Robert D. Richardson Jr.'s discussion of *Walden* as "the earned affirmation of a man who had to struggle almost constantly against a sense of loss, desolation, and decline that grew on him age" (*Henry Thoreau*, 256).

18. See John Hildebidle's comments on this passage, which he reads in the context of Thoreau's struggle with the emerging new discourse of Science (*Thoreau*, 102–11).

19. See Sattelmeyer, "The Remaking of *Walden*." For detailed information on the *Walden* manuscript, see Clapper, "The Development of Walden."

20. For perceptive analyses of the profusion of symbolic associations of the pond, see Paul, *The Shores of America*, 332–45; and Lyon, "Walden Pond as Symbol."

21. Robert Milder has provided an informative discussion of the evolution of this chapter in Thoreau's development of the *Walden* manuscript (*Reimagining Thoreau*, 144–51).

22. Paul, *The Shores of America*, 343–45.

23. Boudreau, *The Roots of Walden and the Tree of Life*, 117; Richardson, *Henry Thoreau*, 310–13, quotation from 312. Other important readings of the sand foliage passage include Charles R. Anderson's emphasis on the centrality of the "leaf metaphor" (*The Magic Circle of Walden*, 243) and its connection to Thoreau's reading of Goethe; and Milder, *Reimagining Thoreau*, 151–60. The particular linguistic context of the passage has been helpfully worked out by Philip F. Gura (*The Wisdom of Words*, 124–41) and Michael West (*Transcendental Wordplay*, 183–96).

ROBERT OSCAR LÓPEZ

Thoreau, Homer, and Community

This essay will seek to add to Thoreau studies by examining new connections between Thoreau's *Walden* and Homer's *Iliad*. In the process, it will also build on the work of other Thoreau scholars, to reflect on his conflicted thoughts about community and friendship in *Walden*. What Thoreau got out of reading Homer and how he felt about human relationships are more interconnected than one might guess. One can, for instance, come to notice Thoreau's conversation with the ghosts of ancient Greece in *Walden*, by beginning with a question that strikes at the notion of community: when Thoreau speaks, with whom is he speaking?

In *Walden*, Thoreau's ideal discourse community is hard to define. One important reason for this is that Thoreau usually does not seem sure about who is listening to him. He seems more certain about the wide range of social forces that he would prefer to escape. His position on social life appears unambiguous in *Walden* when he says, "wherever a man goes, men will pursue and paw him with their dirty institutions and, if they can, constrain him to belong to their desperate odd-fellow society" adding that "I preferred that society should run 'amok' against me, it being the desperate party."[1] It worries the author of *Walden* that men and women, if given the chance, institutionalize each other and halt their progress toward a truly free consciousness. As Lewis Leary puts it, Thoreau "advocated consciousness, yes; perception, certainly;

From *Nineteenth-Century Prose*, vol. 31, no. 2 (Fall 2004), pp. 122–151. © 2004 by San Diego State University.

but manipulation, no."[2] Of these three, manipulation is the only mechanism that involves live communication among people, rather than individuated and private thought. Community endangers both consciousness and perception insofar as all social intercourse is tainted by the prospects of manipulation and, therefore, corruption.

It would be rash to conclude that, because of his fear of human manipulation, Thoreau spits on all notions of human community. He is not a total misanthrope. He believes that noble virtues are available to anyone, in any locale or era where individuals find opportunities to cultivate their better instincts. As Bob Pepperman Taylor says of Thoreau, he "firmly believes that truth, heroism and virtue are universal attributes found in great individuals in all historical settings."[3] This idealism about human capability is closely linked to Thoreau's desire to be firmly rooted in the present rather than transfixed by the gleaming prestige of the past. Even though Thoreau is wary of his peers, he tries his best not to express his wariness as a smug preference for organic communities of an earlier golden age. He is hostile to historical nostalgia and refuses to grant to antiquity a higher place in the social order than his own time. The famous and enduring last words of *Walden* are that "The sun is but a morning star."[4] The book's finale is a statement of proportionality. In thinking about the sun being as small as one dot of light, perhaps the reader can appreciate the enormous timeline that human potential inhabits.

Time is clearly on the author's mind in *Walden*, though his thoughts on human beings' relationship to history are complex and multilayered. Thoreau had a complex affection for dead geniuses like Homer, to be examined below, but this reverence for ancient ideas is still tempered by his desire to dismiss the grandiose claims of history's crumbling ruins and rotting tombs. Thoreau wants to stand outside of, and to condescend to, history itself:

> Time is but the stream I go a-fishing in. I drink at it; but while
> I drink I see the sandy bottom and detect how shallow it is.[5]

The past holds nothing necessarily magical. It is a natural reflection of everything he knows already. That is why Thoreau writes in *A Week on the Concord and Merrimack Rivers* that "the history we read is only a fainter memory of events which have happened in our own experience."[6]

Eventually, though, his rejection of history fails, and he lapses into Homer worship, despite all attempts to see the claims of the past as shallow. These strides to treat history irreverently do not work, I will argue, due to his incurable bitter edge when Thoreau thinks about the human community accessible to him in the present tense. The ancients fill a gap left by the mediocrity of Thoreau's contemporaries. When he writes in *Walden* that "I never received more than one or two letters in my life ... that were worth the postage," he is not only confessing but also causing his alienation from other people, in the very act of writing such an affront to anyone who took the time to try to contact him.[7] As Stanley Cavell describes it, Thoreau "must undertake to write absolutely, to exercise his faith in the very act of marking the word,"[8] even where this exercise requires that he reject other human beings before they have been given the chance to reject him. All humanity must be dismissed, glibly if not cruelly, for the individual to find pure enlightenment. The ideal of meditation without compromising distractions becomes a desire for an absence of spoken language and a distrustful attitude toward conversation. Thoreau writes toward the end of his week in a riverboat with his soft-spoken brother:

> [T]he most excellent speech finally falls into Silence.... Silence is the universal refuge, the sequel to all dull discourses and all foolish acts, a balm to our every chagrin, as welcome after satiety as after disappointment.[9]

Thoreau is not necessarily looking for an escape from all conversation—only from the triviality of noise and chatter. The problem is that he never hears any discussion around him that can rise to his threshold of worthy dialogue. The imperfections of spoken exchanges ("dull discourses") drive him to silence. There is still a powerful appetite for better conversation, but it becomes internal and private. In the vast majority of circumstances, for Thoreau, the self is the most viable partner in discussion:

> I should not talk so much about myself if there were anybody else whom I knew as well.[10]

The arguable word in the above sentence, though, is "about." Talking *about* one's self is not exactly controversial, but talking only *to* one's self is, because without an audience, a book's authority dwindles down to the level of an easily forgotten journal.

Thoreau's ambivalent feelings about membership in a discourse community are evident in his mixed feelings about his target audience. The audience for a published book (with all its final polish and institutional authority) is different from the audience for a loosely organized journal. Since Thoreau produced both types of literary oeuvres, he could not have been unaware of the difference. Leonard Neufeldt has pointed out that Thoreau's "Journal turned out to be his largest work by far and, in his estimation, possibly his most important project as a writer."[11] Robert Sattelmeyer, agreeing that the Journal "became the major work of Thoreau's imaginative life," views the inception of Thoreau's personal writings as particularly important because of the fact that his friendship with Emerson both precipitated and was strengthened by his dedication to journal-keeping.[12] Yet despite the breadth of Thoreau's journals, Neufeldt points out that "Thoreau's 'failure' to be definitive on the purpose of his journalizing is part of a pattern noticeable throughout."[13] It was common for many different types of people in nineteenth-century Concord to keep journals—perhaps too common. If everyone who kept a journal fell into the sacred category of "author," then, as Neufeldt's research reveals, "authority" would be a badge conferred on Concord's "clergy, teachers, naturalists, businessmen, lawyers, housewives, unmarried women, students, and farmers [who] left journals behind ranging from a few page fragments to Bronson Alcott's fifty neatly bound volumes of approximately five million words."[14] The jump from the world of journals to the world of books involves an escape from the common din of the former into the respectable exclusivity of the latter. Perhaps with the respect of a published book comes an easier command of the audience's attention, readers' greater willingness to listen to the author and take him seriously, and ultimately a larger discourse community. The fact that Thoreau struggled to publish *A Week on the Concord and Merrimack Rivers* and *Walden* could reflect a hunger for that larger discourse community even as he sometimes hints, as noted above, that it is beneath him to jostle for society's approval.

The underlying crisis of *Walden* is perhaps not a search for a "redemption of language" as Stanley Cavell's work stresses,[15] but, I would propose, an unsatisfying search for an appropriate community to receive whatever meaning the writer's consciousness can generate. Stanley Cavell says that "*Walden* shows that we *are* there; every tongue has confessed what it can; we have heard everything there is to hear.... What is left to us is the accounting."[16] Cavell's argument would imply that Thoreau was certain that there was nothing left to confess and nothing left to hear; it assumes that Thoreau had truly given up entirely on talking and listening to people. But the reality of Thoreau's relation to other human beings is much more ambivalent. Thoreau wants to be heard and respected; he also wants companions but needs them to be free of hypocrisy and manipulation by having no conflict of interest. Such an argument oddly requires that they have no interest in him at all. He prizes neutrality as a condition for any acceptable social relationship (be it with friends or with a living audience), even though to most people the neutrality he prescribes would very well look like coldness, detachment, or indifference, none of which is conducive to friendship. "Individuals, like nations," Thoreau writes in *Walden*, "must have suitable broad and natural boundaries, even a considerable neutral ground between them."[17] The author wants to be social, but requires that any society with which he associates remain at a cold distance. He reveals his own uncertainty about how close an intimate friend should be suffered to approach, when he adds that "If we would enjoy the most intimate society with that in each of us which is without, or above, being spoken to, we must not only be silent, but commonly so far apart bodily that we cannot possibly hear each other's voice in any case."[18]

His ambivalence about the value of a conversational community ultimately drives Thoreau to abandon his glib irreverence toward history, and to choose as his closest companions canonized ghosts like Homer. Live humans are too prone to speak, whereas the words of an ancient voice can still reach Thoreau in perfect silence. This is the difference, in his mind, between "garrulous and noisy eras, which no longer yield any sound" and the "Grecian or silent and melodious era" that is somewhere, but nowhere, and "ever sounding and resounding in the ears of men."[19]

It is no secret that Thoreau had persistent difficulty with notions of community and neither made nor kept friends easily. Harmon Smith notes in *My Friend, My Friend* that Emerson, one of his most important confidants, "found Thoreau's natural combativeness more and more difficult to deal with as the years passed."[20] Likewise, Sattelmeyer notes of the Thoreau–Emerson relationship that "by 1850, each was writing about the estrangement as accomplished, and looking at the other with a mixture of disappointment, anger, and resignation."[21] With living, breathing humans who come to him with their own compromises and political biases, Thoreau rarely finds any lasting satisfaction—not even in deciding he does not need them. "No word is oftener on the lips of men than Friendship," he ruminates in *A Week on the Concord and Merrimack Rivers*,[22] even though his prognosis for the true value of human companionship remains bleak. "To say that a man is your Friend, means commonly no more than this, that he is not your enemy," he notes soon after, adding that "[i]n our daily intercourse with men, our nobler faculties are dormant and suffered to rust."[23] The fact that he still desires a friend with whom he can chat is made clear, even if he makes long complaints about such a companion still being unfound among the living. "Think of the importance of Friendship in the education of men," he writes. "It will make a man honest; it will make him a hero; it will make him a saint."[24] In *Walden*, Thoreau ridicules townspeople for "the gossip which is incessantly going on there ... as refreshing in its way as the rustle of leaves and the peeping of frogs."[25] At other times he admits that he is prone to the same rustle and peeping. In the same chapter he writes that "I love society as much as most ... am naturally no hermit, but might possibly sit out the sturdiest frequenter in the bar-room, if my business called me hither."[26]

Solitude would be the prettier way to characterize Thoreau's situation; but since he never reconciles himself fully to a life without human company, the word "estrangement" is more apt. The ongoing estrangement from the social world around him, as well as with its languages, could very well be a key reason for his occasional turn to the Greeks. Robert D. Richardson, Jr. points out that Thoreau's grounding in Latin and Greek was not necessarily outstanding, given the curriculum at Concord Academy and Harvard (where Thoreau attended) in the 1830s,[27] and that it is perhaps Thoreau's voracious absorption of modern languages that marks him as exceptional among his peers. In *Henry Thoreau: A Life of the Mind*, Richardson writes that "Thoreau is always thought of as well educated and well read in the classics—and no one has ever written a better defense of them—but it is not always recalled that he could read French, German, and Italian with ease, and, more important, that he was both inclined and prepared to think of literature in a broad, multicultural sense."[28] Notwithstanding Thoreau's aptitude for living languages, however, his intellectual trajectory from his youthful journals to the writing of *Walden* suggests that Greek and Latin often appeal to him precisely *because* they are not the languages in which other people speak anymore. Dead languages do not taint words with the alienation possible in social relationships with people who talk back to him. It is perhaps no coincidence, for instance, that in the fall of 1839, when Henry Thoreau and his brother John were both romantically interested in Ellen Sewall—and John seemed closer to winning the rivalry—Henry distracted himself from his hurt feelings by working on a translation of Aeschylus' *Prometheus Bound* and essays on the Roman satirist Persius.[29] Antiquity soothes Thoreau's injured pride, his resentments, and his annoyances with peers.

Even when Thoreau is not conversing with ancient writers, there are abundant traces in his writings of difficult emotions left over from unsatisfying interactions with other people. Human rejection, as a sign that the role of conversational companion has been inadequately filled, is an indispensable component in Thoreau's writing—and it is important to remember that the rejection is working in both directions. A perennial condition of his texts is that the reader can be driven to buck Thoreau's preaching and send him back to his ancient grotto with a dismissive flourish and a closing of his book. His posture is both defensive and offensive when he writes in the closing pages of *Walden* that "It is a ridiculous demand England and America make, that you shall speak so that they can understand you. Neither men nor toadstools grow so."[30] Who is spurning the other, and who—the reader or the author or both—is being disregarded? Rejection becomes simultaneous, a circle of chicken and egg with no traceable starting point. Indeed, despite the beauty of his prose, more than a few who read *Walden* find it difficult to like Thoreau's character enough to heed him. And this is a serious problem, given that, as Stanley Cavell says, "the hero of this book is its writer."[31] Bob Pepperman Taylor cites Thoreau's social downfall as his self-righteousness, something that sours many devotees who first embrace and then discard him after finding his moral self-referentiality untenable:

> As I began to age, with family and job and all the other trappings and responsibilities of conventional American adulthood, I found (again like so many others) Thoreau beginning to get on my nerves. He seemed abrasive, self-righteous, arrogant.[32]

Taylor's preface looks like the diary many people could have kept about their evolving relationships to this oeuvre. A tenth grader without much life experience can easily take Thoreau's words that "There is not one of my readers who has yet lived a whole human life"[33] as an inspiration to see the future as boundless. To an adult the same words can feel like a blunt and uninvited criticism with little constructive value. Too much of a conventional adult life is already written, and fixed in a form that possibly merits Thoreau's contempt. Taylor is only one person with very specific circumstances, but who *doesn't* have some very specific circumstance that excludes the subject from Thoreau's ideal discourse? And more importantly, given the fact that Thoreau seems inclined to talk only to the worthies who could transform him into a saint or a hero, with whom exactly is Henry David Thoreau having his elaborate conversation?

Enter the Greeks

At times in *Walden*, Thoreau is having the conversation with the reader, as imperfect as the reader must necessarily be. As William Cain puts it, "*Walden*'s point of view and its social and economic criticism are strenuously individualized: this author is speaking to *you*, and it is your life that he tells you must be changed."[34] At other times, Thoreau is speaking to himself. But there is a special group of people whom Thoreau will find irresistible: those who have never tried to manipulate him, or estrange him, or suffer his estrangement. These latter companions have not only staved off compromises in the past but are guaranteed to make no ugly compromises in the future. These ideal interlocutors are already dead. They are the great geniuses from humanity's distant past. "The works of the great poets have never yet been read by mankind, for only great poets can read them," Thoreau writes in *Walden*, adding that on a pile of the greatest poets' works, "we may hope to scale heaven at last."[35] He pretends not to fetishize their antiquity for its own sake; rather, he claims that his pantheon is based merely on an objective measure of their talent. The authors of great books "are a natural and irresistible aristocracy in every society, and, more than kings or emperors, exert an influence on mankind," he adds.[36]

In particular, the Greeks help Thoreau with some of his most troubling blind spots, such as his chronic naïveté about the cruelty of the animal world. At one point in *Walden*, Thoreau observes a war between black and red ants in the forest. He introduces it by saying, "I was witness to events of a less peaceful character," betraying a hint of a loss of innocence, at which point the allegory of the Trojan War calibrates his prose again, since he redeems the bellicose event by imagining that two of the red ants are Achilles and Patroclus.[37] "I felt for the rest of that day as if I had had my feelings excited and harrowed by witnessing the struggle, the ferocity and carnage, of a human battle before my door," he concludes.[38] The showdown between two races of insects was not a small incident in Thoreau's mind, but rather a haunting one, as evidenced by the fact that two of his books mention it. Years earlier, the war between the ants had worked its way into Thoreau's own poetry in *A Week on the Concord and Merrimack Rivers*:

> Here while I lie beneath this walnut bough,
> What care I for the Greeks or for Troy town,
> If juster battles are enacted now,
> Between the ants upon this hummock's crown?
> Bid Homer wait till I the issue learn,
> If red or black the gods will favor most,
> Or yonder Ajax will the phalanx turn,
> Struggling to heave some rock against the host.[39]

Even as he bids Homer to wait, while he watches the war between black and red ants, Thoreau can articulate the war only by using Homer's tropes. Despite the attempts in both books to shrug off the authority of history and find personal validation in the language of the present tense, Homer's value still overshadows Thoreau, prefixing the terms, the meanings, and the lessons that the war between the ants can offer.

Throughout *Walden* Thoreau wants to claim a personal wholeness simply through his own ability to experience and to observe. Nonetheless, Thoreau must go outside of his views about the redemptive value of the natural world in order to assimilate the violence he witnesses. Homer's tropes of nature, with a piercing clarity that Thoreau finds beyond his grasp, point to an underlying predatory force, not only in animals and birds but in the forcefulness of water, wind, and fire. Thoreau's fascination with the *Iliad* may be a search for the missing component in his own representations of the cosmos. In Homeric time and space, gone is the relaxing and ennobling tranquility of man's experience in nature. Gone is the peace of mind in the setting of untamed rivers and wild forests that Thoreau tries to celebrate as golden silence. Thoreau is too complex to limit himself to the pastoral optimism of Virgil's *Eclogues* or the bucolic idylls of Theocritus—in turning to Homer, he chooses to face the tougher side of the natural world. When Homer likens human relationships to the interaction among animals in the wilderness, the comparison, if anything, adds a brutality and unfeeling aggressiveness to the human side of the equation. For instance, in Book XVII of the *Iliad*, as Menelaus battles Hector for the body of Patroclus, Athena wishes to embolden Menelaus. To keep him from relenting, she instills in him μυιης θαρσος, *myies tharsos*, or "the courage of a gadfly," eager to bite since it finds the blood of men λαρον, *laron*, or "sweet."[40] Homer's choice of attaching the genitive-possessive form of the word *myia* meaning "fly," to *tharsos* meaning "courage," precludes human beings from claiming romantic virtues like bravery as their unique entitlement. For Homer, the divinely inspired force that causes mosquitoes to suck the blood from someone's bare arm equals the masculine adrenaline that leads men to clash on the battlefield. Everything human is also animalistic; everything animal also has its traces of humanity. Homer's Greek threatens Thoreau's project of withdrawing from the corruptions of society and finding purer contemplation in nature. If the *Iliad* is any index, nature will only show him all the deleterious influences that drove him away from the manipulations of social life in the first place.

It is not only when Homer likens humans to animals that their bloodthirstiness and violence increase. When people behave like naturally occurring elements, their terror expands. In Book XX, as Achilles goes on his mad rampage to drive the Trojans from the beachhead, he is compared to θεσπιδαες πυρ, *thespidaes pyr*, or "all-consuming forest fire," as well as a wind that scatters everything in confusion and goads the fire even further.[41] The natural world mirrors human aggression and cruelty so well, precisely because in all forms of physical existence, whether living or inanimate, there is an innate order of strong and weak. Violence is ubiquitous. Many of Homer's most memorable similes, usually beginning with Greek lead-in words like ως, *hos*, or "just as," match relationships of vicious and tranquil beings to the mysteriously imbalanced social relationships among humans. In Book XXII, as Achilles chases down Hector at the walls of Troy, they are likened to a κιρκος, *kirkos*, or hawk, and a τρηρωνα, *trerona*, or dove (the accusative form). The strength of the simile lies in the fact that nature traps both the hunted and the hunter in a game of flight and pursuit that can only delay, but never abort, the inexorable murder of one by the other.[42] Homer reminds Thoreau that if he takes his fellowship with nature too seriously, it will not be a retreat at all. He will see in events like the war of the ants everything that disgusts him about the social conflicts of town life.

The Greeks, though dead and invisible, rupture Thoreau's isolation; they bring to him a humanity outside of himself that he must come to terms with. Thoreau almost never allows the value systems of others to impinge or make any demands on his own. "The only obligation I have a right to assume is to do at any time what I think right," he claims in "Civil Disobedience"[43] with a confidence that "what I think right" flows from a pure, palpable, coherent, and distinct self. But the Greeks, present cognitively while absent physically, repeatedly threaten the integrity of that self. In *Walden*, he admits that only one item, of all the possessions that he may have lost to visitors in his unlocked cabin, still felt lacking to him:

> Yet though many people of every class came this way to the pond, I suffered no serious inconvenience from these sources, and I never missed anything but one small book, a volume of Homer, which perhaps was improperly gilded ... I am convinced, that if all men were to live as simply as I then did, thieving and robbery would be unknown. These take place only in communities where some have got more than sufficient while others have not enough."[44]

Homer is the failure in Thoreau's wholeness. Homer's book is the only thing that he "missed." This statement could imply that it was either the only thing stolen, or the only theft that caused him any grief. Either way, Homer ruptures the self-sufficiency and self-referentiality of Thoreau's world in *Walden*. Homer's epic, the site of Thoreau's excess, surpasses simplicity (being gilded) and throws the equilibrium between him and his neighbors out of balance. It is his, but it is also alien enough to him that it can be taken away.

Homer's disruption of Thoreau's independence appears in another section of *Walden*, when Thoreau is cataloguing the "Visitors" whom he has entertained at Walden Pond. Not surprisingly, he has had few visitations that he considers noteworthy. At one point Thoreau reminisces that "Many a traveller came out of his way to see me and the inside of my house, and, as an excuse for calling, asked for a glass of water. I told them that I drank at the pond, and pointed thither, offering to lend them a dipper."[45] Walter Harding does not conclude from this statement that Thoreau experienced Walden in the total absence of human company. Diaries and letters belonging to members of the surrounding community point to a healthy stream of visitors (including notables like Emerson, Hawthorne, and the Alcotts). "The only guests that Thoreau did not welcome," Harding clarifies, "were the curious—and there were plenty of them."[46] The fact that so many people tried to pry into his solitary life at Walden reveals that Thoreau was interacting enough with the larger community to get something of a reputation. Life in Walden was not a total withdrawal from society. Nonetheless, the fact that Thoreau wanted to exclude the curious, as Harding claims, still reflects a powerful desire to withdraw from human relationships, even if he found it impossible to do so completely. In discouraging all but a small circle from seeking his friendship, he seals his world off from any intruder who might compromise his independence. At one point he says that in the winter months, "For human society I was obliged to conjure up the former occupants in the woods," a statement that reveals simultaneously his loneliness and his ostensible ability to cure his loneliness with his imagination.[47]

At a rare and pivotal moment while at Walden, one person enters his life and excites Thoreau more than anything that he can conjure with sheer mental concentration. Almost half of "Visitors" is devoted to describing Alek Therien, a French-Canadian woodchopper, close to Thoreau in age, who truly attracted Thoreau's affection. It is this individual whom Harding says Thoreau "immortalized" in *Walden* by dwelling so long on their ambivalent friendship.[48] Thoreau writes:

> He interested me because he was so quiet and solitary and so happy withal; a well of good humor and contentment which overflowed at his eyes.[49]
>
> ...
>
> I occasionally observed that he was thinking for himself and expressing his own opinion, a phenomenon so rare that I would any day walk ten miles to observe it, and it amounted to the re-origination of many of the institutions of society.[50]

Therien's role in the unfolding of *Walden* is crucial for many reasons. He seems to be the only living person whose character is virtuous enough to hold the author's attention for several pages. Thoreau sincerely seems to like him; he notes that "he thoroughly believed in honesty and the like virtues."[51] Thoreau's confession is uncharacteristically emotional, revealing a loss of command over his own passions. He admits, after all, that he would walk ten miles to observe the man's honesty; and he also states with a small bit of concern that "it amounted to the re-origination of many of the institutions of society," as if hinting that Therien's charm threatens to compromise Thoreau's isolation. But the long reflections on this unique friend end with a cold disavowal, when Thoreau concludes disapprovingly that "If I suggested any

improvement in his mode of life, he merely answered, without expressing any
regret, that it was too late." Ultimately, the man's failure to match Thoreau's
intellect leads to an ungenerous assessment:

> Yet his thinking was so primitive and immersed in his animal life,
> that [...] it rarely ripened to anything which can be reported.[52]

It is informative to trace this ambivalent contact with the woodsman to the
first point of interaction. The Canadian man is introduced into the narrative
not by his own name, but by Homer's:

> Who should come to my lodge this morning but a true Homeric
> or Paphlagonian man,—he had so suitable and poetic a name that
> I am sorry I cannot print it here,—a Canadian, a woodchopper
> and post-maker.... He, too, has heard of Homer.[53]

"Alek" is certainly a name with "poetic" potential since "Alexander" is the
name for Paris, the Trojan prince and abductor of Helen, in the *Iliad*. For
important reasons to be examined below, however, Thoreau does not want
to draw any parallels between Alek Therien and Paris. Instead he prefers to
compare his friendship with Therien indirectly to the friendship between
Achilles and Patroclus. Although Thoreau alludes to there being some reason
for leaving the man's identity anonymous, within the text of *Walden* Homer's
name replaces Alek Therien's name as the way to mark and to value this
unexpected acquaintance:

> To him Homer was a great writer, though what his writing was
> about he did not know. A more simple and natural mind it would
> be hard to find.[54]

Homer authorizes Thoreau's love for the stranger. While Thoreau states
that Therien knows enough English to converse with an American, it is the
Greek language that at first unites them. He notes, "Some priest who could
pronounce the Greek itself taught him to read his verse in the Testament in
his native parish far away; and now I must translate to him, while he holds the
book, Achilles' reproof to Patroclus for his sad countenance."[55]

   Thoreau's quoting of this passage bears directly on the meaning
of the Canadian's arrival. "Achilles' reproof to Patroclus" comes from the
opening of Book XVI of the *Iliad*. To analyze the significance of this section,
I have block-quoted Thoreau's version of his translation and juxtaposed it
against my translation of the original Greek from Homer's text. What is not

included in the allusion is just as important as what appears in *Walden*. In my translation from the Greek, the words that Thoreau chooses to omit from his gloss are in bold

> *Walden*:
> ... I must translate to him, while he holds the book, Achilles' reproof to Patroclus for his sad countenance.—"Why are you in tears, Patroclus, like a young girl?"
> —"Or have you alone heard some news from Phthia?
> They say Menoetius lives yet, son of Actor,
> And Peleus lives, son of Aeacus, among the Myrmidons,
> Either of whom having died, we should greatly grieve."[56]

> *Iliad*:
> **And so, they were waging wars around the ship with well-built benches, when Patroclus came before Achilles, the shepherd of those people, gushing warm tears just as a spring, bubbling up from black depths, pours dark water down a steep side of rock. Bright, swift-footed Achilles, seeing him, was wonder-struck, and calling to him directed these winged words to him:**
> "Why such crying from Patroclus, just like a tenderly young girl **who, rushing beside her mother, begs to be embraced and picked up, and clutching at her mother's skirt, rushing at her, blocks her way? She keeps gazing at her with tearful eyes until she is picked up ... Just like that girl, Patroclus, you pour heavy tears.** Is there perhaps some announcement for the Myrmidons, or for myself? Well, as such what news do you release from Phthia? They say Menoitos, the son of Actor, still lives, and Peleus son of Aeacus still lives among the Myrmidons. Greatly would we be grieving, you know, over either of those having died. **Or is it you're lamenting the Achaeans, who are getting destroyed on the hollow ships on account of their own offenses—speak up! Hide not in your thoughts, so that we both can know.**[57]

It is highly unlikely that this passage of *Walden* is strictly objective translation. The *mise en scène* for his reading of Achilles' reproof of Patroclus hints that Thoreau's interaction with Therien is at once a parallel to, a translation of, an interpretation of, and a revelation of, the meaning of Achilles' words to Patroclus. First one ought to consider the mysterious physicality of the moment. Thoreau translates while the woodsman holds the book—the book has collapsed the "considerable neutral ground" that, only three pages earlier, Thoreau has emphasized as a necessary buffer to keep human interaction from collapsing into meaningless chatter. Is the woodsman sitting and Thoreau standing? Are they both standing, and if so, does the author have to hook his arms around Therien's shoulder to get a good look at the book? Or are they sitting, side by side, so that one man's left arm brushes the other's right. Whatever the configuration, Therien, regardless of his various faults that Thoreau will catalogue, has ripped a vulnerable hole in Thoreau's safe zone. They are touching and—could it be?—*feeling* each other. Would this not cheapen Thoreau's ideal of silent abstraction? Would it not cheapen the "natural aristocracy" to which Homer belongs, by giving it into the crude hands of a simple-minded man who does not understand him as well as Thoreau does?

The reading of the book is already a dramatic moment in itself. Thoreau is making a friend and touching another human being, allowing himself to become entangled. It is no minor detail, then, that at this point of male bonding, bordering on outright homoeroticism, the passage of the *Iliad* that he is reading deals with Achilles and Patroclus, classic archetypes of friendship. Thoreau's sexual orientation is open to different interpretations, though one should proceed with caution in trying to apply labels of "straight" or "queer" to him, since one might run the risk of sexualizing relationships that could just as easily be viewed as intense social interest between companions. The value of pondering the extent of eroticism in Thoreau's interaction with Therien lies, perhaps, not in whether one can prove that he was really "gay" all along, but rather what it tells us about Thoreau's view of bodily closeness and emotions such as longing, affection, and jealousy—sentiments that *Walden* as a whole prefers to skirt rather than to confront. Walter Harding, analyzing Thoreau's hostility toward marriage (and women in general) after being rejected by Ellen Sewall and Mary Russell, characterizes Thoreau's negotiation with his sexuality by proposing that "Thoreau was able to sublimate his love for the opposite sex in a worship of the world of nature and, as he once put it, falling in love with a shrub oak."[58] Thoreau found that his love for Ellen Sewall and Mary Russell ended, respectively, in rejection and frustration.

Harding's heteronormative spin on Thoreau's libido is not airtight, however. Robert Richardson points out that in 1839, Thoreau wrote a poem to Ellen Sewall's younger brother Edmund in the "conventions of Elizabeth love poetry" designed to "articulate rather than repress the strong surge of affection Thoreau felt for this 'gentle boy.'"[59] While the fact that Edmund was only eleven and Thoreau was twenty-two would cause the twenty-first-century reader some alarm, the age difference between the author of the love poem and its object may have actually made the entire exercise safer within the social norms of the 1830s. Richardson claims that since "it never crossed their minds that there might have been a physical attraction or longing behind all this, there was no reason for writer or reader to express or conceal the emotional attraction," adding that "as in the case of Whitman, a strongly affectionate nature was in some ways freer to express itself (when it chose) before Freud made us so complexly self-aware of all the possible implications of our feelings."[60]

Richardson is somewhat more comfortable than Harding with the possibility that Thoreau's erotic life included occasional attractions to the same sex. If homosocial or homosexual attraction was a dimension of Thoreau's interior life, then it developed somewhat early in his adulthood (at least by 1839) and possibly co-existed with his love for women like Ellen Sewall. Neither Richardson nor Harding, though, chooses to explore the full range of possibilities in Thoreau's admiration of Therien, who becomes a character in *Walden* in the mid-1840s, the point at which, as Walter Harding states, Thoreau "slipped into the pattern of the confirmed bachelor."[61] There is no dramatic age difference between the author of *Walden* and the Canadian wood-chopper to render the relationship sexually "safe" the way that the eleven years of difference between Thoreau and Edmund Sewall made the 1839 love poem safe. The heightened attention to Therien in the text of *Walden*, allusions to Achilles and Patroclus, and the details about the two men huddling together to read from the same book, leave this scene of the book open to speculations about homoeroticism. Whether Thoreau desired Therien as a friend or as something more, clearly Thoreau desired him, and his longing is significant regardless of the final verdict about the author's sexual orientation. The chapter "Visitors" in which this scene appears focuses on Thoreau's struggle to balance his ideals with his need for human company—and that is what Book XVI of the *Iliad* is about as well. The *Iliad's* basic plot lines depend upon Patroclus' death inspiring Achilles to kill Hector, so loyalty between male friends forms the crux of the entire epic.

The friendship between Achilles and Patroclus is something that Homer can depict, but that Thoreau cannot express in terms of his own experience in *Walden*. Thoreau has gone to great lengths to avoid allowing anyone to control his passions as much as Patroclus controlled those of Achilles. The story of their relationship, which Thoreau is obsessed with, weakens his position from within—first, intellectually, because he knows Homer's theme shatters his ideal of "considerable neutral ground"; and second, personally, because his fascination with the story has brought him into the arms of a charming woodsman whom Thoreau desires as a friend but cannot accept on qualitative grounds. This section of *Walden* is a vivid case of literature acting as a pander. Dante, one of the few post-antiquity authors whom Thoreau classes as a genius,[62] includes in the *Divine Comedy* a warning about the compromising effects of literature. In Canto V of the *Inferno*, Paolo and Francesca are sentenced to be blown around by strong winds for having been lustful and adulterous. Francesca laments that it was the physical experience of reading about the affair of Lancelot that caused her and Paolo to approach each other too closely. She explains that "One day, to pass the time away, we read of Lancelot—how love had overcome him. We were alone, and we suspected nothing. And time and time again that reading led our eyes to meet, and made our faces pale, and yet one point alone, defeated us."[63] Reading a book together, according to Dante's schema, is doubly threatening to one's piety, because both the dreamy fancies of the story itself, and the physical proximity that results from sharing the same book, can assault even the strongest person's resistance to temptation. This, then, is perhaps the danger of the *Iliad* to Thoreau, as he reads to Therien. It is both sexuality and passionate devotion between friends (set in the troubling context of larger social institutions clashing with individual conscience) that the *Iliad* poses as its temptation.

Thoreau idealizes the *Iliad* based on its aesthetic grandeur and then finds himself unable to translate the central theme, close friendship, into real life. Even his translation from Greek into English, while linguistically impeccable, fails, because he says that Therien, after hearing it, remarks "That's good" and nothing more, going on his way to bring a bundle of oak bark to a sick man.[64] The woodsman shows more interest in charity than Thoreau does, and seems more connected than Thoreau to other people in Massachusetts.

Also important are the nuances of the Greek in *Iliad* XVI. The first word of the book is ως, *hos*, a particle that usually introduces similes and stands in to say, "meanwhile." The word ως leads to a backdrop, either through a comparison or through narration of simultaneous events. It smacks of connectedness, relatedness, the inability of events or thoughts to be truly isolated. The first lines of Book XVI frame the moment by stating: "and so, as the men were making war around the ship with well-carved benches." At this point in Homer's epic, Achilles has tried to stay out of the war based on his individual perception of what is just. He burns with righteous anger over Agamemnon's ostensible misdeeds toward him. But the petty rivalry of other men continue even as Achilles sulks; the story, the cosmos, and the society of the *Iliad* all connect the sulking individual to the greater drama of social life with the simple word *hos*. And what is the moment that has required this framing? It is the arrival of the weeping Patroclus, who comes with the intent of forcing Achilles out of his isolation. Patroclus, using pathos and affect, means to drag Achilles back into the fray, despite Achilles' insistence that his independent conscience entitles him to stay out of the battle.

The passage in Book XVI is full of words that emphasize the raw physicality of passionate contact. Not only is Patroclus crying, but he is also touching Achilles' body, so much that Achilles emphasizes repeatedly his similarity to a distraught daughter clinging to her mother's body. Achilles' comparative phrase ηυτε κουρη νηπιη, *eyte koure nepie*, or "like a girl of tender age," should be enough to drive home the point. Yet he repeats it even more insistently by declaring, "τη ικελος Πατροκλε," *te ikelos, Patrokle*, or "Patroclus, that girl do you resemble." Achilles' redundant likening of Patroclus to a weeping girl (and his corollary comparison of himself to Patroclus' mother) is based on the physical experience of Patroclus' desire for contact. There is the reference to the girlish way of grabbing a mother's skirt, ειανου απτομενη, *heianou haptomene*, or "having taken hold of her mother's dress" and even more importantly, the word describing what Patroclus and little girls desire: ανελεσθαι, *anelesthai*, or "to be swept up and held." Strangely, Thoreau omits the fleshy references to bodily contact and the analogy of Achilles/Patroclus to mother/daughter. He skips directly to the dry description of Myrmidons, the sons of Aeacus and Actor, and the grief one would show to fallen fighters. Though the lines about Patroclus' touching Achilles probably speak more directly to what is on Thoreau's mind, he chooses to skip the most intimate exchange and includes, instead, arcane place names, clumsy genealogies, and frigid portrayals of grief. Grief is thematically less menacing than the delicate compromises that come with wanting to be held, coddled—loved— by someone who may not share the same vision of right and wrong.

The aporia in *Walden* cannot be interpreted, however, as Thoreau's decisive conclusion that human intimacy is irrelevant, because the text of *Walden* reveals (perhaps unwillingly) through its *mise en scène* that intimacy has prompted this passage as Thoreau's body is pressed close to the woodsman's while he reads the *Iliad*. Just as Patroclus' demand for Achilles' physical attention is jarring in the *Iliad*, so Thoreau is jarred by Therien's body, one might suggest, into telling only half the story and leaving it to the reader to excavate the real significance of the allusion. If this gloss on the *Iliad* is an unintentional disclosure of Thoreau's internal tension about human intimacy, so too is the strange fact that Thoreau summarizes the first twenty lines of Book XVI by calling it "Achilles' reproof to Patroclus." What in Achilles' words is truly a rebuke? Patroclus' tears are compared to the deep, warm water that comes from a spring. Achilles likens him to a delicate and tender little girl, a taunt based on behavioral norms, but he does not respond to Patroclus' eagerness by cursing him or pushing him away. Rather, he asks "what news do you bring?" And then, rather than spurning the intimacy, he demands even more connectedness, by issuing the command, "speak, do not hide things in your mind; speak so that we both can know." Achilles' reproach is directed not at Patroclus but rather at Agamemnon, whom Achilles accuses of acting unjustly. Rather than scolding Patroclus, Achilles seems more interested in finding out what could cause such a lapse in his friend, whom he considers so close to himself that anything in the other's mind is an equal entitlement of his own.

This chapter of *Walden* may have been a subtle turning point for Thoreau; if so, it would be appropriate, since the passage he translates marks the crucial turning point in the *Iliad*. Up until Book XVI, Achilles has done, in effect, what Thoreau has done up to that point in *Walden*. Based on bitterness and disappointment over his unfair treatment by Agamemnon, Achilles has sworn off all intercourse with the larger society of the Greeks to protest the latter's injustice. The image of a man withdrawing from his people to protest the society's moral corruptions would have resonated powerfully for the self-described hermit of Walden Pond. Thoreau's withdrawal from society would not have involved such a hostility to bourgeois marriage, were it not for the fact that he fell in love with and proposed to the same woman, Ellen Sewall, as his brother John. Emerson prodded Thoreau unsuccessfully to overcome his bitterness about Ellen Sewall. In their social circle, Thoreau's stubborn grudge against bourgeois marriage had achieved, as Harmon Smith describes it, "the status of myth," and "his celibacy was always referred to in terms of the crushing blow Ellen's rejection had dealt him."[65] Marrying, for Thoreau, would have meant entering all the trappings of society that *Walden* disdains. His refusal to marry, conversely, went hand in hand with his refusal to engage in many of the social events that occupied contemporaries like Emerson. It meant staying out of circulation—and that is (in quite a different context) what Achilles is doing in the first fifteen books of the *Iliad*.

Angry over his disagreements with Agamemnon about ownership of the captive woman Briseis, Achilles has withdrawn from the war and from almost all social activities. He has carved out a space of self sufficiency where he entertains himself with Patroclus and detaches himself from the implications of the Trojan War. In Book IX, Odysseus visits Achilles and Patroclus in their reclusive tent and begs them to reenter the war; but Achilles remains steadfast about abstaining, and he persuades Patroclus to follow suit. In Book XVI, Achilles and Patroclus develop a difference of opinion, and the plot line of the *Iliad* turns. Patroclus grieves for the Greeks who have died, while Achilles stays stubborn about his withdrawal and refuses to sympathize with them. In the line immediately after Thoreau stops his translation, the true reproof between Achilles and Patroclus occurs, but it is the reverse of what Thoreau represents: Patroclus harshly criticizes Achilles rather than vice versa, and the cause for Patroclus' harsh judgment of his friend is based on Achilles' refusal to abide by the dictates of community. Patroclus cannot insulate his emotions, as Achilles does, from the suffering of the Greeks whom they are refusing to help. Patroclus scolds his friend:

> You have become unworkable, Achilles!
> May the anger that you guard over never seize me.
> You—cursed in your virtue! I ask: how will another, one of
> your posterity, be profited, if, let's suppose, you fail to protect
> the Argives from a disgraceful death?[66]

Patroclus' response to Achilles focuses most critically on the malfunctioning link between Achilles' private world and the public world that obligates both of them. The words in Greek all point to a distortion in Achilles' system of logic. It has become too individuated and lacks reasonable input from outside. According to Patroclus, Achilles has become αμηχανος, *amechanos*, or "dysfunctional," a negation of the verb that means to devise, construct, or put into use. The verb *phylassein*, usually meaning to guard or protect, is instead used by Patroclus to describe Achilles' actions toward his own χολος, *cholos*, or "anger" personified. Rather than worrying as he should about the fate of his friends and his own children, Achilles, driven by self-righteousness, bestows upon his own emotions (and the most destructive ones at that) the nurturing tendencies that he should instead be directing toward other men. Whereas Achilles wishes, in the earlier analogy, to liken himself to Patroclus' mother, Patroclus refuses the metaphor, coldly and brutally, instead placing Achilles in a linguistic no man's land, where no words that imply a harmony with the social world ought to be applied logically at all. The very notion of "virtue" or "honor" that Achilles believes entitles him to retire into a private world and disregard the problems plaguing the others, is tied by Patroclus' speech to a curse, at the moment that he brazenly addresses his friend through a vocative, crying "you—cursed in your honor!" Patroclus uses the strange word αιναρετη, *ainarete*, a brutal compound wedding the adjective αινος, *ainos*, or "grim," with αρετη, *arete*, the important Greek word for virtue or honor. The stubbornness of Achilles' attachment to his individual conception of honor has blinded him to the importance of community and, as Patroclus' words hint, made him a grim and undesirable human being.

Achilles must choose at this point. He may sacrifice his position and succumb to the exhortation of his closest friend, or else he may hold steady in his conscience and risk losing the other's company. Achilles' dilemma represents the danger of friendship and the conversation that friends bring. Friendship with heightened emotions produces anxiety in Thoreau and makes him flee from social settings in search of silence and secluded discussions with ancient ghosts. Friends make demands, argue, and pressure one to make ideological compromises. Friendship is always a possible window through which the hypocritical and corrupted ideas of larger society will infiltrate the sanctuary of individual conscience.

Thoreau would have probably understood Achilles' protest against the Greeks as a matter of conscience. Achilles, Homer makes clear, does not abstain from the war out of fear, but out of his own sense of moral rectitude. He responds to Odysseus' pleas to join the war, in Book IX, by making a rational argument incorporating philosophical observations about human nature:

> What obligates the Argives to make war with Trojans?
> What moreover brought the people of the Atreides to this place
> and has them huddling and assembling?
> Or was it not on account of Helen with her beautiful hair?
> Or, of all the men who live, are the only ones who love their wives
> The sons of Atreus? After all, any good and sensible man
> Loves and concerns himself with the woman who is his.[67]

Achilles consistently offers rational arguments for his decision. In Book XVI, even his love for Patroclus is not enough to derail his principles. Despite his best friend's personal attacks, he stands firm on his logic, drawing boundaries of relevance in his surroundings, and refusing to back down from them.

> But this soreness enters my heart and soul
> When a man, who exceeds in power, would desire to block a
> man similar to him
> And snatch back his prize![68]

Citing his actions based on a rational analysis of Agamemnon's use of authority, Achilles remains in his self-imposed isolation, bucking even his best friend's most desperate pleas. He ends up losing Patroclus, avenging Patroclus, bringing about Hector's death, and thereby making the central story line of the *Iliad* possible. Immediately following his rhetoric of detachment, Achilles still refuses to go to battle but places his armor on Patroclus and sends him to combat with specific instructions not to storm Troy. Hector slays Patroclus in battle and steals Achilles' arms, thereby precipitating the moment of grief that afflicts Achilles, jolts him out of his isolation, and prompts him to rejoin with the Greeks. Thoreau says that he kept Homer's *Iliad* on his table in Walden, sustaining himself through his heavy days of work with "the prospect of such reading in the future."[69] The *Iliad* is something he seems to leave aside at times, when there is work to be done, and then revisits later. There is a climax to his study, though—a "prospect" for a future time when the epic's wisdom will come to him in its purest and most enlightening form. But what exactly is the wisdom that he hopes to glean from Homer? The *Iliad* is nothing without the crucial break in Achilles' isolation and his final surrender of perfect independence, all because his love for Patroclus makes his self-referential ideology impossible to sustain. In the *Iliad* death is everywhere, and upon death, the meaning of a human's life is permanently translated into the way he is remembered by his community. Patroclus' funeral games are necessary because Achilles can only memorialize his love publicly, in a social environment. Then the epic ends with the funeral of Hector, and the beautiful lamentations made by three women who recount their respective relationships to him: his mother Hecabe, his wife Andromache, and his friend Helen. Hector is defined purely according to his reputation as it endures in the memory of those socially related to him. He is respectively his mother's favorite son, the world's most faithful husband, and Helen's best friend. Thus Thoreau's fondness for the *Iliad* could be an obsession with social connectedness and may have reflected back, in one way or another, on the unresolved status of the self-reliant integrity he seeks in *Walden*. Without the collapse of Achilles' self-referential ethics and his subsequent submission to the standards of a larger community, there is no story; rather there would be only endless war devoid of higher meaning.

If one removes the fantastic acts of gods, the *Iliad* portrays humanity in two molds, both senseless and irrational: either violence or affection. The social brings threats of extermination or kindness in excess of one's natural needs. In the *Iliad*, nature is a mirror, but it shows only what the battlefield shows: a grid of grudges and passions, culminating in violence, that tie together the animal world as they unify the human world. No reader can say with any certainty what lessons for his own life Thoreau gleans from the narrative, because Thoreau performs no exegesis in *Walden*. His analyses are internal and private. It is tempting to suppose that he saw in Achilles' change of heart the inevitable in himself: at some point, he would have to engage society at large, even with its imperfections.

Yet the *Iliad* is still a brutally physical book, and a book about war. It represents a set of challenges to Thoreau's integrity; but ultimately it does not win him over. Thoreau never lends the lumberjack his armor, nor lays down his life for Therien's sake. The encounter with his Homeric friend from Canada culminates with Thoreau's dismissing the man as too simple, too brutish, too mired in his animal nature. There is still a natural tendency in Thoreau that resists war. The man who wrote *Walden* and the avid reader of Homer's *Iliad* is still the same author who spent the night in jail because he opposed the war against Mexico. The lesson of Achilles and Patroclus must have had an impact on Thoreau, but he also must have wanted his version of their drama to be about sacrificing one's liberty for the sake of a universal humanity, and not about avenging a friend. The theme of friendship and interpersonal loyalty in the *Iliad* needed to morph, for Thoreau, into a more generalized concern for other people, for a community much larger than acquaintances and neighbors, for society and humanity itself—an entity that could obligate him based on principle and conscience rather than on personal affection. The *Iliad* teaches its readers a great deal about the twin themes of love and violence, but Thoreau was one reader determined to rewrite the epic with a non-violent way of expressing love. Homer and Thoreau each came upon a turning point where their heroes—in Homer's case Achilles and in Thoreau's case himself—had to emerge from isolation and consummate their memberships in a larger discourse community. What came of the turning point, however, differed dramatically. Homer gave the world Book XVI and pushed gore and violence to new heights. Thoreau, determined to do better than his Greek forefather, gave the world "Civil Disobedience."

NOTES

1. Henry David Thoreau, *Walden*, in *The Works of Henry David Thoreau* (Ann Arbor: State Street Press, 2001), 477.

2. Lewis Leary, "Your Mind Must Not Perspire: Thoreau on Observation, Perception and the Role of Consciousness." *Cast of Consciousness: Concepts of the Mind in British and American Romanticism*, ed. B. Taylor and R. Bain (New York: Greenwood Press, 1987), 158.

3. Bob Pepperman Taylor, *America's Bachelor Uncle: Thoreau and the American Polity* (U of Kansas P, 1996), 31.

4. Thoreau, 604.

5. *Ibid.*, 416.

6. Henry David Thoreau, *A Week on the Concord and Merrimack Rivers* (Ann Arbor: State Street Press, 2001), 91.

7. Thoreau, *Walden*, 413.

8. Stanley Cavell, *Senses of Walden* (U of Chicago P, 1992), 29.

9. Thoreau, *A Week*, 123.

10. Thoreau, *Walden*, 344.

11. Leonard Neufeldt, "Thoreau in his Journal," in *Cambridge Companion to Thoreau*, ed. Joel Myerson (Cambridge UP, 1995), 107.

12. Robert Sattelmeyer, "Thoreau and Emerson," in *Cambridge Companion to Thoreau*, ed. Joel Myerson (Cambridge UP, 1995), 25.

13. Neufeldt, 108.

14. *Ibid.*, 109.

15. Cavell, 92.

16. *Ibid.*, 30.

17. Thoreau, *Walden*, 452.

18. *Ibid.*, 452.

19. Thoreau, *A Week*, 124.

20. Harmon Smith, *My Friend, My Friend: The Story of Thoreau's Relationship with Emerson* (U of Massachusetts P, 1999), 2.

21. Sattelmeyer, 28.

22. Thoreau, *A Week*, 69.

23. *Ibid.*, 70–71.

24. *Ibid.*, 71.

25. Thoreau, *Walden*, 473.

26. *Ibid.*, 451.

27. Robert D. Richardson, Jr.'s study of Thoreau's reading habits, *Henry Thoreau: A Life of the Mind* (U of California P, 1986), points out that the curriculum at Concord and Harvard both emphasized the classics to such a degree that Thoreau's grasp of ancient languages "sounds impressive, but it was, of course, required of all students and was taught in a less than promising atmosphere." Because of the brutality of the classical teaching methods, Richardson muses that "Thoreau's interest in classics thus grew almost in defiance of his formal schooling. But grow it did" (24).

28. Richardson, 13–14.

29. *Ibid.*, 5.

30. Thoreau, *Walden*, 597.

31. Cavell, 5.

32. Taylor, ix.

33. Thoreau, *Walden*, 603.

34. William Cain, "Henry David Thoreau, 1817–1862: A Brief Biography," in *A Historical Guide to Henry David Thoreau*, ed. William Cain (Oxford UP, 2000), 31.

35. Thoreau, *Walden*, 422.

36. *Ibid.*, 421.

37. *Ibid.*, 522.

38. *Ibid.*, 523–24.

39. Thoreau, *A Week*, 99.

40. Homer, *Iliad*, ed. E.H. Warmington, M.A. (Harvard UP, 1967), XVII.570–72. This is the standard version of the *Iliad* known to classicists as the "Loeb Classical Library." It includes a translation into English by Dr. A.T. Murray, but all translations from Greek to English, used in this essay, were made by the author.

41. *Ibid.*, XX.490.

42. *Ibid.*, XXII.139–40.

43. Henry David Thoreau, "Civil Disobedience," in *The Works of Henry David Thoreau* (Ann Arbor: State Street Press, 2001), 321.

44. Thoreau, *Walden*, 477. An interesting irony is that Walter Harding argues that Alek Therien, who figures importantly in the second half of this essay, actually borrowed the volume and never returned it.

45. *Ibid.*, 459.

46. Walter Harding, *The Days of Henry Thoreau* (Princeton UP, 1982), 196.

47. Thoreau, *Walden*, 544.

48. Harding, 190.

49. Thoreau, *Walden*, 456.

50. *Ibid.*, 459.

51. *Ibid.*, 459.

52. *Ibid.*, 459.
53. *Ibid.*, 454.
54. *Ibid.*, 455.
55. *Ibid.*, 454.
56. *Ibid.*, 455.
57. Homer, XVI.1–20.
58. Harding, 104.
59. Richardson, 58.
60. *Ibid.*, 58.
61. Harding, 110.
62. Thoreau, *Walden*, 422.
63. Dante Alighieri, *Inferno*, in *Divine Comedy*, tr. A. Mandelbaum (New York: Alfred A. Knopf, 1995), V.127–32.
64. Thoreau, *Walden*, 455.
65. Smith, 160.
66. Homer, XVI.29–32.
67. *Ibid.*, IX.337–42.
68. *Ibid.*, XVI.52–54.
69. Thoreau, *Walden*, 419.

BIBLIOGRAPHY

Cain, William "Henry David Thoreau, 1817–1862: A Brief Biography." In *A Historical Guide to Henry David Thoreau*. Ed. William Cain. Oxford UP, 2000. 11–57.

Cavell, Stanley. *Senses of Walden*. U of Chicago P, 1992.

Dante Alighieri. *Inferno*. In *Divine Comedy*. Tr. Allen Mandelbaum New York: Alfred A. Knopf, 1995.

Harding, Walter. *The Days of Henry Thoreau*. Princeton UP, 1982.

Homer. *Iliad*. Ed. E.H. Warmington. Harvard UP, 1967.

Leary, Lewis. "Your Mind Must Not Perspire: Thoreau on Observation, Perception and the Role of Consciousness." In *Cast of Consciousness: Concepts of the Mind in British and American Romanticism*. Ed. B. Taylor and R. Bain. New York: Greenwood Press, 1987. 151–59.

Neufeldt, Leonard. "Thoreau in his Journal." In *Cambridge Companion to Thoreau*, ed. Joel Myerson. Cambridge UP, 1995. 107–123.

Richardson, Robert D., Jr. *Henry Thoreau: A Life of the Mind*. U of California P, 1986.

Sattelmeyer, Robert. "Thoreau and Emerson." In *Cambridge Companion to Thoreau*. Ed. Joel Myerson. Cambridge UP, 1995. 25–39.

Smith, Harmon. *My Friend, My Friend: The Story of Thoreau's Relationship with Emerson*. U of Massachusetts P, 1999.

Taylor, Bob Pepperman. *America's Bachelor Uncle: Thoreau and the American Polity*. U of Kansas P, 1996.

Thoreau, Henry David. "Civil Disobedience." In *The Works of Henry David Thoreau*. Ann Arbor: State Street Press, 2001. 317–340.

———. *Walden*. In *The Works of Henry David Thoreau*. Ann Arbor: State Street Press, 2001. 341–604.

———. *A Week on the Concord and Merrimack Rivers*. In The Works of Henry David Thoreau. Ann Arbor: State Street Press, 2001. 1–124.

ERIC G. WILSON

Thoreau, Crystallography, and the Science of the Transparent

In an 1842 letter, Sophia Hawthorne describes an afternoon during which her husband Nathaniel led Emerson and Thoreau down to a frozen Concord River for some ice-skating:[1]

> Henry Thoreau is an experienced skater, and was figuring dithyrambic dances and Bacchic leaps on the ice—very remarkable, but very ugly, methought. Next him followed Mr. Hawthorne who, wrapped in his cloak, moved like a self-impelled Greek statue, stately, and grave. Mr. Emerson closed the line, evidently too weary to hold himself erect, pitching headforemost, half lying on the air.[2]

One wonders what possessed Emerson and Thoreau to accompany Hawthorne to the ice. While Hawthorne deports himself with classical decorum (playing the straight man), the formerly dignified Emerson flails against gravity, each instant threatening to thud on the grains, and Thoreau turns rambunctious adolescent, struggling to recover a grace he perhaps never enjoyed.

But then we recall: Emerson and Thoreau, despite their skaterly forms, had long been interested in ice. Six years before, Emerson while walking over a frozen Concord common had turned transparent eyeball—becoming

From *Studies in Romanticism*, vol. 43, no. 1 (Spring 2004), pp. 99–117. © 2004 by the Trustees of Boston University.

nothing, to see all. This crystal vision later shimmered in "The Snow-Storm," a poem on the vitality of ice. Likewise, Thoreau had already spent hours recording frozen phenomena: the rime on his morning window, the blue-gray bubbles in a cake of Walden ice.

Why would Thoreau, hungry for *life*, be concerned with frozen wastes? One answer: he was aware of a particular science that emerged in the late eighteenth century: crystallography, the study of the qualities of crystals, especially their structure and growth. Beginning to understand with unprecedented precision the laws of crystal formation, scientists of the age, such as Emanuel Swedenborg and René-Just Haüy, recognized in the crystal not only an intrinsically interesting specimen but also a special revelation of the secret virtues of matter. Staring into the transparent corridors of these minute prisms—frozen or otherwise—these eighteenth-century observers were indeed searching for nothing less than the portal to the monads of the universe and the powers by which these primal patterns combine.

Thoreau was interested in ice crystals for precisely this reason—the hoar frost on the morning window could constitute a numinous disclosure of the laws of life. Envisioning the currents of life in the crystal, Thoreau further embraced the bit of ice as a poetic model—a transparent prism troping unseen light into dazzling spectrums. Accordingly, I shall study Thoreau's representations of ice not only to shed fresh light on his general theories of seeing, nature, and language but also to illuminate his particular obsessions in *Walden*: "transparency," "formation," and "extravagance."

In 1842, in his first published essay, Thoreau wonders why "[v]egetation has been made the type of all growth" since "in crystals the law is more obvious." "[W]ould it not be as philosophical as convenient to consider all growth," he continues, "but a crystallization more or less rapid?"[3] This remarkable suggestion—that ice is the primary form of organic development—could well be only the clever trope of a budding poet. However, when we are reading a writer who spent his days recording facts, we should always first take him literally. No doubt, his own close studies of the homologies between crystals and leaves inspired him to make such an assertion. Moreover, he knew that he was reinforcing with his own eyes what had already been conjectured by several European natural philosophers during the eighteenth and early nineteenth centuries.

Before he became the visionary who would profoundly influence New England transcendentalism, Swedenborg was a metallurgist, chemist, and mining engineer who possibly originated the science of crystallography.[4] Remarkably, the young Swedenborg discovered in crystals what he would later find in everything after his conversations with angels in 1745: the invisible world revealed. Indeed, even in his early scientific works, Swedenborg advanced the insight that Emerson and Thoreau would later admire—the finite, visible world corresponds to an infinite, unseen one. In Emerson's words, Swedenborg throughout his life found that "[e]ach law of nature has the like universality; eating, sleep or hybernation, rotation, generation, metamorphosis, vortical motion, which is seen in eggs as in planets." "These grand rhymes," Emerson continues, "delighted the prophetic eye of Swedenborg."[5]

Swedenborg's crystallography is at the core of this analogical vision. In his first book, the *Principles of Chemistry* (1721), he notes that the hexagonal shapes of ice combine and spread in the same way that vegetables bud and branch. Just as botanical seeds under the influence of heat and water press outward into leafy encrustations, so aqueous globules in freezing temperatures solidify into transparent stars. Swedenborg discovers a similar process when he studies how water produces crystals of salt. For Swedenborg, both crystallizations are remarkable, for they illustrate the transformation of amorphous spheres into cubes.[6]

In the context of Swedenborg's cosmogony, these same crystals become windows to the secret mechanisms of life. According to Swedenborg in his *Principles of Chemistry* as well as in his 1722 *Miscellaneous Observations on Natural Things* and his 1734 *Philosophical and Mineralogical Works*, the process by which infinite spirit originates and sustains the finite universe is essentially crystallization, the transformation of shapeless energy into regular structures, called "crustals." For Swedenborg, the universe began when infinite spirit condensed its force into a single, transparent, spiraling point. (Think of a single eddy in an immense ocean.) Overwhelmed by the boundless energy it contains, this point—a portal between infinity and the finite—whirls eventually into the first crustal: a vortex comprised of inner motion and a highly tenuous, transparent crust. (Now picture a tornado and call its outer shape a crust.) The force of this powerful motion eventually explodes the outer crust into fragments that likewise churn into translucent spherules of energy, or crustallized eddies. These spheres are primary particles. They in turn combine to form elements—gravity, magnetism, ether, and air—that organize the particles into a vast solar vortex. Eventually, this solar rotation, like the first point of infinity, flies apart at its edges, and the resulting fragments constitute the chaos described at the beginning of Genesis. The abyss—yet another huge vortex—at some point divides into planets, among which is the earth, a more stable and opaque crustillization that frequently freezes into crystals—nebulous spheres transformed into cubes and hexagons.[7]

At least five salient points emerge from this theory. One, Swedenborg rejects Newton's atoms moving mechanically in a void and instead believes that the universe is comprised of motion organized in geometrical forms. Two, particles and elements, though organized by crusts of varying degrees of plasticity, are transparent in their pristine forms. They become opaque only when combined into irregular patterns. Three, events are polarized—distributed motion and discrete pattern, centripetal and centrifugal forces. Four, the universe is analogical. The original infinity cohering into a primal point is homologous to the solar vortex condensing into a sun, the first chaos organizing into planets, mushy seeds pressing into leaves, and globes of water stiffening into crystals. Five, each part, properly seen, is a window to and a mirror of infinity: as geometrical patterns of spirit, both beholder and beheld refract and reflect the first light.

The crystal, then, is no different in kind from any other being in Swedenborg's universe: everything is a geometrical form of infinite motion. The crystal is, however, distinct in degree, for it reveals in the clearest of lights the cosmic processes that remain hidden in more opaque, lubricious events. In other words, the crystal is capable of revealing hidden correspondences between visible and invisible forms, and thus constitutes an early instance of Swedenborg's theory of correspondence: the visible world as glassy template of an invisible one. Indeed, in these scientific treatises, Swedenborg laid foundations for his later effort, to use Emerson's words, "to put science and the soul, long estranged from one another, at one again" (*Representative Men* 63).

Composing his 1850 essay on Swedenborg, Emerson likely recalled an 1839 article in *The New Jerusalem Magazine*, "Swedenborg's Scientific Merit," in which he would have found that Swedenborg originated the science of crystallography (see note 4). But Emerson did not need to go to this periodical to learn about the science of crystal. By the turn of the nineteenth century, several natural philosophers of whom he was aware were developing Swedenborg's dynamical crystallography in three directions: the "molecular," the "electromagnetic," and the "organic."[8]

As Emerson learned from John Herschel's 1830 *Preliminary Discourse on the Study of Natural Philosophy*, crystallography was emerging as a method for ascertaining the atomic nature of matter.[9] According to Herschel, in the late eighteenth century Haüy theorized that crystals are comprised of "integral molecules" that aggregate into larger crystalline shapes according to mathematical rules.[10] Forwarding this theory, Haüy betrayed a Newtonian heritage—he assumes that matter is made of atoms that combine mechanically—that Eilhardt Mitscherlich would later attempt to correct through a more intense attention to chemistry. Mitscherlich in the early nineteenth century suggested that crystals are distinct from uncrystallized bodies not through their integral molecules but by way of their chemical compositions. For Mitscherlich, crystals are best studied as a collection of spherical atoms held together by electrical affinity. Still, though this theory improves on Haüy's by being more sensitive to chemical complexity, it nonetheless, as Herschel notes, relies on the notion that matter is comprised of minute particles that aggregate through "mutual attractions and repulsions," otherwise called *"molecular forces."* Seen this way, crystals are "little machines" geometrically embodying the blind forces of the cosmos.[11]

While Emerson was learning of this mechanical model of the crystal, which recalls Swedenborg's geometries of the crystal, he was also becoming aware of a more dynamical theory of crystalline matter based on the emerging science of electromagnetism. By 1807, Humphry Davy had discovered that chemical relations are electromagnetic: charged elements combine or separate through agreement or disagreement in galvanic charges. This finding—of which Emerson learned in Davy's *Elements of Chemical Philosophy* (1812)[12]—inspired the British scientist to conjecture that matter might be comprised of "physical points endowed with attraction and repulsion" and therefore capable of being "measured by their electrical relations."[13] Like Swedenborg before him, Davy embraced the crystal as a rich revelation of nature's polarized powers, wondering if the "laws of crystallization" and the "electrical polarities of bodies" are "intimately related."[14] Some years later—as Emerson was well aware[15]—Davy's student Faraday likewise turned to the crystal in order to substantiate his own theories of electromagnetism. In 1831, Faraday discovered electromagnetic induction, a finding that did away with Newton's (and Haüy's) notion of matter by revealing material as a field of electromagnetic waves.[16] Throughout the rest of his days, Faraday labored in his *Experimental Researches in Electricity* (1831–1852) to understand the implications of this finding—which Emerson himself hailed in 1834 as the disclosure of the "secret mechanism" of "life" and "sensation."[17] In the course of these efforts, Faraday frequently turned to the crystal, for he found in its transparent lattices "beautiful" manifestations of the "electrical condition" (*Experimental Researches* ¶ 1689).

While Davy and Faraday approached crystals from the angles of chemistry and physics, Goethe and Schelling studied crystallization from a more biological point of view. In botanical and zoological studies later perused by Emerson,[18] Goethe laid out his primary scientific idea: nature develops through the agency of archetypal forms that metamorphose into diverse phenomena. As Goethe claimed in his 1790 *The Metamorphosis of Plants*, the primal plant form is the leaf.[19] Four years earlier, in an article on the intermaxillary bone, he proposed that the archetypal zoological phenomenon is the vertebra.[20] Even earlier, observing geological phenomena in an 1784 essay, Goethe concluded that granite is the primal rock form, a first crystallization of an original liquid fire.[21] Just as one leaf develops into all plants, and a single bone emanates into every animal, so a granite crystal is the seed of the earth's rocks. Appropriately, Emerson draws on these studies in his essay on Swedenborg, using Goethe's analogical theory to illustrate Swedenborg's homologies (*Representative Men* 60–61). Emerson also no doubt had in mind a key passage in Goethe's 1820 *On Morphology*: "Nature has no system; she has—she is—life and development from an unknown center toward an unknowable periphery." Yet, Goethe immediately adds that a centripetal power counters nature's boundless, centrifugal forces.[22] This centripetal balance is another way of conceiving the archetype, the formative principle of formless energy. In Goethe's cosmos, unbounded life organizes itself into polarized eddies, variously accelerated: round bone, eye of leaf, and quartz spheroid.

As Emerson knew from his philosophical studies,[23] Schelling, like Goethe, rebelled against mechanism by endorsing a theory of a single field of energy that is not merely blind electricity but rather a living, developing, conscious power. As Schelling argues in *Ideas for a Philosophy of Nature* (1797), an abysmal "Absolute" realizes itself by manifesting itself to itself in dynamic, evolving polarized processes between antinomies such as ideal and real, infinite and finite, subject and object, irritation and satisfaction, attraction and repulsion. Each polarized form is not only a visible pattern of the invisible principle of life but also a marker of this principle's consciousness of itself. Galvanized stones are ciphers of spirit at a low level of awareness. Breathing plants reveal spirit at a higher level of consciousness. Animals, who negotiate between pain and pleasure, show spirit to be capable of rudimentary thought. Humans, comprised of finite body and infinite mind, perfect the spirit by self-consciously reflecting the spirit back to itself.[24] Given this cosmology, in which an amorphous vitality manifests itself in solid forms, it is not surprising that Schelling especially emphasized the process of crystallization. In *On the World Soul* (1798), he argues that nature tends toward crystallization as a primary form of individuality: rock or ice crystals are primitive organizations of life that will one day evolve into more individualistic structures, such as plants, animals, and humans. Crystals are early humans; humans are evolved crystals.[25]

If Emerson through his reading became aware of theories of crystallography, Thoreau through his own observations connected to cold crystal *facts*. This is not to say that Thoreau was not versed in theories of the crystal. In the 1840s, he was learning of Goethe's theory of archetypal forms in the *Italian Journey* (1786) and of Schelling's *Naturphilosophie* in J. B. Stallo's *General*

Principles of the Philosophy of Nature (1848).[26] Likewise, he was familiar with Swedenborg, favorably alluding to the Swedish seer in *A Week on the Concord and Merrimack Rivers*.[27] Moreover, he probably learned about Davy's and Faraday's electromagnetic crystals from his conversations with Emerson. Still, Thoreau valued experience over authority.[28] Unlike Emerson, content to glean his crystallography from treatises, Thoreau went regularly to the ice, where, fascinated by the reticulated tetrahedrons, he gathered facts and ideas. Studying these lattices almost daily during the Concord winters, Thoreau in the end found them much more interesting and important than did Emerson. He not only crafted numerous descriptions of their forms and functions. He also found in them a symbol of his most persistent idea: nature is a form of turbulence, an agitated poem, a crystal whose interiors storm.

Embracing the ice as a revelation of life, Thoreau combines heterogeneous offices. He is a scryer, studying crystals to find the destiny of the cosmos, the rhythm by which everything—pond, loon, human—moves. He is an optical theorist, searching in the frozen lens for laws by which light bends into colors, by which his own eyes curve thoughts and feelings into images. He is a physicist and chemist, in the crystalline shape looking for the principles by which matter moves and combines. A biologist as well, Thoreau also sounds the ice for the laws of life—the processes by which living things function—and life itself—the original abyss beyond its concrete forms. Merging these offices, Thoreau is above all a poet—a scribbling magus, a scientist armed with tropes—transforming cosmos into logos, ice crystals into crystalline symbols.

Thoreau began his studies of crystals on December 24, 1837, only months out of Harvard and a few pages into his journal (begun at Emerson's suggestion). He notices some "curious crystallizations" in the "side of the high bank by the leaning hemlock."

> Wherever the water, or other causes, had formed a hole in the bank—its throat and outer edge ... bristled with a glistening ice armor. In one place you might see minute ostrich feathers, which seemed the waving plumes of the warrior ... in another the glancing fan-shaped banners of the Lilliputian host—and in another the needle-shaped particles collected into bundles resembling the plumes of the pine, might pass for a phalanx of spears.
>
> The whole hill was like an immense quartz rock—with minute crystals sparkling from innumerable crannies.
>
> I tried to fancy that there was a disposition in these crystallizations to take the forms of the contiguous foliage.[29]

Grasping for tropes to picture these curious prisms, Thoreau strangely mixes war implements and organic forms. The crystals appear as plates of shining armor, ostrich feathers waving like plumes, fans turned miniature banners, and pine needles become spears. While the crystals *seem* to be static, Thoreau sees in them activity—growth and flight, the energy of soldiers before the attack. Yet, in the midst of this tension, the ice suddenly explodes. The bank turns quartz. It shimmers innumerable sparks. Warmed, Thoreau imagines the crystals as closely linked leaves.

These crystals attract Thoreau for several reasons. First, he is simply fascinated by their bristling shapes. Two, these frozen shapes inspire him to create his own forms—a series of tropes in which he likens crystals to feathers, banners, and spears. Three, as Thoreau fashions his tropes, he senses fiery energy lurking in the calm crystals. Four, he realizes that these coruscating crystals, not dead, might hold the key to the "disposition" to grow like foliage.

In addition to these salient features—which recall Goethe and Schelling—we observe two other points. Thoreau perceives the frost a highly specific way, noticing in its particular geometries, lattices, reticulations, textures, and colors analogies to other palpable, finely rendered images, like feathers and leaves. This concrete vision is not an end in itself: Thoreau's particular attention serves as a seed from which richer visions grow; or, to change the metaphor, as a pebble splashing a pond into concentric circles. From his initial descriptions of the ice, he rises to a more general metaphor—ice as plane of quartz shimmering with a pervasive fire—and then to an even more general trope—the crystals as revelations and vehicles of life itself. The ice *activates* Thoreau's mind. It stimulates in him imaginative acts of perception that open into intuitions of holistic energies coursing not only through crystals but also stones and leaves.

Thoreau's agents of transformation in this process require further explanation. Instead of leaping from part to whole, Thoreau *works* his way from particular to general by way of analogies, by the power of tropes. He focuses his attention on the minute forms of the crystal. He *feels* a relationship between this prism and a ubiquitous energy, but he cannot *think* exactly what this relationship is. Inspired by the crystalline shape and his desire to grasp a whole beyond the parts, he forges correspondences. The transparent reticulations suggest the networks in the leaf, which in turn point to imbrications of the feather, and the feather opens into more complex human productions: not only elegant armor and instruments of war but also, as we shall see, musical chords and poetic rhymes. Each successive trope serves as a *magnifying lens*, a crystal in its own right, through which Thoreau sees his way to the next level.

One thinks here of Emerson's 1841 "Circles," in which Emerson claims that the eye is the first circle, while the horizon it forms is the second. Each more general vista, each wider horizon, constitutes a further circle that includes and transcends those that came before it. Notably, when he views crystal, Thoreau's first horizon is comprised of inanimate elements, nonliving atoms and molecules; his second is composed of cells, plant cells, which contain atoms and molecules; his third circle is made of cells combined into organs—the bird-wing; and his fourth sphere opens into the human being, who adds self-consciousness to the atoms, cells, and organs that comprise him. Thoreau's concentric vision does not stop here but extends outward to even more universal regions.

Thoreau returns to these connections in his 1842 "A Natural History of Massachusetts." Recalling a walk on an icy morning of 1837 that was favorable for "crystalline botany," he likens crystals to foliation:

> When the first rays of the sun slanted over the scene, the grasses seemed hung with innumerable jewels, which jingled merrily as they were brushed by the foot of the traveler, and reflected all the hues of the rainbow, as he moved from side to side. It struck me that these ghost leaves, and the green ones whose forms they assume, were the creatures of but one law; that in obedience to the same law the vegetable juices swell gradually into the perfect leaf, on the one hand, and the crystalline particles troop to their standard in the same order, on the other. As if the material were indifferent, but the law one and invariable, and every plant in the spring but pushed up into and filled a permanent and eternal mould, which, summer and winter forever, is waiting to be filled.
>
> This foliate structure is common to the coral and the plumage of birds, and to how large a part of animate and inanimate nature. The same independence of law on matter is observable in many other instances, as in the natural rhymes, when some animal form, color, or odor has its counterpart in some vegetable. As, indeed, all rhymes imply an eternal melody, independent of any particular sense....
>
> Vegetation has been made the type of all growth; but as in crystals the law is more obvious, their material being more simple, and for the most part more transient and fleeting, would it not be as philosophical as convenient to consider all growth ... but a crystallization more or less rapid? (53–54)

Thoreau is initially drawn to the frost-covered blades. They shimmer like "innumerable jewels" and reflect the "hues of the rainbow." Inspired by this image of kaleidoscopic gems, he elevates to a new trope: he envisions the blades as phantom adumbrations of leaves. He generalizes further. He conjectures that these frosty revelations and the more sappy ones in summer pattern one law. Rising to increasingly holistic insights, he wonders if *all* material forms are manifestations of this law. If so, the favored form of this principle is the crystal, an archetypal structure common to all nature. The crystalline form is the "rhyme" scheme of nature. It gathers into poetic harmony not only vegetable forms (leaves) and animal shapes (feathers) but also colors and odors. These crystal assonances and alliterations point to an "eternal melody," the music of the spheres humming beyond fleshy ears. Crystals, not leaves, should be "the type of all growth," for in crystals being is more brightly revealed.

Crystal shapes again captivate Thoreau. Their anatomies once more inspire him to create increasingly general tropes. These tropes empower him to intuit the primal form of life. Yet, Thoreau here recognizes new potencies. In likening the illuminated frost to jewels reflecting the rainbow, Thoreau shows that ice is a prism refracting white light into the diverse colors of the spectrum. The morning ice is a mediator between undifferentiated brightness and the different hues of the world, and thus a threshold between the one and the many (Ishmael's "colorless all color" and Hopkins' pied beauty). The crystal as prism bends, or turns, white light into diverse colors that hide and reveal the transparent brightness immanent in their opaque hues. This troping of colorless beams into kaleidoscopic fulgurations is "characterized by a translucence ... of the eternal in the particular. It always partakes of the reality which it renders intelligible; and while it annunciates the whole, abides itself as a living part of that unity of which it is representative."[30] These last words come from Coleridge's definition of the symbol in *Statesman's Manual* (1816) and suggest that the ice crystal as prism is a symbol of the symbol, an organic exemplification of what literary symbols sometimes achieve—"a living momentary revelation of the Inscrutable"[31]—to use Goethe's words in *Maxims and Reflections*. Smitten by the poetics of nature (gazing at the crystal turn unsullied light into dazzling spectrums), Thoreau aptly creates his own tropes, turns of transparent feelings into words.

The crystal's colors point to a ubiquitous brightness. Its "foliate structure" suggests a form repeated throughout the universe. "Rhyming" with other structures—leaves and feathers—the crystal opens into a cosmic poem or symphony that expresses the eternal law through which vital energy becomes cogent form. Though this law is beyond observation and description ("independent of any particular sense"), it nonetheless partially reveals its virtues in a recurring "foliate structure" common to frost (stable crystals), leaves (crystals that flutter), feathers (jewels that fly), and even humans (with minds like diamonds). Like Goethe's archetypes and Schelling's primary polarities, this crystalline form organizes—differentiates—the infinite, undifferentiated energy of life. Precipitations of holistic power, Thoreau's crystals are thus prototypical patterns of all growth—mergings of centrifugal vitality and centripetal cohesion, unity and diversity, mystery and solution.

These two remarkable sequences on frost—from 1837 and 1842—are not exceptional but reveal virtues of ice that persistently fascinated Thoreau. For instance, in February of 1851, Thoreau fixates on "fleets of ice flakes" that reflect the sun like "mirrors" and embody nature's "art." Likewise, in January of 1852, Thoreau likens ice to "foliage" as well as "the characters of some oriental language." Later that month, the snow inspires him to conclude that there is "a vegetable life as well as a spiritual and animal life in us." In January of 1853, Thoreau marvels over a frozen waterfall spangled with "egg shaped diamonds" and "branch fungus icicle[s]." Snow crystals in January of 1856 motivate this insight: "the same law that shapes the earth-star shapes the snow star ... [E]ach of these countless snow-stars comes whirling to earth, pronouncing ... Order, *kosmos*."[32]

Thoreau's early and abiding studies of crystals yield to him particular insights on vision, nature, and language. Beholding the morning frost, he sees *through* the shimmering lattices to the primal crystalline form organizing the amorphous force of life. He realizes: the crystal is not only in the ice but also in trees, birds, and men. Hence, everything, properly viewed, is a crystal—a transparent portal through which one might discern invisible powers criss-crossing the cosmos. Viewing the world through a crystal lens, Thoreau penetrates the hidden law by which the one becomes the many, energy turns to form. He understands that holistic life functions in polarized patterns, gatherings of centrifugal power and centripetal stability, turbulence and geometry. Organic forms, Thoreau further realizes, resemble poetic forms. Crystal structures—whether they thrive in ice, leaves, wings, or brains—are tropes, turning invisible energy (white light) into visible images (pied spectrums). Specifically, they are synecdoches, parts partaking of and revealing the whole, opaquely transparent windows partially disclosing the mysterious power of which they—and everything else—are made.

Thoreau's crystallography, then, not only offers an intrinsically interesting interpretation of frozen shapes. It also provides potent hermeneutical tools for illuminating three of Thoreau's most persistent concerns in *Walden*: "transparency," "formation," "extravagance," registers, respectively, for "optics," "organicism," and "poetics." Even though Thoreau in *Walden* is more interested in leaves than crystals, he nonetheless is drawn to the pond because it is a "great crystal" on the "surface of the earth."[33] The crystalline virtues of Walden water—thawed or frozen—constitute some of the primary goals of Thoreau's Walden quest.

As Thoreau announces throughout "The Ponds," he values Walden water for its "crystalline purity," its especial pellucidity. "The water," he observes, "is so transparent that the bottom can be easily discerned at the depth of twenty-five or thirty feet." Sailing over the unfrozen pond, he can "see many feet beneath the surface the schools of perch and shiners, perhaps only an inch long." From the pond's frozen surface, he can discern and retrieve a lost axe, even though it rests some twenty-five feet below (177–78). Likewise, he finds that "such transparent and seemingly bottomless water" not only reveals its depths below but also reflects the clouds above. Hence, to float on this translucent surface is also to fly in the air, and to watch fish become birds (189–90). Disclosing the deeps and marrying opposites, the pond moreover comprises a standard of beauty. It—along with White Pond—is "much more beautiful than our lives," "much more transparent than our characters" (199). Hyaline like "precious stones," these liquid surfaces are better able to reflect and thus to intensify light than are more opaque bodies. They are "Lakes of Light," fiery concentrations of the ubiquitous luminosity often unnoticed in the loose atmosphere. Frozen, Walden water features similar virtues. As Thoreau claims in "House-Warming," the pond's first ice—"being hard, dark, and transparent"—"affords the best opportunity that ever offers for examining the bottom where it is shallow" (246). In "Pond in Winter," the transparency of the blue ice inspires him to consider "ice" as "an interesting subject for contemplation," for frozen water seems to remain "sweet forever" while thawed "soon becomes putrid" (297).

Like the morning ice Thoreau earlier observed, the crystalline water—frozen or thawed—constitutes a special means of vision as well as the ideal end of vision. First of all, the transparent surface—which Thoreau actually calls "earth's eye" (186)—allows him to view depths, interpenetrations, brightnesses, and durations that he would not normally perceive. Looking through the sheet of thawed water, using it for his eyes, he apprehends the pond's "bottomless water"; notices marriages between muck and clouds, bounded form and boundless space; discerns the sun's rays more intensely revealed; and apprehends mergings of time (blue ice) and eternity (eternal sweetness). Sounding from the frozen surface, he recovers things otherwise lost, such as his axe and the pond's deepest bottom—which, though measurable, inspires thoughts of abyssal depths.

If the pond's transparency facilitates such visions, it also symbolizes the ideal ends of these acts of seeing. As Thoreau intones in "Pond in Winter," soon after he has measured the bottom, he is "thankful that this pond was made deep and pure for a symbol" (287). Though he does not say exactly what the pond symbolizes, he suggests that it points to crystalline qualities that all beings secretly possess. To see forms not merely as self-contained units of opaque matter but also as transparent patterns of holistic energies—this is one of Thoreau's primary quests at Walden Pond. He attempts to translate his activities—ranging from digging to bathing to fishing to planting—as well as the phenomena he studies—such as loons and owls and leaves that blow— into windows through which he can see constant laws and mirrors in which he can view his own essential nature. In essaying to discover covert crystals in opaque elements, Thoreau tries to find in *everything* what he perceived in the pond: interpenetrations between surface and depth, finite and infinite, time and eternity, darkness and light.

Thoreau's mode of seeing—he turns his crystal glass to the world in hopes of turning the world to glassy crystal—is richly instanced in the thawing-bank sequence in "Spring," a revelation of the process by which distributed life flows into discrete form—by which energy crystallizes into pattern. Standing before the melting mud, Thoreau fixates, again, on foliated shapes, leaf-crystals.

> Innumerable little streams overlap and interlace one with another, exhibiting a sort of hybrid product, which obeys halfway the law of currents, and halfway that of vegetation. As it flows it takes the forms of sappy leaves or vines, making heaps of pulpy sprays a foot or more in depth, and resembling ... the laciniated lobed and imbricated thalluses of some lichens; or you are reminded of coral, of leopards' paws or birds' feet, of brains or lungs or bowels, and excrements....
>
> When I see ... this luxuriant foliage, the creation of an hour, I am affected as if in a peculiar sense I stood in the laboratory of the Artist who made the world and me,—had come to where he was still at work, sporting on this bank, and with excess of energy strewing his fresh designs about. I feel as if I were nearer to the vitals of the globe, for this sandy overflow is something such a foliaceous mass as the vitals of the animal body. You find thus in the very sands an anticipation of the vegetable leaf.... The feathers and wings of birds are still drier and thinner leaves.... The very globe continually transcends and translates itself, and becomes winged in its orbit. Even the ice begins with delicate crystal leaves, as if it had flowed into moulds which the fronds of water plants have impressed on the watery mirror. (305–6)

Thoreau studies the mud through his "crystal" eye, discerning in it depths, interpenetrations, brightnesses, and durations that he might not normally discern. Under this gaze, the sliding much becomes more than mere dirt. It opens into the "vitals of the globe," the chthonic surge of ubiquitous being. It reveals interdependencies between bounded (earthy globes) and unbounded (birds unfettered), flux ("sandy overflow") and structure ("vegetable leaf"), chance (the Ur-Artist "sporting") and law (nature's recurring forms). Generally opaque, this muck now shimmers with invisible laws. Creeping in time, finite, it discloses organic processes transcending temporality, infinite—not confined to this or that but present in everything.

Thoreau in this passage senses in the flowing mud what he earlier perceived in the crystal dawn: the law of natural formation. Amid the burgeoning blooms of spring, he aptly apprehends in the leaf, not the crystal, the primal cosmic form. However, the leaves now coalescing the mud are strikingly analogous to the crystals that before organized the water. In both cases—walking on a winter morning or standing, stunned, before the spring thaw—Thoreau witnesses what Goethe saw in plants, bones, and rocks, what Schelling intuited in the universe's polarized rhythms: not simple order, cosmos, nor mere disorder, chaos, but rather a mutual arising of abyss and pattern—*chaosmos*.[34] Envisioning the Artist of the universe metamorphosing much into lobes and globes, Thoreau realizes that this creator is no Yahweh, separating chaos and order, and no Platonic maker, mimicking the static forms of eternity. This demiurge is playful. He sports in the ooze. He strews fresh designs. Yet, he persistently concocts the same basic form: the leaf. In the bloody mire is the incipient leaf. The hawk's flick: leaf ratified. The brain is bulbous lichen. The heart photosynthesizes blood. Everything is ubiquitous sap cohered into a frond. But what is a leaf but a "foliate structure," a verdurous crystal?

Watching chaos turn into form (unseen vitality refract into pied beauty), Thoreau thinks of tropes—of how each reticulated pattern is a symbol of the whole, a word of the abyss. Leaf crystal is *logos*, word frond, water made flesh. Internally, this archetypal pattern is liquid potential (the unformed abyss, a centrifugal energy). It is a "lobe," a word embodying in sound its properties. "*[L]obe*" is "especially applicable to the liver and lungs and the *leaves* of fat, (λείβω, *labor*, *lapsus*, to flow or slip downward, a lapsing; λοβος, *globus*, lobe, globe; also lap, flap, and many other words)." This sap presses into a more stable material form (a balance of centrifugal and centripetal forces), rendered linguistically by the liquid "B" stiffening into the more solid "F" or "V." Externally, the lobe forms "a dry thin *leaf*, even as the *f* and *v* are a pressed and dried *b* ... with a liquid *l* behind it pressing it forward" (306).

The natural process by which water takes the shape of the crystalline leaf is enacted by the word "leaf." The word "leaf," like a biological leaf, is nature's "constant cypher." It bears the sense and sound of universe. Fluid, figured by "l" pushing into "b," and form, "f" and "v," "leaf" reveals the cosmic polarity between turbulence and pattern. Liquid "l," alveolar sonorant, flowing into bilabial voiced stop "b," and forming eventually into labiodental voiceless spirant "f," the word sounds the rhythm by which the world ceaselessly hums. All events, ceaselessly metamorphosing imbrications of liquid energy and solid organization, are thus "translations" of lobes into crystals or crystals into lobes. Some of these "translations" are moments of "transcendence," transmutation from simple to complex, conscious to intelligent. The ice crystal contains and transcends the water; the leaf includes and surpasses the crystal; the feather subsumes and outreaches the green serrations.

Moved by nature's tropes—leafy crystals and crystalline botany—Thoreau desires to participate in organic process by creating his own transparent leaves: the pages of *Walden*. For Thoreau, studied in winter's convoluted crystals and spring's intricate leaves, linguistic transparency is not discursive pellucidity, not Bacon's plain style or Locke's clear communication. On the contrary, for Thoreau a lucid style should reveal the manifold paradoxes and powers coursing through the gracefully turbid universe. To understand Thoreauvian transparency is to feel the force of a seeming contradiction troubling the pages of *Walden*: the book's persistent call for simplicity in a bewilderingly complex style. Though Thoreau spends most of "Where I Lived, What I Lived For" urging "Simplicity, simplicity, simplicity," he concludes his book by fearing, "chiefly lest [his] expression may not be *extra-vagant* enough, may not wander far enough beyond the narrows limits of my daily experience" (91, 324). Yet, this ostensible clash is in fact perfectly logical. The "simplicity" of nature is not its accessibility or clarity but rather its strangeness, its sublimity. Recall: "simple" emerges from the Indo-European root *sm-*, which means "same-fold," and from the Latin *simplus*, signifying "single." Hence, to be simple is literally to be undifferentiated and thus beyond diversity—abyssal, ungraspable, sublime. The simplicity of nature, then, is not only its elegant laws—its harmonious geometries—but also its "mysterious," "unexplorable" powers—its infinite wildness (317–18).

Ice crystals and spring leaves alike reveal nature's simplicity, nature's extravagance—order and wildness, mystery and solution. Their transparency is luminous darkness. Mimicking the muddy demiurge, Thoreau creates his own transparent crystals, his own extravagant leaves. For instance, in the melting-bank passage quoted above, his diction yields a series of disorienting polarities. The "Artist who made the world" inhabits a "laboratory"—a site of disciplined labor—but spends his "work" time by "sporting"—frolicking with random glee. Yet, this "excess of energy"—overflowing the tubes of his lab—is nonetheless ruled by "law," a principle that admits no superfluity. How can this artist be both scientist and jester? How can his creations be orderly and chaotic? Moreover, we wonder how the "atoms" produced by this artist "learn" his laws? How can an element consciously accrue knowledge? Certain individual words likewise disconcert. When Thoreau stares at the melting bank, he is "affected as if in a *peculiar* sense" he stood before the primal artist. "Peculiar" here clearly means "unique" or "special" but also suggests "odd" or "eccentric" as well as "possessive" ("peculiar" derives from French and Latin roots concerned with the ownership of private property). Hence, standing before the mud, Thoreau is both "proper"—at home, as it were, on his property, self-possessed on his possession—and "strange"—displaced from the norm, not-at-home in the familiar world. Double, he watches the "Artist who made the world" "*still* at work." As in Keats's "Ode on a Grecian Urn," "still" as adverb connotes both "without movement" and "up until this time"—tranquility and perpetual motion. Agitated yet calm, this Artist strews about fresh "*designs.*" A "design" is of course a composed pattern, a planned artifice, but also, etymologically, a movement from meaning—a motion from (*de*) the stable sign (*signum*). On the one hand, these various tensions are paradoxes, surface contradictions that are nonetheless true—Thoreau's extravagantly simple cosmos in an interplay between chance and law, spontaneity and structure, comfort and weirdness, perpetual motion and unmoving calm, meaning and meaninglessness. Yet, on the other hand, these semantic gaps remain unclosed, irreducible contradictions: laws cannot be random, atoms are not able to study, well-adjusted men are not strange to themselves, an artist cannot be still and also moving, and designs are not both present and absent at the same time.

Thoreau's passage instances the linguistic extravagance strewn throughout *Walden*. Though many parts of the book—like "Economy"—are "philosophical" in style, logical and lucid, and though other parts of the text—like "Winter Animals"—are "scientific" in form, concrete and journalistic, some sequences are wildly "poetic," complex, dense, strange, almost surreal. These latter sites, curiously, are more transparent than the former—more capable of revealing nature's complex simplicity.

To read *Walden* is to walk in the woods. For much of the walk—peregrinating through a disquisition on "grossest groceries" or a description of a squirrel—one is on familiar ground, treading without much strain or surprise. Yet, at certain turns—at the melting-bank passage, the final paragraph of the book, or the occasional sentence fraught with puns and paradoxes—the walker unexpectedly encounters fiery quartz, a leaf on fire. In the transparent lattices, he sees strange distortions, kaleidoscopic flickerings, ubiquitous light bent into diverse hues. He returns to the brown earth and finds that all is different. What seemed ordinary is now weird, a bright confusion.

This is the virtue of crystal, be it ice or quartz, foliated leaf or transparent prose. It is a special revelation of what is always already true of everything else but hidden, lurking under opaque surfaces. While all beings are in some way crystals—polarized geometries of unbounded energy some are more limpid than others, and thus more capable of revealing the processes by which they are animated. Figuring this cosmic poetics, Thoreau alternates between relatively untroubled, discursive sequences and sudden eruptions of semantic turbulence. The discursive sections are opaque crystals—ordinary, stable facts. The unexpected sparks and fires are crystals of extreme transparency: shocking apocalypses of the abyss on which we all float.

For Thoreau, to be transparent is also to be trans-parent—beyond the father, through the mother. Though he was studied in Emerson's numerous meditations on transparency, he in the end broke from his intellectual patriarch by going to the ice to see for himself, in his own peculiar fashion. Beholding the dawn frost, staring long at frozen opacities, he discovered directly, in the open air, what Emerson gleaned from books: to gaze through the crystal is to pass through to the origin, the matrix, the obscure womb that is nonetheless muse to all leaves, and jewels.

NOTES

1. This essay is related to the section on crystals in my book, *The Spiritual History of Ice: Romanticism, Science, and the Imagination* (New York and London: Palgrave/Macmillan, 2003). While in the book I focus on how Thoreau marries hermetic scrying and scientific crystallography—the occult and the factual—in his various descriptions of ice, here I attend to Thoreau's scientific senses of crystal and how they relate specifically to *Walden*.

2. Sophia Hawthorne, qtd in Rose Hawthorne Lathrop, *Memories of Hawthorne* (Boston: Houghton Mifflin, 1897) 53.

3. Thoreau, "Natural History of Massachusetts," *The Portable Thoreau*, ed. and intro. Carl Bode (New York: Viking/Penguin, 1962) 53–54.

4. In an anonymous article in the *New Jerusalem Magazine* 8 (Nov. 1839): 118–19, entitled "Swedenborg's Scientific Merit," it is reported that John-Baptiste André Dumas, a famous nineteenth-century French chemist, praised Swedenborg as the originator of crystallography. Most historians of science, however, claim this honor for Haüy.

5. Ralph Waldo Emerson, *Representative Men, The Collected Works of Ralph Waldo Emerson*, vol. 4, eds. Robert Spiller, Joseph Slater, et al. (Cambridge, MA and London: Belknap P of Harvard UP, 1971–) 62.

6. Emanuel Swedenborg, *Some Specimens of a Work on the Principles of Chemistry, with Other Treatises*, trans. Charles Edward Strut (London: William Newbery, 1847) 26, 37–38.

7. Swedenborg, *The Principia*, trans. Augustus Clissold (London: William Newbery, 1846) 45–54.

8. In designating these three "schools" of crystallography, I am largely following John G. Burke's *Origins of the Science of Crystals* (Berkeley and London: U of California P, 1966) 11–51. I should here note that it is likely that the crystallographers comprising these three schools had not been exposed, as Emerson had, to Swedenborg's scientific work.

9. As we know from Emerson's sermons, Emerson had read Herschel's book by 1831, when he compared it favorably to Milton's *Paradise Lost* (*The Complete Sermons of Ralph Waldo Emerson*, 4 vols, eds. Albert J. von Frank, et al. [Columbia: U of Missouri P, 1989–92] 4: 157).

10. John F. W. Herschel, *A Preliminary Discourse on the Study of Natural Philosophy*, foreword Arthur Fine (Chicago and London: U of Chicago P, 1987) 240–45.

11. Herschel 240–45. For an excellent discussion of Mitscherlich and Haüy, see also Burke 78–79, 120–25.

12. Emerson read Davy's work assiduously throughout the late 1820s and early 1830s, and praises the scientist often in his journal and early lectures. For instance, in an 1836 lecture, he lauds Davy's "sublime conjecture" that there is "hut one matter in different states of electricity" that might yield a vision of a "central unity" (*The Early Lectures of Ralph Waldo Emerson*, 3 vols, eds. Stephen E. Whicher, Robert E. Spiller, and Wallace E. Williams [Cambridge, MA: Harvard UP, 1959–72] 2: 29). For a detailed discussion of Emerson's relationship to Davy in particular and the science of electricity in general, see Eric Wilson, *Emerson's Sublime Science* (London and New York: Macmillan/St. Martin's, 1999) 76–97.

13. Sir Humphry Davy, *Elements of Chemical Philosophy*, vol. 4, *The Collected Works of Sir Humphry Davy*, ed. John Davy (London: Smith, 1839–40) 39–40.

14. Davy 40. See also Burke 150–51.

15. As I have argued in *Emerson's Sublime Science*, Emerson followed Faraday's discoveries closely throughout his career, and showed particular enthusiasm for his electromagnetic theories in the early 1830s (76–97).

16. Michael Faraday, *Experimental Researches in Electricity*, *Great Books of the Western World*, eds. Robert Maynard Hutchins, et al. (Chicago: Encyclopedia Britannica, 1952) ¶ 27.

17. Emerson, *The Journals and Miscellaneous Notebooks of Ralph Waldo Emerson*, 16 vols, eds. William H. Gilman and Ralph H. Orth, et al. (Cambridge, MA and London: Belknap P of Harvard UP, 1960–82) 4: 94.

18. Emerson was reading Goethe's scientific works closely in the 1830s. He mentions them often in his early lectures, showing special enthusiasm for Goethe's view that "[t]he whole force of the Creation is concentrated upon every point"; thus, massive "agencies of electricity, gravity, light, [and] affinity combine to make every plant what it is" (*Early Lectures* 1: 72). For a discussion of Emerson's relationship to Goethe's science, see *Emerson's Sublime Science* 61–67.

19. Johann Wolfgang Goethe, *Metamorphosis of Plants*, *Goethe: The Collected Works: Scientific Studies*, vol. 12, ed. and trans. Douglas Miller (Princeton, NJ: Princeton UP, 1988) 76–97.

20. Goethe. "An Intermaxillary Bone Is Present in the Upper Jaw of Man As Well As in Animals," *The Collected Works: Scientific Studies* 12: 111–16.

21. Goethe, "On Granite," *The Collected Works: Scientific Studies* 12: 131–35.

22. Goethe, "Problems," The Collected Works: Scientific Studies 12:43–44.

23. An 1835 journal entry suggests that Emerson knew of either Schelling's *Ideas for*

a Philosophy of Nature (1797) or his *System of Transcendental Idealism* (1800)—or perhaps both—for he accurately summarizes Schelling's main tenets in an extended journal entry (*Journals and Miscellaneous Notebooks* 5: 30).

24. F. W. J. Schelling, *Ideas for a Philosophy of Nature*, trans. Errol E. Harris and Peter Heath, intro. Robert Stern (Cambridge: Cambridge UP, 1988) 17–18, 44–49, 83.

25. Schelling, *Von der Weltseele* (Hamburg, 1798) 189, 219. See Burke for this discussion of Schelling's crystallography 149–51.

26. Robert Sattelmeyer, *Thoreau's Reading: A Study in Intellectual History* (Princeton, NJ: Princeton UP, 1988) 26–27.

27. Thoreau praises Swedenborg in *A Week on the Concord and Merrimack Rivers* for being able to see, empirically, spiritual powers (*The Writings of Henry David Thoreau*, ed. J. Lyndon Shanley [Princeton, NJ: Princeton UP, 1981–] 325). However, as Walter Harding and Michael Meyer note in *The New Thoreau Handbook* (New York: New York UP, 1980), Thoreau once said that he had little "practical" use for the Swedish mystic (98).

28. Laura Dassow Walls in *Seeing New Worlds: Henry David Thoreau and Nineteenth-Century Natural Science* (Madison: U of Wisconsin P, 1995) provides an excellent discussion of the contrasts between Emerson's "rational holism," a mode of observation ground on theory, and Thoreau's "empirical holism," a concrete way of seeing (53–93).

29. Thoreau, *The Journal of Henry David Thoreau*, 5 vols., eds. John C. Broderick, et al. (Princeton, NJ: Princeton UP, 1981–) 1: 22.

30. Samuel Taylor Coleridge, *The Collected Works of Samuel Taylor Coleridge*, gen. ed. Kathleen Coburn, 14 vols. to date (Princeton: Princeton UP, 1969–) 6: 30.

31. Goethe, *Maxims and Reflections*, qtd. in Max L. Baeumer, "The Criteria of Modern Criticism on Goethe as Critic," *Goethe as a Critic of Literature*, ed. Karl J. Fink and Max L. Baeumer (New York and London: UP of America, 1984) 10.

32. Thoreau, *The Journal of Henry David Thoreau* 3: 190; 4: 238–39; 4: 279; 5: 456; *Journal*, vol. 8, *The Writings of Henry David Thoreau*, ed. Bradford Torrey (Boston: Houghton Mifflin, 1906) 88.

33. Thoreau, *Walden*, *The Writings of Henry David Thoreau* 199. All additional citations from *Walden* will come from this edition and be designated by a page number in parentheses.

34. Walls beautifully describes Thoreau's primary vision in *Walden*: Thoreau "opened his eyes and saw, in the streets, fields, and forests, chaos: not the ancient void out of which man created pristine order, but a new insight into the imbrication of all order with disorder, disorder with the emergence of order, the *self*-organizing power of a chaotic nature quite apart from human desire or even presence" (238).

STEVEN HARTMAN

"The life excited":
Faces of Thoreau in Walden

> My work is writing, and I do not hesitate, though I know that no subject
> is too trivial for me, tried by ordinary standards; for, ye fools, the theme
> is nothing, the life is everything. All that interests the reader is the depth
> and intensity of the life excited.
> —Thoreau, *Journal*, 18 October 1856 (*J* 9: 121)[1]

At the end of *Walden* the Thoreau persona speculates on his reasons for
choosing to leave the woods at the end of the Walden experiment: "I left the
woods for as good a reason as I went there. Perhaps it seemed to me that I
had several more lives to live, and could not spare any more time for that
one" (*W* 323). It seems unlikely somehow that the writer who penned these
lines could have imagined at the time just how many lives he would live, and
continues to live, not as a universally understood historical or literary figure,
but as an enormously variable icon in the culture that has both inherited
and shaped him. From a life less than ordinary yet by no means dramatic we
have inherited a figure in Thoreau who is variously heroic (and sometimes
villainous), an archetype of the environmental hermit, the conscientious
objector, the alienated misanthrope, the nature-mystic and the political
subversive, among many other roles—this metaconstruct is more hydra-
headed, in fact, than it is Janus-faced. This essay focuses not so much on any
one (or few) of these particular faces as on the range of ways through which

From *The Concord Saunterer*, (*New Series*) vol. 12/13 (2004/2005), pp. 341–360. © 2003 by The
Thoreau Society.

Thoreau makes his own mutability a pronounced feature in *Walden*, the book which has served more than any other of his principal works to influence Thoreau's evolving public image.

A brief taxonomy of Thoreau's faces in *Walden* may suggest the scope and complexity of the author's literary representations of himself. Already in the very first paragraph of the work Thoreau represents himself in a variety of capacities. He appears to us as a member of society and also as someone outside its pale: "*At present* I am a sojourner in civilized life *again*" (*W* 3, emphases added) (the italicized adverbials can only imply that he was *not* a sojourner in civilized life during his two years at Walden Pond). He assumes the form of a narrating character who is rooted in factual history but who nevertheless exhibits some fictional traits: "I … earned my living by the labor of my hands only" (*W* 3) (a perfunctory knowledge of the historical Thoreau's life during this period is enough to throw this claim into doubt). Moreover, this narrator is not only the figure undertaking the experiment in self-sufficiency in the narrative about to unfold but a distinct editorial speaker looking back at his former self after this event: "When I wrote the following pages, or rather the bulk of them, I lived alone, in the woods, a mile from any neighbor, in a house which I had built myself, on the shore of Walden Pond, in Concord, Massachusetts" (*W* 3). This last sentence sets up another duality in Thoreau's textual persona: namely, he is both the biographical subject portrayed in *Walden* and the implied author behind this portrait.[2] This is in fact the very first line in the text of *Walden*. Its temporal frames of reference are striking, for they situate Thoreau simultaneously at the time of the Walden experiment, at the time of the book's composition (both during and after the experiment if we are to take the speaker at his word) and, finally, at a moment which postdates virtually all of the *Walden* text except the present utterance. In other words, the editorial comment in the book's first sentence creates the impression that *Walden*'s opening line of narrative may also have been one of the last lines its author composed.

It hardly seems necessary to belabor the point. Thoreau's complex self-representation in the opening passage of *Walden* seems too savvy to be the haphazard product of chance. For the subtle ways in which it manipulates characterization, perspective, voice modulation and psychic distance, it may not be a unique specimen in our literature, but it is a particularly fine one. The opening paragraph itself includes only sixty-nine words in three sentences, but its brevity and apparent straightforwardness mask a playfulness at work in Thoreau's rhetoric. In effect, the author destabilizes readers' most basic preconceptions about who is speaking, from which vantage point and in what form, only to turn this instability to his own advantage. Thoreau does this by sneaking a variety of identities (or categories of identity) into a single hypostatic figure—his textual self. Or it might be just as correct to say that he superimposes multiple layers of identity over his narrating persona.

An unusual imaginative space opens up in *Walden* where many varied and even contrary faces find room to exist in a single indispensable figure. That many readers (both sympathetic and resisting) manage to take this persona seriously as a unified, credible consciousness, even when they may have great difficulty reconciling some of his self-negating attitudes or views, seems a good measure of Thoreau's success in pulling off his *textual con*, a phrase not intended to be disparaging in any way, but suggesting nevertheless the necessity of a certain guileless cooperation on the part of Thoreau's readers.[3]

The *author* is an essential component of Thoreau's textual persona in *Walden*. This is explicit in the text itself. In the opening pages of the book, Thoreau continually reminds his audience (whom he identifies, ideally, as poor students) that they are in fact reading a book and that he is its architect. Even this authorial component of Thoreau's textual persona has several distinct faces, including (at various points) the lecturer, the preacher, the critic, the philosopher, the historian, and the poet-dramatist. In the pages that follow *Walden*'s opening paragraphs Thoreau extends and expands upon the guises under which he initially appears to include a whole gallery of distinct types.

A look at the ways in which Thoreau characterizes or accounts for himself at an *explicit* level in *Walden* may provide a useful starting point for an examination of more subtle forms of self-representation in the work.[4] We can begin by looking solely at the classes of occupation to which Thoreau admits he belongs. In "Economy" Thoreau describes how he supplemented his income during his stay at Walden Pond by working as a surveyor, a carpenter and a day-laborer, noting that he has "as many trades as fingers" (*W* 58).

This turns out to be something of an understatement. If we are to take the narrator at his word elsewhere in the work, he either is or has been a student (52), a plowman (55), a teacher (69), a (retail) tradesman (69), a gardener (83 *et passim*), a builder (85 *et passim*), a homesteader (157), a hunter (210 *et passim*), a fisherman (211 *et passim*) and a lecturer (271), among other things.

To this list we can easily add another catalogue of explicit self-classifications based not on Thoreau's various occupations but on his *pre*occupations, habits, customs, proclivities, self-judgments or simply his situation. Like those of the first group, the categories of identity in this grouping tend to be signaled by Thoreau in the form of virtual equations, as in "I am by nature a Pythagorean" (162) or in a manner not far removed from such formulations. He informs us that he is a friend of flora and fauna (42 *et passim*), a traveler (53), a squatter (49 *et passim*), a (failed) philanthropist

(73), the worst man he has ever known (78), a worshipper of the sunrise (88), a citizen of the world (119), a heathen (266), a hermit (270) and, my favorite, a human insect (332). The numerous faces that coalesce in this expanding figure of Thoreau are further augmented by the many descriptors he applies to himself, not as transient characterizations relevant to specific situations or circumstances, but as relatively stable or constant traits. In turn he informs us that he is callous (29), (full of) shortcomings (49), inconsistent (49), hypocritical (49), guilty of some excesses (59), abstemious (61), serene (129), more favored by the gods than other men (131), frugal (142), repulsed by the eating of flesh (which is unclean) (214), coarse and indifferent (217), unconcerned about the obscenity of his *words* (as opposed apparently to his deeds) (221), impure (221), stiff-necked (241), and *extra-vagant* (324).

This catalogue of curious epithets is drawn entirely from Thoreau's *explicit* self-equations and characterizations. If we were to open this list up to include additional qualities that are not explicit but strongly implied or otherwise manifest in the Thoreau narrator's various postures, it would include a whole other range of descriptors, such as earthy, wild, curious, observant, opinionated, intolerant, sympathetic, hopeful, scornful, impudent and restless.

Many of Thoreau's self-characterizations are mildly ironic, but beneath their wry gloss most of them are still largely credible at face value in the context of *Walden's* narrative. None of the preceding lists is comprehensive, nor do they need to be. There is no need, in fact, for us to read especially deeply into any of these specific categories of identity. Their significance lies not in their individuation, such as it is, but in their subtle insinuation of Thoreau's slippery, mutable identity as a theme in its own right. *Walden* bears this preoccupation out more profoundly in other ways, some of which are bound to affect how we regard and make sense of Thoreau. The following sustained passage from very early in the *Walden* text playfully foregrounds the narrator's protean or composite identity:

> For a long time I was reporter to a journal, of no very wide circulation, whose editor has never yet seen fit to print the bulk of my contributions....
>
> For many years I was self-appointed inspector of snow storms and rain storms, and did my duty faithfully; surveyor, if not of highways, then of forest paths and all across-lot routes, keeping them open....
>
> I have looked after the wild stock of the town, which give a faithful herdsman a good deal of trouble by leaping fences; and I have had an eye to the unfrequented nooks and corners of the

farm.... I have watered the red huckleberry, the sand cherry and the nettle tree, the red pine and the black ash, the white grape and the yellow violet, which might have withered else in dry seasons. (*W* 18)

In this lightly satiric passage Thoreau's taxonomy of identities—as husbandman, shepherd, surveyor, steward of public byways, rustic haunts and spaces wild, self-appointed meteorologist, journalist and editor[5]—may seem little more than a digression. Yet because the passage focuses almost exclusively on the narrator's many self-styled roles it foreshadows *Walden*'s preoccupation with this very theme. At this point in the work Thoreau's narrator has only just begun to establish himself as a textual entity, so the mutability of his identity is not likely to strike the reader as an especially salient feature of *Walden*. Yet as the work progresses the theme becomes more and more prominent as the narrator's roles expand in range and number. In turn the reader is obliged to define and redefine Thoreau throughout the work.

The faces of Thoreau which emerge in *Walden* are not limited to the roles his persona assumes in the work at the level of explicit self-identification—we also find these roles evinced in the narrator's sentiments, stances, gestures, attitudes or manner. The Thoreau that we have inherited, being in large measure an extension of the *Walden* persona, is much more than the sum total of what the narrator *claims* to be. In fact, many of his other faces—the uncompromising individualist, the esthete, the lover of purity, the spiritualist, the close observer and eulogist of nature—are established in the work through largely indirect means, though this makes them no less palpable.

A number of these faces are merely extensions of various speaker personae[6] in the lecture materials around which he fashioned his narrative. Others are equally stylized extensions of traditional literary genres and forms: for instance, the Socratic dialogue of "Brute Neighbors," which introduces two faces—the hermit and the poet; the rant of "The Ponds," which unleashes a Jeremiah; or the work's many elements of pastoral, which give us a shepherd inhabiting a liminal borderland between civilization and the wild. Substituting one bucolic setting for another, Thoreau transforms his shepherd self into a husbandman and turns the conventional flock into a beanfield: "Mine was, as it were, the connecting link between wild and cultivated fields; as some states are civilized, and others half-civilized, and others savage or barbarous, so my field was, though not in a bad sense, a half-cultivated field" (*W* 158).

Not without reason does Leo Marx see this pastoral element as the controlling model of the work as a whole (Marx 243–45), though he does so virtually to the exclusion of other equally important literary modes that coalesce in *Walden*,[7] which is actually something of a generic Swiss army knife. One of the faces which emerges unexpectedly in Thoreau's narrative is that of the modified epic hero. The very same chapter that gives us the most obvious adaptation of the pastoral mode ("The Bean Field") is also rife with mock-heroic elements. Obviously these are included for light comic relief, but that does not disqualify them as important indicators of the heroic framework Thoreau constructs piece by piece throughout the work. Perhaps more important are the many references Thoreau makes throughout *Walden* to heroic literature, especially in its third chapter, "Reading," which Stanley Cavell interprets as something of a user's manual positioned early in the book so that readers will understand how the author expects them to read it (Cavell 3–35). There are, of course, other important indicators, such as Thoreau's symbolic act of withdrawing to Walden Pond, of declaring independence, on July 4th—a gesture meant to recall *the* defining moment in American history. As an individual reenactment of this event, Thoreau's own declaration of independence sets him up as a typological representative of the American people. Thus Thoreau invites us to view his actions in sweeping symbolic terms, as epic expressions of the culture's (latent) potential for virtuous accomplishment.

In *Walden* Thoreau seeks to define the American ethos, both as it is and as it could be. An amalgam of the poet, the hero, and the cultural historian, his narrator speaks out as a dissenting member of the polis to an essentially flawed civilization, while also presuming to speak *for* that civilization in a variety of capacities. In the guise of the cultural historian he tries, like Emerson, to expose the runaway materialism and spiritual blight of his own age. Yet in the role of the poet-dramatist he also seeks to extol the virtues latent in this same crass civilization, to uncover the potential for enlightenment its members possess should they learn to recognize and observe the all-important differences between ends and means. "If I seem to boast more than is becoming," Thoreau admits in the first chapter of *Walden*, "my excuse is that I brag for humanity rather than for myself; and my shortcomings and inconsistencies do not affect the truth of my statement" (*W* 49). This last aim is epic in design and scope, but to accomplish it Thoreau needs a dramatic embodiment of those latent virtues, an enlightened hero whose idealized words and actions can capture archetypically the moral essence of a people.

Only days after taking up full-time residence at Walden Pond Thoreau had contemplated America's need for such a native hero in his journal:

> I am glad to remember tonight as I sit by my door that I too
> am at least a remote descendant of that heroic race of men of
> whom there is tradition. I too sit here on the shore of my Ithaca,
> a fellow-wanderer and survivor of Ulysses. How Symbolical,

significant of I know not what the pitch pine stands here before my door unlike any glyph I have seen sculptured or painted yet—One of Nature's later designs. Yet perfect as her Grecian art. There it is, a done tree. Who can mend it? And now where is the generation of heroes whose lives are to pass amid these our northern pines? Whose exploits shall appear to posterity pictured amid these strong and shaggy forms? (*PJ* 2: 156–57)

We are not likely to encounter questions more obviously rhetorical than this last one. The answer is already evident in the comparisons Thoreau courts with Ulysses, in his advertised pedigree as a "descendent of that heroic race of men of whom there is tradition" (156). On the very first page of *Walden* the author persona asks those readers who are not particularly interested in him personally to pardon his self-absorption. He highlights his dual role as both the architect of the book and the true subject of its discussion. "In most books, the I, or first person, is omitted; in this it will be retained; that, in respect to egotism, is the main difference. We commonly do not remember that it is, after all, always the first person that is speaking. I should not talk so much about myself if there were any body else whom I knew as well" (*W* 3).

As discourse subject Thoreau is also a thematic and figurative vehicle, a quirky self-styled "Everyman" or Bunyanesque "Pilgrim" constructed for an age in which allegory is no longer a viable form, its conventions functionally obsolescent. Indeed, Thoreau's earnest allegorical designs would be fairly ludicrous if they were not concealed within a largely realistic narrative filtered through the perspective of his own manifestly flawed literary persona. This figure inspires admiration, nervousness, consternation, antipathy, ridicule and even pity. Reviews of *Walden* when the book first appeared were quite favorable on the whole, but many of these positive assessments also had a sort of nervous chuckle about them, a quality of barely suppressed bewilderment. *Walden*'s author, wrote one reviewer, is "absolutely haunted by the singular desire of placing himself before the reader's eyes in the most unfavorable light possible" (Scharnhorst 33). While many contemporary reviewers enjoyed and were willing to recommend *Walden*, they did not know entirely what to make of its unusual tenor. The intervening years have not neutralized the book's (especially its narrator's) capacity to generate conflicting reactions in its readers, some of them wantonly starry-eyed, others resistant, even vitriolic. Certainly this extraordinary spread of responses, as Lawrence Buell describes it (Buell 314), owes much to our express desire to explain the figure's unorthodox qualities in conventional terms. But it owes just as much to the sleight of hand by which Thoreau tricks us into thinking in conventional terms to begin with. Thoreau constructs the gallery of faces for his textual self not by over-identifying formalistically with any specific literary antecedents, but by raiding as many of them as he profitably can and suffusing what he manages to come away with in his own text, his own textual persona, which is a hybrid of conventional character types. If *Walden* is indeed a literary Swiss army knife, then each of its generic components, while indispensable to the integrity of the whole, cannot on its own define that whole. This is no less true of its mutable narrator.

"The struggle in me," Thoreau wrote in the *Journal* during his first spring at Walden Pond, "is between a love of contemplation and a love of action—the life of a philosopher & of a hero. The poetic & philosophic have my constant vote—the practice hinders & unfits me for the former" (*PJ* 2: 240). In a number of contexts Thoreau seems to assume that the *poetic* and the *heroic* represent different, possibly even antipodal, ways of engaging the world.

The assumption is not strange, nor is his express desire to reconcile these aspirations in himself. At a purely textual level this desire becomes realized in his narrative persona, an amalgam of both forms of engagement. Through his many metaphors of dawn, his ubiquitous imagery of rebirth, Thoreau casts himself time and again in the role of an ideal poet-hero.

The preeminence of the auroral hour is emphasized in the *Journal* and in *Walden*; in both works Thoreau applies auroral metaphors to himself frequently. Dawn is when Thoreau bathes, undergoing a ritual of rebirth, and the day is at its best because his life is beginning anew, continually anew, with endless possibility ahead for *knowing* more, *being* more, *seeing* more and *doing* more. Whether in the form of spring, dawn, awakening or rebirth, the auroral hour is the ideal state or season toward which Thoreau is constantly inclined: "I have been as sincere a worshipper of Aurora as the Greeks. I got up early and bathed in the pond; that was a religious exercise, and one of the best things which I did.... Morning brings back the heroic ages" (*W* 88).

This ideal state, moreover, is explicitly identified with an ongoing process of self-reform. "Morning is when I am awake and there is a dawn in me. Moral reform is the effort to throw off sleep" (*W* 90). In *Walden* Thoreau tends to address his culture's (latent) potential for improvement through self-reform in the form of positive exhortations and parables. A number of these, like the previous example, make use of auroral imagery. His culture's shortcomings, on the other hand, are exposed through the narrator's frequently caustic criticism of his close-minded neighbors, whose *domestic* lives are often associated with morbidity and death.

These are the rhetorical counterweights of Thoreau's discussions throughout *Walden* and, to some degree, "Resistance to Civil Government." The rhetoric of advocacy implies its opposite: the rhetoric of denunciation.

Thoreau's use of inclusive pronouns (*we, us* and *our*) often signals the former technique. "Any prospect of awakening or coming to life to a dead man makes indifferent all times and places. The place where that may occur is always the same, and indescribably pleasant to all *our* senses" (*W* 134, emphasis added). In contrast, denunciations are most often signaled by a particular use of the third-person through which Thoreau effectively distances himself and us as readers from a corresponding gallery of deficient types: the farmer, the merchant and the villager, to name but a few. Each of these types is subsumed under one of his favorite dismissive labels, the ever-handy "mass of men"[8] (*W* 8 *et passim*; *RP* 66 *et passim*). If the parables in which these straw figures appear do not make their deficiency of virtue abundantly clear, then Thoreau is not above throwing in the odd heavy descriptor, such as "unclean and stupid" (*W* 195) or "clumsy" (*W* 6), to drive the point home.

At the level of heroic dramatization, *Walden's* author-narrator effectively denies a complicity in the wayward tendencies of his neighbors through his symbolic withdrawal from their sphere of influence and affairs, an act which is not only the premise but one of the culminating effects of *Walden's* narrative. Though to all appearances it is thrust upon him, Thoreau's occupation of very much the same space in "Resistance to Civil Government" occurs when he is placed in jail. "I saw that, if there was a wall of stone between me and my townsmen, there was a still more difficult one to climb or break through, before they could get to be as free as I was. I did not for a moment feel confined, and the walls seemed a great waste of stone and mortar. I felt as if I alone of all my townsmen had paid my tax" (*RP* 80). Of course, the *appearance* of his forced imprisonment is just that—the incarceration is precipitated by his own calculated refusal to meet his civic obligations as defined by the community. His imprisonment, then, is as much a voluntary act of withdrawal as his relocation to Walden Pond. In both cases he chooses to break his compact with society on his own terms. His adopted position of exteriority is not compromised by the literal interiority of the prison cell in "Resistance." As Thoreau's descriptions make clear in the essay, the usual senses of "freedom" (69 *et passim*) and "imprisonment" (77) do not apply. These terms should be read in an inverted sense, as should each of the conceptual oppositions (such as exteriority/interiority) based on the dichotomy of liberty and captivity. His townsmen/jailers, remarks the Thoreau narrator, "thought that my chief desire was to stand the other side of that stone wall. I could not but smile to see how industriously they locked the door on my meditations, which followed them out again without let or hindrance, and *they* were really all that was dangerous" (80).

By taking up residence in this exterior space (whether in his jail cell or at Walden Pond), Thoreau lays claim to a moral high ground where he can stand

and dress down the ubiquitous mass of (straw) men without being implicated in their follies, whether they merely "labor under a mistake" (*W* 5), "lead lives of quiet desperation" (*W* 8), "discontented[ly] ... and idly complain" (*W* 16) or "serve the state ... not as men mainly, but as machines" (*RP* 66). Another way of putting this is to say that (with a few notable exceptions) Thoreau represents the antipode of almost all that he condemns in his objectified neighbors. Following this logic, one of the most important effects of his frequent denunciations is an implied construction of his own virtue.

Thoreau's literary persona in *Walden* is an unstable textual entity insofar as his evident characteristics undergo a constant realignment throughout the work. It would probably be much more accurate to refer to this persona in the plural. The Thoreaus of *Walden* and "Resistance" are certainly not the same personae, though they have much in common with one another— the two works are, after all, cross-referential—and each has furnished the metaconstruct that shares the author's name with some of its most salient faces. The operative word is *faces*, for each of these personae is in fact a plurality of characters, and without question *Walden*'s narrator shelters the broadest and most diverse constituency of Thoreau identities.

"*Walden*, presented as memoir," writes Joyce Carol Oates, "is a work of artful self-invention." Thoreau's "subtle and ambiguous ... appropriation of the journal genre" in his masterwork is "an artfully composed and semi-fictionalized portrait of 'Henry David Thoreau' as a hero free of all personal history and identity" (Oates 32). It is an intriguing proposition, to think of Thoreau's reinvention of himself as an effect of generic innovation. Yet there is more to Thoreau's "artful self-invention" than his savvy manipulation of established literary forms and their conventions, and it would probably be unwise to think of *Walden*'s protean narrator as somehow just a by-product of Thoreau's attempt to reinvent himself on the printed page. Either possibility may help to account for any number of interesting decisions Thoreau made in the process of composing *Walden*, as well as many features that readers continue to find interesting in the work for entirely different reasons. But the very conceptual framework from which Thoreau draws his meaningful sense of purpose as an artist may help to explain these choices and features equally well, not least his protean self-representation in *Walden*.

In the early pages of *Walden* Thoreau meditates on the stars as "the apexes of what wonderful triangles! What distant and different beings in the various mansions of the universe are contemplating the same one at the same moment!.... Could a greater miracle take place than for us to look through each other's eyes for an instant? We should live in all the ages of the world in an hour; ay, in all the worlds of the ages. History, Poetry, Mythology!—I know of no reading of another's experience so startling and informing as this would be" (*W* 10).

This idealized view of the human potential for self-realization informs *Walden* at a number of levels. It is not uncommon for such a view to find expression in Thoreau's writings in combination with tropes emphasizing the timelessness of poetry (or art)—a fairly conventional notion if timelessness is taken to mean *permanence*. Yet as the preceding passage implies, Thoreau's timeless poetry is something else. A correlative of mythology and history, it is timeless because it exists somehow *out of time*.

Not that Thoreau is entirely clear about how this works. "That time which we really improve, or which is improvable," he states matter-of-factly in *Walden*'s third chapter, "is neither past, present, nor future" (*W* 99). We could well ask just where (or when) that improvable time *is* to be found. But we will not get a ready answer in this particular passage. Like so many of Thoreau's enigmatic utterances, the statement is offered at face value, with no explanation or elaboration in context, and his narrative moves on without looking back.

Thoreau often speaks of poetry, history and mythology as timeless in a sense equally unconventional, not to mention more than ordinarily abstract. He aligns them with one another as virtually inexhaustible *banks* of epistemological wealth insofar as they store, accrue and make available to the culture the most essential human knowledge. They represent, in other words, the ultimate repositories of our evolving knowledge, as well as the most significant means by which this knowledge is transmitted from one generation to the next. In Thoreau's scheme, poetry, history and mythology tend to transcend the ephemeral media with which they are typically associated. "The true poem is not that which the public read," Thoreau writes in *A Week on the Concord and Merrimack Rivers*. "There is always a poem not printed on paper, coincident with the production of this, stereotyped in the poet's life. It is what he has become through his work. Not how is the idea expressed in stone, or on canvas or paper, is the question, but how far it has obtained form and expression in the life of the artist. His true work will not stand in any prince's gallery" (*A Week* 343).

Of course, Thoreau is speaking here about something much more involved than mere lines arranged, however successfully, on a page. The artist's "life" and "work" are inseparably bound up in his conception of poetry, and this may be essential to our understanding of Thoreau's literary projects *in toto*; it certainly sheds some interesting light on the variety of creative biography advanced in a work like *Walden*.

The questions that most disturb, puzzle and confound us, Thoreau (over)states in *Walden*, "have in their turn occurred to all the wise men; not one has been omitted; and each has answered them, according to his ability, by his words and his life" (*W* 108). As thus conceived, poetry comprises both the "words" and the "life" of the artist. Though it may well find expression in verse, *true poetry* (*A Week* 343) is by no means limited to that medium. Similar notions attach to the rubrics of *mythology* and *history* as Thoreau uses them, for the three are clearly interrelated in his system of operative abstractions and metaphors. Yet the exact nature of their correlation is somewhat trickier to pin down. Is it one of equivalency, complementarity, symbiosis? Or of hierarchy, dependency, causality? Depending on where we look in Thoreau's writings, we are apt to find more than one possibility confirmed.

In one journal entry Thoreau speaks of poetry as "exaggerated history" (*PJ* 2: 204). Elsewhere mythology is defined as "ancient history or biography," the "oldest history still memorable" (*PJ* 2: 381). Together these definitions seem to suggest a specific implicational order in which one epistemological bank implies the existence of the next in a chain (mythology → history → poetry). In other contexts, however, Thoreau seems to invert or otherwise shake up this order, and we needn't look further than this last journal entry to find an example: "Mythology ... is the fruit which history at last bears—The fable so far from being false contains only the essential parts of the history" (381). In a lengthy aside in *A Week on the Concord and Merrimack Rivers* Thoreau claims that the hidden significance of fables—identified as "the ethics running parallel to ... poetry and history"—is far less remarkable than the readiness with which fables "may be made to express a variety of truths ... still older and more universal ... than any whose flesh and blood they are for the time made to wear" (*A Week* 61). As if anticipating his readers' doubts, or possibly their confusion, Thoreau then asks: "But what signifies it?" A fitting question, to which he offers the following hyperbolic answer:

> In the mythus a superhuman intelligence uses the unconscious thoughts and dreams of men as its hieroglyphics to address men unborn. In the history of the human mind, these glowing and ruddy fables precede the noonday thoughts of men, as Aurora the sun's rays. The matutine intellect of the poet, keeping in advance of the glare of philosophy, always dwells in this auroral atmosphere (61).

Thoreau's preoccupation with history, mythology and poetry is not in itself unusually significant. These subjects are, after all, standard fare in Western literature. Far more significant are Thoreau's repeated attempts to explicate the dynamics among or between these banks of knowledge in the process of working out his own role as a poet. As we have begun to see, his various articulations of this problem disclose, in the aggregate, anything but an airtight logic. If mythology is the oldest history still memorable, and poetry is exaggerated history, what then are we to make of Thoreau's claim that the poet's intellect *precedes* philosophy and the "noonday thoughts of men" (61), dwelling instead in the same "auroral atmosphere" (61) from which myth flowers? Perhaps Thoreau's meditations on this subject are so apparently circular because he is attempting to articulate what is in some measure inexpressible in perfectly rational terms, a notion that he entertains himself in the "Conclusion" of *Walden*:

> I desire to speak somewhere *without* bounds; like a man in a waking moment, to men in their waking moments; for I am convinced that I cannot exaggerate enough even to lay the foundation of a true expression.... The volatile truth of our words should continually betray the inadequacy of the residual statement. Their truth is instantly *translated*; its literal monument alone remains. The words that express our faith and piety are not definite (*W* 324–25).

Enigmatic words. The words of a writer grasping after the unattainable in a poetic idiom sonorous but far from definite indeed, except that in this case it seems to illustrate what Thoreau emphasizes at the start—his "desire to speak ... *without* bounds."

Thoreau's poetic exaggeration is rooted in his often idiosyncratic use of otherwise semantically stable terms and concepts. Thoreau often bends language to serve a variety of purposes, some of them highly unusual and many of them problematic. It is worth remarking the presence of certain prominent metaphors and abstractions in the preceding passage: the auroral "waking moment" as incipient artistic or philosophical awareness, the "literal monument" as an imperfect measure of artistic production, and "truth" as an ideal constant against which art's ephemeral forms are found wanting (*truth*, of course, is yet another staple item in Thoreau's poetic and rhetorical vocabularies, an umbrella value for the wisdom that history, poetry and mythology presumably convey). Many of these very elements appear with remarkable frequency in Thoreau's writings, especially *Walden* and the *Journal*, becoming virtual leitmotifs.

Statuary imagery ("the literal monument") is often employed emblematically when Thoreau seeks to distinguish between an essential or timeless art and its concrete correspondent in the world of here and now— other emblems representing a variation on the same concept include the canvas, the painting (or picture) and, of course, the book. Yet Thoreau is never entirely consistent even in his use of fine-arts tropes. In the following passage from the opening chapter of *Walden* the artistic literal monument in the form of a painting or a bust stands emblematically not for art's material shadow but for its higher or undistilled essence:

> We have adopted Christianity merely as an improved method of *agri*-culture. We have built for this world a family mansion, and for the next a family tomb. The best works of art are the expression of man's struggle to free himself from this condition, but the effect of our art is merely to make this low state comfortable and that higher state to be forgotten. There is actually no place in this village for a work of *fine* art, if any had come down to us, to stand, for our lives, our houses and streets, furnish no proper pedestal for it. There is not a nail to hang a picture on, nor a shelf to receive the bust of a hero or a saint (*W* 37–38).

In more than one sense we can look at a work like *Walden* as Thoreau's most fully actualized attempt to "furnish [a] proper pedestal" for "the bust of [such] a hero or a saint." This heroic, sainted figure, molded as a potential archetype, is a stylized projection of himself. Thoreau fashions this idealized literary self from the raw materials of his own life. Yet as he conceives of it, and frequently speaks of it, *life* is only partly what the biographical record is capable of revealing or confirming about a historic figure; it is at least as much a product of the imagination. In Thoreau's expanded sense of these concepts, *imagination*—no less than *life*—is readily identifiable with "a superhuman intelligence" (*A Week*, 61) comprising both writers and their audiences and involving the imaginative acts in which each engages collaboratively—*creative writing* and *creative reading*, in other words, in senses extending even beyond what Emerson had envisioned in "The American Scholar" (94).

As we find this conception applied in his own case, Thoreau's *life* becomes fully realized only in or through his writings. This requires the active participation of readers who must negotiate, in Lawrence Buell's words, "the actual or supposed events" of Thoreau's significant history as well as the attendant "myths of authorial stance and voice" (Buell 312) to which they give rise. In its most wide-open sense Thoreau's *life* becomes inseparable from the traditions of reader response by which his works are interpreted and through which authorial myths are shaped, reinforced, validated and reshaped. When these myths become well enough established they in turn exert a renewed influence on subsequent readings of his works, and the process continues full-circle.

There is, of course, an inevitable and perturbing circularity to the logic of this idea, especially insofar as both the myths and the interpretations are doubtlessly based to some degree on preconceptions about Thoreau's life at the same time that they are credited with helping to shape this life. Yet Thoreau himself helps to sanction this interpretive paradox in numerous ways. For instance, in one journal entry containing an extended meditation on the Persian poet Saadi,[9] Thoreau underscores the "insignificant" difference between the "personal" (or *individual*) life of a poet and the more enduring "historical" life of that figure as "embowelled" by posterity:

> Sadi entertained once identically the same thought that I do—and thereafter I can find no essential difference between Sadi and myself. He is not Persian—he is not ancient—he is not strange to me. By the identity of his thought with mine he still survives. It makes no odds what atoms serve us. Sadi possessed no greater privacy or individuality than is thrown open to me. He had no more interior & essential & sacred self than can come naked into my thought this moment. Truth and a true man is something essentially public not private. If Sadi were to come back to claim a *personal* identity with the historical Sadi he would find there were too many of us—he could not get a skin that would contain us all.... By living the life of a man is made common property. By sympathy with Sadi I have embowelled him. In his thoughts I have a sample of *him* a slice from his core ... but I could not have got this without being equally entitled to it with himself. The difference between any man and that posterity amid whom he is famous is too insignificant to sanction that he should be set up again in any world as distinct from them (*PJ* 5: 289–90).

Written while *Walden* was still undergoing significant revisions, Thoreau's meditation on Saadi plays upon some interesting oppositions: the notion of individual selfhood and intellectual property versus that of a collectively animated self which is "common property"; the notion of experiential selfhood versus that of textually constructed selfhood; and finally the notion of literary meaning as stable as opposed to fluid. This last dichotomy pits a reductive conception of meaning as immutable—fossilized as it were at a specific historical moment when the writer composes his or her work or authorizes it for publication—against a very different sense that can only be seen as supertemporal and non-finite. The product of a dynamic relation among authors, texts and their readers, literary meaning in this last sense continually evolves, building upon preexisting constellations of meaning that have become, in effect, inseparable from the text. In this last particular Thoreau would seem to be anticipating the reception-theory school of reader-response criticism by well more than a century.

The entity that emerges in Thoreau's description of the "historical Sadi" is "embowelled" vis-à-vis the active, mediating influence of imaginative readers, and this of course suggests any number of ready parallels with our own posthumously animated Thoreau. This connection is scarcely less than explicit in Thoreau's own discussion, for his ostensible meditation on Saadi turns out to be a *de facto* meditation on himself, as the next extended paragraph in the entry makes clear:

> I only know myself as a human entity—the scene, so to speak, of thoughts & affections—and am sensible of a certain doubleness by which I can stand as remote from myself as from another. However intense my experience—I am conscious of the presence & criticism of apart of me which as it were is not apart of me— but spectator sharing no experience, but taking note of it—and that is no more I than it is you.—When the play—it may be the tragedy—is over, the spectator goes his way. It was a kind of fiction—a work of the imagination—so far as he was concerned. A man *may* be affected by a theatrical exhibition; On the other hand he *may not* be affected by an actual event which appears to concern him never so much (*PJ* 5: 290).

Just as he finds "no essential difference between Sadi and [him]self" (289) Thoreau acknowledges that his own readers have an equal stake in his "identity" (289). In fact, the metaphors equating his "experience" (290) with dramatic and fictional forms readily suggest a notion of public spectacle wholly consistent with the imaginative life showcased in a work like *Walden*. The "theatrical exhibition" (290) functions as an elaborate metaphor for Thoreau's literary production, performance and reception. The most peculiar and revealing feature of Thoreau's rhetoric in this entry is his functional attempt to confuse or admix the three ordinarily distinct categories of identity upon which his theatrical conceit depends. These identities are those of the author (or playwright), the audience (or spectator) and the actor (or character). Through some rather complex associative wordplay each of these roles is projected on his readers and assumed by Thoreau himself. Thoreau's role as author is implicit, just as the existence of "the play—it may be the tragedy" (290)—implies a playwright. He speaks of himself synecdochically as both the actor and the stage—"the scene ... of thoughts and affections" (290)—yet he also acknowledges that he is the spectator observing this scene.

Far from being merely a representation of Thoreau's detached critical faculty, his "spectator" (290), or second self, is an entity capable of standing entirely aloof from the figure on that stage, "sharing no experience, but taking note of it" (290).

This is precisely the point at which Thoreau brings his own audience into the mix. His second self, he says, "is no more I than it is you" (290). By directly addressing his posthumous readers in the form of the second-person *you*, Thoreau implicates them in the metaconstruct of his own identity,[10] which involves not one but each of the roles—author, spectator and dramatic persona—indispensable to his theatrical conceit. In all of its playful ingenuity, this conceit merely reinforces the thesis of Thoreau's earlier meditation on Saadi: "The difference between any man and that posterity amid whom he is famous is too insignificant to sanction that he should be set up again in any world as distinct from them" (290). Likewise, Thoreau's description of his own complex doubleness elicits a self that is bounded neither by time nor by space, defying the natural limitations of any life as conventionally conceived.

"Here I am 34 years old," Thoreau admits in the *Journal* three years before *Walden*'s publication, "and yet my life is almost wholly unexpanded. How much is in the germ! There is such an interval between my ideal and the actual in many instances that I may say I am unborn.... Life is not long enough for one success. Within another 34 years that miracle can hardly take place" (*PJ* 3: 313). A similar doubt over what he can reasonably expect to accomplish in the allotted years of his lifetime is evident in another journal entry from eight months earlier:

> I have no more distinctness and pointedness in my yearnings than an expanding bud—which does indeed point to flower & fruit to summer & autumn—but is aware of the warm sun & spring influence only. I feel ripe for something yet do nothing—cant discover what that thing is. I feel fertile merely. It is seed time with me—I have lain fallow long enough. (*PJ* 3: 143–44)

Despite the note of impatience discernable in both of these passages, language in each of the entries strongly suggests Thoreau's belief that a reckoning will inevitably occur ("How much is in the germ!"; "I feel ripe for something"). The key to this reckoning, as Thoreau imagines it, can be found in his greatly expanded conception of his own *life*.

To a certain extent Thoreau's expanded conception of his life can be seen as a reflection of the very broad semantic range "life" exhibits as a lexical item in his operative poetic vocabulary. In Thoreau's writings terms like *life*, *self* and even *work* often categorically express ways or modes of *being*. They are not exactly interchangeable as linguistic signs, yet they are to some degree inseparably bound up in one another, for each approximates a superordinate value that is expressible only through the imperfect aid of metaphor in an ideal context, "somewhere *without* bounds" (*W* 324). These terms approximate this value less on their own than in combination with one another and in this respect they have much in common with *history, poetry* and *mythology* as we find Thoreau invoking these abstractions. In one of Thoreau's most far-reaching senses *life* or *a life* might be defined as a personified configuration of attitudes, values, beliefs and accomplishments (whether real or reputed) which endures and even thrives so long as others identify with it, legitimate it, enshrine it, and actively *use* it. Of course, nowhere in Thoreau's writings will we find *life* defined in exactly these terms, but in the aggregate his many idiosyncratic applications of the term point strongly to such a comprehensive definition.

Such a sense of the term is compatible with an observation Thoreau made in his journal during his first year in residence at Walden Pond, wherein he notes that he has at least one advantage over his neighbors who must look to theaters and society for amusement: "my life itself is my amusement and never ceases to be novel—the commencement of an experiment—or a drama which will never end" (*PJ* 2: 243). In approaching Thoreau's writings we cannot get around scrutinizing some of his favored metaphors, images and tropes—the lexicon of what we might call his poetic idiolect. Evident patterns in his modes of metaphoric expression reveal a great deal about his habits of thought, just as incongruencies in these patterns may help to reveal limitations or even innovations in his thinking. "It is the faculty of the poet to see present things as if, in this sense, also past and future, as if distant or universally significant. We do not know poets, heroes, and saints for our contemporaries, but we locate them in some far-off vale, and, the greater and better, the further off we [are] accustomed to consider them" (*J* 13: 17).

The grand abstractions of mythology, poetry and history find embodiment in Thoreau's idealized figures of the hero, the poet and the saint. In turn he continually superimposes these figures on his own literary persona. Their timeless universality, a defining feature, is self-applied time and again, as is their quality of virtue. If the poet speaks *for* civilization, then the hero acts archetypically *on behalf of* it: "All poets and heroes," Thoreau asserts in *Walden*'s second chapter, "are the children of Aurora, and emit their music at sunrise" (*W* 89). Thoreau's virtual identification of poets *and* heroes represents an admixture of the *deviser* and the *device* that is omnipresent in *Walden* in the form of the narrator himself, the poet-creator and hero-persona of the work. If *Walden* draws heavily on the resources of poetry, mythology and history, then it also represents Thoreau's most coherent and self-contained literary effort to feed back into these timeless banks of knowledge. By projecting so many faces onto his textual persona Thoreau attempts to be Homer, Achilles and Herodotus all in one, while also setting himself up as something of a philosophical "counter-friction to stop the machine" (*RP* 74) of prevalent systems of thought (Paley's doctrine of political expediency, for instance, or Adam Smith's materialistic economic philosophy) whose implications he clearly views as harmful.

These, of course, are a great many robes for any one figure to wear simultaneously, yet Thoreau attempts to don some or all of them at once throughout his writings. Nowhere do so many faces coalesce as completely or successfully in a single figure than in *Walden*'s narrator. "In any weather, at any hour of the day or night, I have been anxious to improve the nick of time, and notch it on my stick too; to stand on the meeting of two eternities, the past and future, which is precisely the present moment" (*W* 17). This eternal present is the setting for Thoreau's "drama which will never end" (*PJ* 2: 243), the myth enacted and reenacted in perpetuity—or as long as new generations of readers willingly partake in it. Emerson may not have been far from the truth when he wrote of the "sleepless insight" by which Thoreau perceived the material world as a means and a symbol ("Thoreau," 433). Thoreau's extraction of "a larger meaning than common use permits" (*W* 100) from the transient material world extends in the end to include his own life. Becoming "the life excited" (*J* 9: 121),[11] it is a life animated (*embowelled*, Thoreau might say) only in and through his writings. In fact, with *Walden* firmly at their center, Thoreau's literary projects constitute the essence of his life[12] as we have inherited it. In their totality these works attempt to construct a story not just of Thoreau's life but of the entire human race—a story that is progressive yet out of time, because like all myths it is always happening. "No truth was ever expressed but with this sort of emphasis—so that for the time there was no other truth.... We give importance to this hour over all other hours" (*PJ* 2: 204).

NOTES

1. The Princeton edition of Thoreau's *Journal* (*PJ*) is cited in this article, with the exception of materials dated after 3 September 1854, which are drawn from the 1906 edition of the *Journal* (*J*).

2. We should not necessarily equate this implied author with the editorial voice of the "sojourner in civilized life" after the two years at Walden Pond, nor even with the circumstantial Thoreau implied on the title page's attribution of authorship. While this last authorial Thoreau is certainly implicated in the literary artifact of *Walden*, his very existence does not depend upon its existence. The same cannot be said of the conventional

authorial figure evoked within the literary construct of *Walden*, who is but one of many coexisting identities subsumed within Thoreau's protean narrator.

3. By populating *Walden* with so many different representations of himself, Thoreau reinforces a more comprehensive strategy for literary meaning formation. The resulting meaning is tied to a totalizing vision of Thoreau and of his works constructed through the dissolution of expected boundaries: an erasure of absolute lines between fact and fiction, between author and character, between texts based on life and a life made out of texts. Such focuses exceed the scope of the present discussion considerably, but they are addressed in greater detail in Hartman (see especially 61–65, 82–103 & 140–173).

4. The sorts of explicit references I mean usually take unambiguous forms at the most superficial level of expression, though this does not rule out ironic or metaphoric utterance. In a few cases the characterizations are scarcely less than explicit, as in Thoreau's description of himself as a gardener/husbandman: "I have always cultivated a garden" (*W* 83). The statement may not equate "Thoreau" with "gardener" as a subject complement, but readers are hardly apt to interpret it otherwise.

5. The "journal, of no very wide circulation" may well be an oblique reference to *The Dial* under Margaret Fuller's editorship, but it may just as likely be an ironic allusion to Thoreau's own *Journal*. *The Dial* had already been defunct for a decade by the time *Walden* went to print, and this fact is not exactly consistent with Thoreau's use of the present perfect and the adverbial "yet" ("whose editor has never *yet* seen fit to print the bulk of my contributions"—emphasis added). The ambiguity concerning the journal and its editorship is almost certainly ironic. More noteworthy in the present discussion is Thoreau's projection of himself in the first person and third person simultaneously. As both the dutiful reporter and the reluctant editor he assumes two distinct semantic and grammatical roles that cannot logically refer to the same entity in this particular phrase, except through the aid of irony. The maneuver reveals something of Thoreau's tendency to regard himself at a certain remove, not as a coherent single identity but as a metaconstruct containing numerous identities.

6. A single persona should not be assumed for these materials.

7. While based in part on Marx's treatment of *Walden* in *The Machine in the Garden*, this observation rests at least equally on his assertive defense of *Walden* as a defining work of American pastoral in his 1999 dispute with Lawrence Buell in the *New York Review of Books*. (See Marx, "Struggle" and "Full Thoreau" as well as Buell and Marx, "Exchange.") No recent public exchange on Thoreau more clearly demonstrates *Walden*'s undiminished potential to inspire not only conflicting readings, but serious ideological *struggles* (to use Marx's own term) where much more is at stake than a loss of face for the contending critics.

8. As a rhetorical foil Thoreau's objectified *mass of men* appears in *Walden* and "Resistance to Civil Government" not less than twenty times in either this exact phrasing or in nearly identical form (as "masses of men" or "most men"): see *W* 6, 8, 16, 17, 35, 46, 91, 104 (twice), 106, 150, 165, 210, 213 and 215; see *RP* 66, 68, 70, 81 and 86. Far too numerous to cite individually, the most common variation on this foil is undoubtedly the word "men," appearing either on its own (as in "But lo! men have become the tools of their tools," *W* 37) or as a constituent of a compound (as in "townsmen," *W* 5 *et passim*). Predictably, this word also appears in many contexts where no deficiency of character is hinted at and where consequently it signals no such foil. The great majority of the twenty variations on mass of men just cited, on the other hand, clearly signal negative examples.

9. Muslih-ud-Din (Saadi), thirteenth-century author of *The Gulistan*, or *Rose Garden*—Thoreau spells his name "Sadi."

10. For clarification of this term (*metaconstruct of his own identity*), see note 5. Identifying the "you" of this passage not simply with Thoreau's readers but with his *posthumous* readers may seem anything but self-evident, but textual markers elsewhere strongly suggest a more specific audience than the general postulated reader of rhetorical convention when Thoreau directly addresses readers by using the second-person pronoun. For a fuller discussion of this feature in Thoreau's rhetoric, see Hartman (152–59).

11. This life is unquestionably a literary construct; it is "All that interests the reader" (*J* 9: 121).

12. In this last instance, *life* has a semantic range that extends far beyond even the metaphorical sense in "the life excited"; Thoreau's life in this superordinate sense of the term is inseparable not just from the figure projected in his writings but from the writings themselves.

Works Cited

Buell, Lawrence. *The Environmental Imagination: Thoreau, Nature Writing, and the Formation of American Culture*. Cambridge, MA: Harvard UP, 1995.

Buell, Lawrence and Leo Marx. "An Exchange on Thoreau" (Buell's letter to the editors and Marx's reply). *New York Review of Books* 46.19 (2 December 1999).

Cavell, Stanley. *The Senses of* Walden. Expanded ed. Chicago: U of Chicago P, 1992.

Emerson, Ralph Waldo. "The American Scholar." *Nature, Addresses and Lectures*. Ed. James Eliot Cabot. New and revised ed. Boston: Houghton Mifflin and Company, 1887. 81–115.

———. "Thoreau." *Lectures and Biographical Sketches*. Riverside ed. Vol. 10 of *Emerson's Complete Works* (12 vols). Boston: Houghton Mifflin and Company, 1890. 419–52.

Hartman, Steven P. *Faces of Thoreau in American Literature*. Ph.D. Diss. University at Albany, State University of New York, 2003. Ann Arbor: UMI, 2003. AAT 3080086.

Marx, Leo. *The Machine in the Garden: Technology and the Pastoral Ideal in America*. New York: Oxford UP, 1964.

———. "The Struggle Over Thoreau." *New York Review of Books* 46.11 (24 June 1999).

———. "The Full Thoreau." *New York Review of Books* 46.12 (15 July 1999).

Oates, Joyce Carol. "The Simple Art of Murder: The Novels of Raymond Chandler." *New York Review of Books* 42.20 (21 December 1995): 32+.

Scharnhorst, Gary. *Henry David Thoreau: An Annotated Bibliography of Commentary and Criticism before 1900*. New York: Garland Publishing, 1992.

Thoreau, Henry David. *A Week on the Concord and Merrimack Rivers*. Edited by Carl F. Hovde, William L. Howarth, and Elizabeth Hall Witherell. Princeton, NJ: Princeton UP, 1980.

———. *Journal. Vol 2: 1842–1848*. Edited by Robert Sattelmeyer. Princeton, NJ: Princeton UP, 1981.

———. *Journal. Vol 3: 1848–1851*. Edited by Robert Sattelmeyer, Mark R. Patterson, and William Rossi. Princeton, NJ: Princeton UP, 1991.

———. *Journal. Vol 5: 1852–1853*. Edited by Patrick O'Connell. Princeton, NJ: Princeton UP, 1997.

———. *The Journal of Henry David Thoreau*. 14 vols. Edited by Bradford Torrey and Francis H. Allen. Boston: Houghton Mifflin, 1906.

———. *Reform Papers*. Edited by Wendell Glick. Princeton, NJ: Princeton UP, 1973.

———. *Walden*. Edited by J. Lyndon Shanley. Princeton, NJ: Princeton UP, 1971.

Chronology

1817	David Henry Thoreau (as he was christened) is born July 12 in Concord, Massachusetts, five years after the marriage of his parents, John Thoreau and Cynthia Dunbar. His father, a kindly and mild-mannered man, the son of a Huguenot immigrant, is employed variously as a store clerk, then owner of a general store, and briefly as a schoolteacher in Boston before settling the family in Concord in 1823. His mother is a vigorous and outspoken activist of English and Scottish descent whose parents had been staunch Tories during the Revolutionary War. Thoreau has three siblings—Helen (1812), John Jr. (1815), and Sophia (1819).
1818	The Thoreau family moves to Chelmsford, Massachusetts.
1821	The Thoreau family moves to Boston, Massachusetts.
1823	The Thoreau family moves to Concord, Massachusetts where John Thoreau and his brother-in-law will establish a pencil-making business, following the discovery of a graphite deposit in New Hampshire.
1827	Young Thoreau first attends school in Boston, then transfers to Miss Phoebe Wheeler's infant academy in Concord, and then enters the Concord Academy. Thoreau writes "The Seasons," his earliest known work.
1833	Thoreau enters Harvard, being chosen over his older brother John. While at Harvard, he redefines his own identity,

reversing his given names to Henry David Thoreau. At Harvard, he is trained in mathematics, classical scholarship, and some natural science during his senior year.

1837   Thoreau graduates from Harvard and, in the fall, teaches briefly at the Center School in Concord, where he is chastised for not administering corporal punishment. Thoreau begins to keep a journal. On November 15, his first publication, an obituary for Anna Jones, an eighty-six-year-old-woman who remembered the Revolutionary War, appears in a Concord paper.

1838   Thoreau and his brother, John, open a private school in the family home, which is soon moved to Concord Academy. Together, they successfully pioneer many innovative teaching methods such as discipline through persuasion and frequent field trips for their students, and the school prospers for several years. On April 11, Thoreau delivers his first lecture at the Concord Lyceum, "Society." He also makes his first trip to Maine.

1839   Thoreau and John take a trip on the Concord and Merrimack rivers.

1840   In July, Thoreau publishes his first essay, "Aulus Persius Flaccus," on the Roman satiric poet, and his first poem, "Sympathy," in the *The Dial*.

1841   Due to John's failing health, the school he and Thoreau established is closed. While searching for a profession, Thoreau works at the family pencil factory where he researches a better formula for the graphite and designs improved machinery for grinding. By the fall, he moves in with the Emerson family where he is to work as a handyman. Thoreau develops a lifelong friendship with Ralph Waldo Emerson, who becomes his mentor, and becomes a regular member of Emerson's "Transcendental Club."

1842   On January 11, John Thoreau dies. On January 27, Emerson's five-year-old son, Waldo, dies. Following these events, Thoreau stops writing in his journal while lapsing into a silence until Emerson intervenes. Emerson has just taken over the editorship of *The Dial* from Margaret Fuller and sets Thoreau to reviewing a stack of natural history books. As a result of this employment, Thoreau publishes an essay in the July *Dial*, "Natural History of Massachusetts," weaving together many entries from his journal around the theme of the healthfulness of nature while extolling "the man of science."

1843   In May, Thoreau moves to Staten Island, New York, to tutor William Emerson's children and scout out the New York literary scene. The arrangement proves disappointing and he detests New York City. However, he meets Horace Greeley, editor of *The New-York Tribune*, who will become an invaluable ally and act as his publicist and literary agent. Thoreau assists Emerson in editing *The Dial* and publishes something in nearly every issue. In July, he and Fuller's brother, Richard, take a trip to Mt. Wachusett, resulting in the essay, "A Walk to Wachusett," published in January in the *Boston Miscellany*. Nathaniel Hawthorne is also interested in Thoreau's work and helps him get his essay, "Paradise (To Be) Regained" in the *United States Magazine and Democratic Review* in November. By mid-December, Thoreau is back in Concord for good.

1844   Thoreau returns to work in the family pencil factory, continuing to make improvements and bringing further success to the business. On April 30, Thoreau, while fishing with Edward Hoar, accidentally sets fire to the Concord Woods when the two try to kindle a fire in an old stump. More than three hundred acres of valuable timber are destroyed. In the fall, Emerson buys fourteen acres of land on the shore of Walden Pond and givens Thoreau permission to squat on in.

1845   In late March, Thoreau begins constructing a cabin at Walden Pond and in May he invites his friends to the house-raising, Emerson, Alcott, and Channing among them. Thoreau moves into the cabin on July 4.

1846   On February 4, he gives a lecture on Thomas Carlyle at the Concord Lyceum. In July, Thoreau is arrested for nonpayment of poll tax. In August, the Concord Women's Anti-Slavery Society meets on his doorstep, with speeches and a picnic afterward. In September, he joins his cousin, George Thatcher of Bangor, Maine, on an excursion up the Penobscot River and is disappointed with the "degradation" of the Indians.

1847   Early in the year, he gives a new lecture, "History of Myself," to audiences in Lincoln and Concord. In March and April, he publishes "Thomas Carlyle and His Work in *Graham's*

Magazine. In September, Thoreau moves out of the Walden cabin and moves into Emerson's house.

1848   On January 26, he delivers a lecture at the Concord Lyceum on "The Rights and Duties of the Individual in Relation to Government," which is published in May as "Resistance to Civil Government" in Elizabeth Peabody's *Aesthetic Papers*. He returns to his family home. In March, he publishes "Ktaadn" in the *Union Magazine*, where it runs in five installments. Late in the year, Thoreau pursues an additional line of work as a professional surveyor.

1849   On May 26, Thoreau publishes *A Week on the Concord and Merrimack Rivers* by James Munroe and Company. It is not very successful and puts a strain on his relationship with Emerson. On June 14, his sister, Helen, dies. On October 9, he and Ellery Channing take a trip to Provincetown on Cape Cod. Thoreau finds the trip exhilarating, especially the bleak landscape.

1850   Thoreau makes his second trip to Cape Cod to gather more material. In July, his friend Margaret Fuller dies in a storm at sea on her way back from Italy. Early in the fall, Thoreau and Channing take a trip to Canada. His written account of the trip is "A Yankee in Canada." Late in the year, he begins to record observations made in his numerous walks. He is elected a corresponding member of the Boston Society of Natural History.

1851   In March, Thoreau rages in his journal about the capture of Thomas Simms, a runaway slave. By midyear, Thoreau is adding to his journal nearly every day as his walks inspired him to look harder and engage more deeply with the natural world.

1853   Thoreau makes a second trip to the Maine woods and publishes "A Yankee in Canada" in *Putnam's Monthly Magazine*. The family has abandoned the manufacture of pencils altogether, and is now shipping packages of plumbago to Boston, New York, Philadelphia, and the Midwest. The American Association for the Advancement of Science attempts to recruit Thoreau, though he declines.

1854   On July 4, Thoreau speaks at a radical meeting in Framingham on "Slavery in Massachusetts." His address earns him a reputation as an abolitionist firebrand. On August 9, Thoreau publishes his masterpiece, *Walden*.

1855	Thoreau visits Cape Cod and contributes to *Putnam's Monthly Magazine*. Some time around May, Thoreau experiences a period of "invalidity and worthlessness" that lasts until September.
1856	Thoreau meets Walt Whitman in Brooklyn.
1857	Early in the year, Thoreau meets a radical abolitionist, Captain John Brown. He travels to Cape Cod and the Maine woods.
1858	Thoreau visits the White Mountains and Mount Monadnock. He contributes to the *Atlantic Monthly*.
1859	On February 3, Thoreau's father dies. In March, Thoreau is appointed to the Harvard College Committee for Examination in Natural History, and he delivers a lecture at the Concord Lyceum, "Autumnal Tints." The town of Concord hires Thoreau to survey the river.
1860	On December 3, Thoreau examines tree stumps in a cold rain and contracts a cold that will lead to his fatal illness.
1861	Thoreau suffers from a persistent cough and his doctor advises him to move to a warmer climate. Instead, he decides to try the allegedly therapeutic air of Minnesota and on May 16 sets out by rail with Horace Mann Jr. His health will weaken steadily through the following months.
1862	In April, Bronson Alcott publishes a tribute to Thoreau in the *Atlantic Monthly* in an essay entitled, "The Forester." Thoreau dies peacefully on May 6. His mother, Cynthia, sister Sophia, and aunt Louisa are in attendance. The schools are dismissed early so that the children of Concord can attend the funeral. In June, the *Atlantic Monthly* publishes posthumously his essay, "Walking, or the Wild."
1864	*The Maine Woods*, edited by Sophia Thoreau and Ellery Channing, is published.

Contributors

HAROLD BLOOM is Sterling Professor of the Humanities at Yale University. He is the author of 30 books, including *Shelley's Mythmaking* (1959), *The Visionary Company* (1961), *Blake's Apocalypse* (1963), *Yeats* (1970), *A Map of Misreading* (1975), *Kabbalah and Criticism* (1975), *Agon: Toward a Theory of Revisionism* (1982), *The American Religion* (1992), *The Western Canon* (1994), and *Omens of Millennium: The Gnosis of Angels, Dreams, and Resurrection* (1996). *The Anxiety of Influence* (1973) sets forth Professor Bloom's provocative theory of the literary relationships between the great writers and their predecessors. His most recent books include *Shakespeare: The Invention of the Human* (1998), a 1998 National Book Award finalist, *How to Read and Why* (2000), *Genius: A Mosaic of One Hundred Exemplary Creative Minds* (2002), *Hamlet: Poem Unlimited* (2003), *Where Shall Wisdom Be Found?* (2004), and *Jesus and Yahweh: The Names Divine* (2005). In 1999, Professor Bloom received the prestigious American Academy of Arts and Letters Gold Medal for Criticism. He has also received the International Prize of Catalonia, the Alfonso Reyes Prize of Mexico, and the Hans Christian Andersen Bicentennial Prize of Denmark.

ETHEL SEYBOLD (1910-2005) is Professor Emeritus of English at Illinois College. She is the author of "The Source of Thoreau's 'Cato-Decius Dialogue'" (1994).

JOHN HILDEBIDLE has been a Professor of Literature at the Massachusetts Institute of Technology. He is the author of *Five Irish Writers: The Errand of*

Keeping Alive (1989), "Prophetic Riddles: The Enigmas of Emily Dickinson" (1998), and an editor of *Modernism Reconsidered* (1983).

ROBERT SATTELMEYER has been Professor of English at Georgia State University. He is the author of "Walden: Climbing the Canon" (2004), "Thoreau and Emerson" (1995), and an editor of *American History Through Literature, 1820-1870* (2006).

GORDON V. BOUDREAU is Emeritus Professor of English at Le Moyne College, Syracuse, New York. He is the author "West by Southwest: Thoreau's Minnesota Journey" (1998), "Herman Melville, Immortality, St. Paul, and Resurrection: From Rose-Bud to Billy Budd" (2003), and "Transcendental Sport: Hunting, Fishing, and Trapping in *Walden*" (1996).

LANCE NEWMAN has been an Associate Professor of Literature and Writing Studies at California State University, San Marcos. He is the author of *Our Common Dwelling: Henry Thoreau, Transcendentalism, and the Class Politics of Nature* (2005), "Wordsworth in America and the Nature of Democracy" (1999), and an editor of *Transatlantic Romanticism: An Anthology of British, American, and Canadian Literature, 1767-1867* (2006).

DAVID M. ROBINSON has been Oregon Professor of English and Distinguished Professor of American Literature at Oregon State University. He is the author of *Emerson and the Conduct of Life: Pragmatism and Ethical Purpose in the Later Work* (1993), *World of Relations: The Achievement of Peter Taylor* (1998), and *The Unitarians and Universalists* (1985).

ROBERT OSCAR LÓPEZ has been an Assistant Professor of English at Rutgers University, Camden Campus. He is currently writing on "Antiquity and Radical Authority" and is the author of articles on Henry David Thoreau, Junot Diaz, Phillis Wheatley, and William Wells Brown.

ERIC G. WILSON has been an Associate Professor of English at Wake Forest University. He is the author of *Coleridge's Melancholia: An Anatomy of Limbo* (2004), "Polar Apocalypse in Coleridge and Poe" (2004), and *The Spiritual History of Ice: Romanticism, Science, and the Imagination* (2003).

STEVEN HARTMAN has been Senior Lecturer in American Literature and Culture in the English Department of Växjö University, Sweden. He is the author of *Dear Allen Ginsberg* (1991) and published articles on Thoreau, Kurt Vonnegut, Michael Ondaatje, Annie Proulx, Derek Walcott, and other writers.

Bibliography

Adams, Stephen, and Donald Ross, Jr. *Revising Mythologies: The Composition of Thoreau's Major Works*. Charlottesville: University Press of Virginia, 1988.

Advena, Jean Cameron. *A Bibliography of the Thoreau Society Bulletin Bibliographies 1941–1969*. Edited by Walter Harding. Troy, N. Y.: Whitston, 1971.

Anderson, Charles. *The Magic Circle of Walden*. New York: Holt, Rinehart, and Winston,1968.

Bennett, Jane. *Thoreau's Nature: Ethics, Politics, and the Wild*. Thousand Oaks, Calif.: Sage, 1994.

Bickman, Martin. *Walden: Volatile Truths*. New York: Twayne, 1992.

Bloom, Harold, ed. *Henry David Thoreau's Walden*. New York: Chelsea House, 1987.

Bonner, Willard Hallam. *Harp on the Shore: Thoreau and the Sea*. Edited and completed by George R. Levine. Albany: State University of New York Press, 1985.

Borst, Raymond R., comp. *The Thoreau Log: A Documentary Life of Henry David Thoreau, 1817–1862*. New York: G. K. Hall, 1992.

Borst, Raymond R. *Henry David Thoreau: A Reference Guide, 1835–1899*. Boston: G. K. Hall, 1987.

Boudreau, Gordon. *The Roots of* Walden *and the Tree of Life*. Nashville: Vanderbilt University Press, 1990.

Bridgman, Richard. *Dark Thoreau*. Lincoln: University of Nebraska Press, 1982.

Buell, Lawrence. "American Pastoral Ideology Reappraised." *American Literary History* 1.1 (1989): 6–29.

———. *Literary Transcendentalism: Style and Vision in the American Renaissance*. Ithaca: Cornell University Press, 1973.

———. *The Environmental Imagination: Thoreau, Nature Writing, and the Formation of American Culture*. Cambridge, Mass.: Belknap Press of Harvard University Press, 1995.

———. *New England Literary Culture: From Revolution Through Renaissance*. Cambridge: Cambridge University Press, 1986.

Burbick, Joan. *Thoreau's Alternative History: Changing Perspectives on Nature, Culture, and Language*. Philadelphia: University of Pennsylvania Press, 1987.

Cafaro, Philip. *Thoreau's Living Ethics: Walden and the Pursuit of Virtue*. Athens: University of Georgia Press, 2004.

Cain, William E., ed. *A Historical Guide to Henry David Thoreau*. New York: Oxford University Press, 2000.

Cameron, Sharon. *Writing Nature: Henry Thoreau's Journal*. New York: Oxford University Press, 1985.

Cavell, Stanley. *The Senses of Walden*. Expanded Edition. San Francisco: North Point Press, 1981.

Collins, Christopher. *The Uses of Observation*. Mouton: The Hague, 1971.

Dombrowski, Daniel A. *Thoreau the Platonist*. New York: P. Lang, 1986.

Drinnon, Richard. "Thoreau's Politics of the Upright Man." *Massachusetts Review* 4.1 (Autumn 1962): 126–138.

Fink, Stephen. *Prophet in the Marketplace: Thoreau's Development as a Professional Writer*. Princeton: Princeton University Press, 1992.

Fleck, Richard. *Henry David Thoreau and John Muir among the Indians*. Hamden, Conn.: Archon Books, 1985.

Friesen, Victor Carl. *The Spirit of the Huckleberry: Sensuousness in Henry Thoreau*. Edmonton, Alta.: University of Alberta Press, 1984.

Garber, Frederic. *Thoreau's Fable of Inscribing*. Princeton: Princeton University Press, 1991.

Gayet, Claude. *The Intellectual Development of Henry David Thoreau*. Uppsala: Almqvist & Wiksell International, 1981.

Golemba, Henry L. *Thoreau's Wild Rhetoric*. New York: New York University Press, 1990.

Gross, Robert A. "Culture and Cultivation: Agriculture and Society in Thoreau's Concord." *Journal of American History* 69 (1982): 42–61.

Hansen, Olaf. *Aesthetic Individualism and Practical Intellect: American Allegory in Emerson, Thoreau, Adams, and James*. Princeton: Princeton University Press, 1990.

Harding, Walter Roy. *The Days of Henry Thoreau: A Biography*. New York: Knopf, 1965. Rpt. Princeton: Princeton University Press, 1982.

———. *The New Thoreau Handbook*. New York: New York University Press, 1980.

Haworth, William L. *The Book of Concord: Thoreau's Life as a Writer*. New York: Viking Press, 1982.

Hildebidle, John. *Thoreau: A Naturalist's Liberty*. Cambridge, Mass.: Harvard University Press, 1983.

Hocks, Richard A. "Thoreau, Coleridge, and Barfield: Reflections on the Imagination and the Law of Polarity." *Centennial Review* (1973): 175–198.

Howarth, William L. *The Book of Concord: Thoreau's Life as a Writer*. New York: Viking Press, 1982.

Johnson, William C. *What Thoreau Said: Walden and the Unsayable*. Moscow, Idaho: University of Idaho Press, 1991.

Lane, Lauriat, ed. *Approaches to Walden*. San Francisco: Wadsworth, 1961.

Marx, Leo. *The Machine in the Garden: Technology and the Pastoral Ideal in America*. New York: Oxford University Press, 1964.

Matthiessen, F. O. *American Renaissance: Art and Expression in the Age of Emerson and Whitman*. London: Oxford University Press, 1941.

McIntosh, James. *Thoreau as Romantic Naturalist: His Shifting Stance toward Nature*. Ithaca: Cornell University Press, 1974.

Metzger, Charles Reid. *Thoreau and Whitman: A Study of Their Esthetics*. Seattle: University of Washington Press, 1961.

Meyer, Michael. *Several More Lives to Live: Thoreau's Political Reputation in America*. Westport, CT.: Greenwood Press, 1977.

Miller, Perry. *Nature's Nation*. Cambridge: Belknap, 1967.

———. "Thoreau in the Context of International Romanticism." *New England Quarterly* vol. 24 (1961): 147–159.

Moldenhauer, Joseph J. "Walden and Wordsworth's Guide to the English Lake District." *Studies in the American Renaissance* (1990): 261–292.

Moller, Mary Elkins. *Thoreau in the Human Community*. Amherst: University of Massachusetts Press, 1980.

Myerson, Joel, ed. *The Cambridge Companion to Henry David Thoreau*. New York: Cambridge University Press, 1995.

———, ed. *Critical Essays on Henry David Thoreau's* Walden. Boston: G. K. Hall, 1988.

Neufeldt, Leonard. *The Economist: Henry Thoreau and Enterprise*. New York: Oxford University Press, 1989.

Ogden, Merlene A. *Walden, A Concordance*. New York: Garland, 1985.

Scharnhorst, Gary. *Henry David Thoreau: An Annotated Bibliography of Comment and Criticism Before 1900*. New York: Garland, 1992.

Paul, Sherman. *The Shores of America: Thoreau's Inward Exploration*. Urbana: University of Illinois Press, 1958.

Paul, Sherman. *Thoreau: A Collection of Critical Essays*. Englewood Cliffs, NJ: Prentice-Hall, 1962.

Peck, H. Daniel. *Thoreau's Morning Work: Memory and Perception in A Week on the Concord and Merrimack Rivers, The Journal, and* Walden. New Haven: Yale University Press, 1990.

Porte, Joel. *Emerson and Thoreau: Transcendentalists in Conflict*. Middletown, CT: Wesleyan University Press, 1966.

Richardson, Robert D. *Henry Thoreau: A Life of the Mind*. Berkeley: University of California Press, 1986.

Robinson, Kenneth Allen. *Thoreau and the Wild Appetite*. 1957. New York: AMS Press, 1985.

Ruland, Richard, ed. *Twentieth Century Interpretations of* Walden: *A Collection of Critical Essays*. Englewood Cliffs, NJ: Prentice-Hall, 1968.

Sattlemeyer, Robert. "The Remaking of Walden." *Writing the American Classics*. Edited by James Barbour and Tom Quirk. Chapel Hill: University of North Carolina Press (1990): 53–78.

———. "'The True Industry for Poets': Fishing with Thoreau.'" *ESQ* 33 (1987): 189–201.

———. *Thoreau's Reading: A Study in Intellectual History with Bibliographical Catalogue*. Princeton: Princeton University Press, 1988.

Sayer, Robert F. *New Essays on Walden*. New York: Cambridge University Press, 1992.

———. *Thoreau and the American Indians*. Princeton: Princeton University Press, 1977.

Scharnhorst, Gary. *Henry David Thoreau: A Case Study in Canonization*. Columbia, SC: Camden House, 1993.

Schneider, Richard J. *Henry David Thoreau*. Boston: Twayne, 1987.

———. "Thoreau and Nineteenth-Century Landscape Painting." *ESQ* 31 (1985): 67–88.

Shanley, J. Landon. *The Making of Walden, with the Text of the First Edition*. Chicago: University of Chicago Press, 1957.

Smith, Harmon L. *My Friend, My Friend: The Story of Thoreau's Relationship with Emerson*. Amherst: University of Massachusetts Press, 1999.

Spiller, Robert E. *Four Makers of the American Mind*. Durham, N. C.: Duke University Press, 1976.

Tauber, Alfred I. *Henry David Thoreau and the Moral Agency of Knowing*. Berkeley: University of California Press, 2001.

Thoreau, Henry David. *Walden: An Annotated Edition*. Foreword and Notes by Walter Harding. Boston: Houghton Mifflin, 1995.

Wagenknecht, Edward. *Henry David Thoreau: What Manner of Man?* Amherst: University of Massachusetts Press, 1981.

West, Michael. "Scatology and Eschatology: The Heroic Dimensions of Thoreau's Wordplay." *PMLA* 89 (1974): 1043–1064.

Wood, Barry. "Thoreau's Narrative Art in 'Civil Disobedience.'" *Philological Quarterly* 60 (1981): 106–115.

Acknowledgments

"Thoreau: The Quest and the Classics" by Ethel Seybold. From *Thoreau: The Quest and the Classics*. Hamden, Connecticut: Archon Books (1969): 1–21. © 1969 by Yale University Press. Reprinted by permission of Yale University Press.

"Naturalizing Eden: Science and Sainthood in *Walden*" reprinted by permission of the publisher from *Thoreau: A Naturalist's History* by John Hildebidle, pp. 97–125, Cambridge, Mass.: Harvard University Press, copyright © 1983 by the President and Fellows of Harvard College.

"From *A Week* to *Walden*" by Robert Sattelmeyer. From *Thoreau's Reading: A Study in Intellectual History*. Princeton, New Jersey: Princeton University Press (1988): 54–77. © 1988 by Princeton University Press. Reprinted by permission of Princeton University Press.

"Springs to Remember" by Gordon V. Boudreau. From *The Roots of* Walden *and the Tree of Life*. Nashville: Vanderbilt University Press (1990): 89–104. © 1990 by Gordon V. Boudreau. Reprinted by permission.

"'Patron of the World': Henry Thoreau as Wordsworthian Poet" by Lance Newman. From *The Concord Saunterer*, vol. 11 (2003): 155–172. © 2003 by The Thoreau Society. Reprinted by permission.

"Living Poetry" by David M. Robinson. From *Natural Life: Thoreau's Worldly Transcendentalism*. Ithaca and London: Cornell University Press (2004): 100–124. © 2004 by Cornell University Press. Reprinted by permission of the publisher, Cornell University Press.

"Thoreau, Homer, and Community" by Robert Oscar López. From *Nineteenth-Century Prose*, vol. 31, no. 2 (Fall 2004): 122–151. © 2004 by San Diego State University. Reprinted by permission.

"Thoreau, Crystallography, and the Science of the Transparent" by Eric G. Wilson. From *Studies in Romanticism*, vol. 43, no. 1 (Spring 2004): 99–117. © 2004 by the Trustees of Boston University. Reprinted by permission.

"'The life excited': Faces of Thoreau in *Walden*" by Steven Hartman. From *The Concord Saunterer*, (*New Series*) vol. 12/13 (2004/2005): 341–360. © 2003 by The Thoreau Society. Reprinted by permission.

Every effort has been made to contact the owners of copyrighted material and secure copyright permission. Articles appearing in this volume generally appear much as they did in their original publication with few or no editorial changes. Those interested in locating the original source will find bibliographic information in the bibliography and acknowledgments sections of this volume.

Index